QUALITATIVE INQUIRY IN EVALUATION

QUALITATIVE INQUIRY IN EVALUATION

From Theory to Practice

**LESLIE GOODYEAR,
JENNIFER JEWISS, JANET USINGER,
AND ERIC BARELA**

JB JOSSEY-BASS™
A Wiley Brand

Published by Jossey-Bass
A Wiley Brand
One Montgomery Street, Suite 1200, San Francisco, CA 94104-4594—www.josseybass.com

Jossey-Bass books and products are available through most bookstores. To contact Jossey-Bass directly call our Customer Care Department within the U.S. at 800-956-7739, outside the U.S. at 317-572-3986, or fax 317-572-4002.

Wiley publishes in a variety of print and electronic formats and by print-on-demand. Some material included with standard print versions of this book may not be included in e-books or in print-on-demand. If this book refers to media such as a CD or DVD that is not included in the version you purchased, you may download this material at http://booksupport.wiley.com. For more information about Wiley products, visit www.wiley.com.

Library of Congress Cataloging-in-Publication Data
Qualitative inquiry in evaluation : from theory to practice / edited by Leslie Goodyear, Eric Barela, Jennifer Jewiss, and Janet Usinger. — 1
     pages cm — (Research methods for the social sciences ; 29)
    Includes bibliographical references and index.
   ISBN 978-0-470-44767-3 (paperback) — ISBN 978-1-118-41815-4 (pdf) — ISBN 978-1-118-41525-2 (epub)   1. Educational evaluation.   I. Goodyear, Leslie, 1966-
   LB2822.75.Q354 2014
   379.1'58 — dc23

                                     2014015898

Printed in the United States of America
FIRST EDITION
PB Printing   10 9 8 7 6 5 4 3 2 1

CONTENTS

PART ONE: The Intersection of Qualitative Inquiry and Evaluation Approaches

PART TWO: Tales from the Field of Qualitative Evaluation   139

CHAPTER EIGHT: BALANCING INSIDER–OUTSIDER ROLES AS A NEW EXTERNAL EVALUATOR   189

Norma Martínez-Rubin and Stuart Hanson

CHAPTER NINE: WHOSE STORY IS THIS, ANYWAY? NAVIGATING AN ETHICAL CONUNDRUM   213

Sharon F. Rallis

FIGURES AND TABLES

FIGURES

TABLES

INTRODUCTION

WHAT IS THIS BOOK ABOUT?

To put it simply, this book is about integrating qualitative inquiry—its approaches, methods, stances, and theories—into the practice of evaluation. What do we mean by "qualitative inquiry" and "evaluation"? We agree with Thomas Schwandt (2007) that qualitative inquiry "aims at understanding the ***meaning*** of human ***action***" (italics in original) (p. 248). It includes many forms of social inquiry such as case study research, naturalistic inquiry, ethnography, and others. Likewise, many definitions of evaluation are in play these days; however, Peter Dahler-Larsen (2012) summarizes them quite succinctly when he defines evaluation as "basically a systematic, methodological, and thus 'assisted' way of investigating and assessing an activity of public interest in order to affect decisions or actions concerning this activity or similar activities" (p. 9).

This book is about the intersection of evaluation and qualitative inquiry; that space in a Venn diagram where qualitative inquiry and evaluation overlap. It is the space where the two colored circles representing qualitative inquiry and evaluation come together to create a new color. That part of the diagram is what we are calling qualitative evaluation. That is what this book is about.

Sometimes, to understand what something is, it is helpful to understand what it is not. This book is not a how-to textbook. This edited volume will not tell you how to develop and implement a qualitative evaluation. Instead, we hope this book will stimulate your thinking on how different evaluation approaches dovetail with qualitative inquiry. In addition, the second part of the book offers "tales of the field" (Van Maanen, 1988) that share the ins and outs of the practice of qualitative evaluation.

WHO IS THIS BOOK FOR AND WHAT DO WE HOPE YOU WILL GET FROM READING IT?

As we surveyed the landscape of available literature, we found a wealth of resources on qualitative research and also on evaluation. However, we found few titles dedicated to an exploration of the intersection of qualitative inquiry and evaluation. This book focuses on that intersection, delving deeply into what it means to carry out qualitative evaluation and examining the practice of qualitative evaluation from various theoretical and practical angles.

This book is geared toward students and evaluators who are relatively new to the practice of qualitative inquiry in evaluation, but who have some foundational knowledge of both evaluation and qualitative inquiry. Its purpose is twofold: as a practical introduction for students and new evaluators and as a reference and resource for practicing evaluators. As an edited volume, this compilation of many voices is meant to spark dialogue among evaluators. Our hope is that the array of perspectives herein provides a window on the world of qualitative evaluation—a travelogue of sorts that describes the terrain and offers examples and lessons learned along the way.

For evaluators who are already using qualitative evaluation approaches, we hope the featured theoretical perspectives and practice considerations will deepen their understanding of the knowledge, skills, and epistemological stances that seasoned qualitative evaluators bring to their work. In short, we hope readers of all backgrounds will find it helpful to "listen in" as the contributing evaluators reflect on the theoretical perspectives that inform their practice and the practice-based experiences that have surfaced new layers of learning about their craft.

Many graduate students receive methodological training in qualitative research but are not adequately prepared to employ those skills out in the field, particularly in the context of an evaluation. In addition, many experienced evaluators with quantitative research backgrounds are interested in learning how to incorporate qualitative approaches into the evaluations they conduct. As many readers are no doubt aware, incorporating qualitative inquiry in evaluation entails much more than simply "doing some interviews" to gather a smattering of quotes to "round out" the quantitative data and analysis. The practicing evaluator must address a substantial number of considerations, and these considerations are not necessarily covered in qualitative research or evaluation textbooks. The chapters in Part 2 of this book illustrate these concepts and tell the tales of practitioners faced with real-world challenges and opportunities as they implement qualitative evaluations.

Going "into the field" to carry out qualitative inquiry— whether facilitating a meeting with evaluation stakeholders or conducting interviews—can be an exciting, uncertain, and even daunting task. We hope this collection of chapters deepens readers' thinking about the endeavor by exploring territory beyond that covered in more methodologically oriented texts and teaching.

HOW TO READ THIS BOOK

As we constructed this volume, we thought about our own experiences as we each entered the field of evaluation and what we have encountered in our practice. We specifically divided the volume into two parts: one focuses on the intersection of evaluation approaches and qualitative inquiry; the other focuses on how evaluators think about and navigate their evaluation practice.

Part 1 of this volume is of particular value to people who are not steeped in evaluation theory. The first set of chapters provides grounding for people who may understand the epistemology of qualitative inquiry, but not necessarily how it dovetails with evaluation approaches. On the flipside, Part 1 also provides grounding for evaluators who want to deepen their exploration of the role of qualitative inquiry in evaluation.

Chapter 1, written by **Thomas A. Schwandt** and **Timothy J. Cash,** provides an historical journey from the advent of qualitative inquiry through its increasing incorporation into the practice of evaluation. Following an overview of the contested definition of qualitative evaluation, they conclude their chapter by describing the three enduring contributions that qualitative inquiry has made in: (1) shaping the ways an evaluation is focused; (2) how values are understood and portrayed; and (3) how evaluations are communicated.

After this orientation, we turn the discussion over to several evaluators who have been leaders in shaping different evaluation approaches and effectively integrating qualitative inquiry. **Michael Quinn Patton** has long been a pioneer in designing evaluations that are actually used by program stakeholders. In Chapter 2, he shares how he thinks about the intersection of utilization-focused evaluation and qualitative inquiry and highlights both opportunities and challenges for practice.

For those entering the realm of using evaluation to affect public policy, **George F. Grob** offers lessons he has learned from many years of work with policy makers at the local, state, and national levels. In Chapter 3, he shares his thoughts and experiences regarding the value of qualitative data in informing policy makers about public programs. His pragmatic approach demonstrates how evaluation operates in the "simultaneously fast paced and glacially slow" arena of policy making.

In Chapter 4, **Katrina L. Bledsoe** argues that although theory-driven evaluation is often associated with randomized controlled trials and the generalizability of programs, to effectively implement theory-driven evaluation, an evaluator must embrace qualitative methods when developing logic models, working with participants to articulate a program's theory, and also when collecting and analyzing data.

Jill Anne Chouinard and **J. Bradley Cousins** are leaders in the development of participatory evaluation. Chapter 5 provides an exploration of the intersections among qualitative inquiry, practical participatory evaluation, and transformative participatory evaluation.

Part 2 of this volume is of particular value to professionals new to the field of evaluation and those who are looking for examples of how qualitative evaluation is done "on the ground." How does one enter an evaluation setting in a manner that portrays professionalism and command of the situation, but also quickly establishes trust? How does one interact with the evaluation funders when their concept of an evaluation design is inconsistent with the questions they want answered? How does one handle an evaluation that gets *off track*? These questions, and more, are addressed through case studies of evaluation practice by evaluators who bring varying degrees of experience to the endeavor.

Part 2 begins with an introductory chapter written by **Laurie Stevahn** and **Jean A. King,** who have spent much of their academic careers guiding students in the development of important skills and competencies for conducting effective evaluations. In Chapter 6, they describe the competencies required to conduct effective evaluations generally, and they delve deeply into the specialized competencies required to conduct effective qualitative evaluations.

In Chapter 7, **Vivianne E. Baur** and **Tineke A. Abma** describe how they used a transformative paradigm with responsive evaluation and hermeneutic dialogue to address power differences in the management of residential units for senior citizens. In addition to discussing how they interacted with the Board that funded the evaluation, this chapter provides a rich description of the strategies these evaluators used to level the playing field and address the unspoken conflicts between the staff and resident council members.

Academically prepared as a health educator and researcher, **Norma Martínez-Rubin** was new to evaluation when she partnered with **Stuart Hanson** to conduct a community assessment of pediatric obesity. Chapter 8 tells the story of how she navigated her own Latina cultural identity and professional background, in light of collecting data and portraying the health-related needs of families living in diverse Southern California communities.

In Chapter 9, **Sharon F. Rallis** describes a situation in which she was caught in an ethical dilemma. As the evaluator of a high-profile, federally funded project, she found herself having to navigate between noted researchers and unhappy public school staff who worked where the project was conducted. This case study provides an opportunity to "listen in" as an experienced evaluator considers how to make sense of—and make the best of—an evaluation that is headed down a problematic path.

The last chapter is written by the editors, **Leslie Goodyear, Jennifer Jewiss, Janet Usinger,** and **Eric Barela**. It brings together our own reflections and experiences as evaluators with those of the other authors featured in this volume. As our four-person editing team slowly but steadily propelled this book forward over the course of several years, we engaged in extensive and deep conversations about what constitutes quality in qualitative evaluation. In the end, we arrived at five elements that we believe are hallmarks of quality for evaluations that employ qualitative inquiry.

The final chapter elaborates on how we arrived at these elements and discusses each in depth. We briefly introduce them here, so that readers may consider how these elements play out in various chapters of the book.

QUALITY IN QUALITATIVE EVALUATION

- Acknowledging Who You Are and What You Bring to the Work

    The evaluator must bring to the process a clear sense of personal identity and professional role. It is a matter of understanding who you are, what you know, and what you need to learn.

- Building Trusting Relationships

    The evaluator needs to engage stakeholders and build trusting relationships from the outset and throughout the evaluation.

- Employing Sound and Explicit Methodology

    High-quality evaluation relies on sound methodology, systematically applied, that is explicitly shared with stakeholders.

- Staying True to the Data

    Conducting high-quality evaluation can only be accomplished by remaining "true" to the data; in other words, hearing participants as they are, not how the evaluator wants them to be.

- Fostering Learning

    Skillful facilitation of the process by the evaluator results in learning by all involved.

As is portrayed in the graphic representation presented in the final chapter, these five elements form a cycle with no set starting point or definitive end point. Like so many things in life—and certainly in the world of evaluation—putting these elements into practice is not nearly as linear or as neat and tidy as the model itself.

We recognize that some readers may be eager to dive deeper into the discussion about the elements of quality before proceeding with the intervening chapters. If that is the case for you, we invite you to flip to the corresponding discussion in the final chapter and then return to main parts of the book. Regardless of what path you decide to take through this edited volume, we hope you will consider how these elements appear not only in the chapters of this book but also in your own evaluation practice.

REFERENCES

Dahler-Larsen, P. (2012). *The Evaluation Society*. Stanford, CA: Stanford University Press.

Schwandt, T. (2007). *Sage Dictionary of Qualitative Inquiry*, 3rd ed. Thousand Oaks, CA: Sage.

Van Maanen, J. (1988). *Tales of the Field: On Writing Ethnography*. Chicago, IL: University of Chicago Press.

ABOUT THE EDITORS

Leslie Goodyear has been a practicing qualitative (and mixed-method) evaluator for nearly twenty years, during which time she has evaluated programs focused on HIV/AIDS prevention, arts, youth development, parenting, youth media, youth civic engagement, afterschool, youth substance abuse prevention, and most recently informal STEM education. In addition to conducting evaluations, she works to build organizational evaluation capacity, provide technical assistance, and build communities of practice for evaluators. Before studying program evaluation at Cornell University, Leslie worked as an early childhood educator and as a frontline and outreach staff person in social service organizations. Her most important evaluation training came in the form of learning to be a crisis counselor and learning to balance the demands of multiple five-year-olds who needed their shoes tied, noses wiped, and questions answered simultaneously. Leslie has a keen interest in how programs are understood, how meaning is made from program experiences, and how that meaning is conveyed to stakeholders so that they can better understand the program experience and make informed decisions. In this vein, she has experimented with new and innovative forms of representation of evaluation findings, including poetry and performance. All of these interests and experiences, and her passion for ethical practice in evaluation, have informed her contributions to the development of this edited volume.

Jennifer Jewiss has been conducting qualitative evaluations for over fifteen years and currently serves as a research assistant professor in the Department of Leadership and Developmental Sciences at the University of Vermont. Jennifer specializes in utilization-focused and developmental approaches to evaluation. She has studied environmental, health, human service, humanities, leadership, and cross-sector initiatives for a wide range of organizations, from small nonprofits to government agencies. Since 2006, much of her time has been devoted to evaluating

US National Park Service initiatives. Her approach to evaluation draws on the power of individual and collective narratives and the value of reflective practice to inform program and organizational development. Her work is often designed to capture a participants-eye-view of a program and to analyze the insights and experiences that illuminate a program's theory in action. Her evaluation practice has been informed and inspired by many years of "roll-up-your-sleeves" involvement in nonprofit organizations, which instilled an enduring appreciation for both the complexity and the rewards of organizational change. Jennifer regularly serves as a methodological consultant to colleagues from various academic disciplines who are new to qualitative evaluation and seeking guidance as they venture into unfamiliar territory. For several years, she also taught a graduate seminar introducing educators and human service professionals to the practice of evaluation. Coaching emerging evaluators as they make the leap into the world of evaluation ranks among the most powerful experiences that shaped her contributions to this book.

Janet Usinger's thirty-year career has been centered on university outreach; her involvement and roles in evaluation have changed over time, however. She began her career as a community-based nutrition specialist for Cooperative Extension. In that role, she developed and implemented nonformal educational programming. During that time, Cooperative Extension was transitioning beyond the "smiley face" evaluations to assessing program impact; she struggled to think about how impact can actually be measured, particularly when the programming was preventive in nature. She then became a consumer of evaluation findings. As an administrator at the state and federal levels, she reviewed program evaluations from program areas as diverse as youth development, natural resources, agriculture production, and nutrition to determine initial and continued funding. At this point, her lens was accountability for the appropriate use of public funds. She then transitioned into an academic position with two primary responsibilities. Continuing in her outreach capacity, she became the principal investigator for a State Gaining Early Awareness and Readiness for Undergraduate Programs (GEAR UP) project. Her evaluation responsibilities have included conducting and coordinating longitudinal qualitative and case studies to understand at a deep and personal level the impact of GEAR UP on adolescents and school climate. In addition, she serves as advisor and mentor to doctoral students who engage in qualitative methods for their research at the University of Nevada, Reno. These four filters—program development and implementation, program funding and accountability, qualitative inquiry to inform program impact, and faculty mentor—have informed her contribution to the development of this volume.

Eric Barela has worked for over a decade as an internal evaluator for a variety of organizations. He is currently chief knowledge and impact officer at Partners in School Innovation, a school-reform nonprofit focused on transforming teaching and learning in underserved urban schools so that every child, regardless of background, thrives. Eric's entire career in evaluation has been in service of public education. Before joining Partners in School Innovation, Eric was an internal evaluator for the Los Angeles Unified School District. Eric's experience in public education has shaped his evaluation philosophy. He approaches every evaluation activity as an opportunity to engage stakeholders in powerful learning. This desire to create learning opportunities for stakeholders led Eric to specialize in qualitative inquiry and a utilization-focused approach to evaluation. He has seen stakeholders reduced to tears when reflecting on qualitative data identifying the processes that led to desired outcomes for students. Because of this power, Eric is also mindful of the need for qualitative evaluators to be clear about data collection and analysis processes, which serve to enhance the credibility of evaluation findings.

ABOUT THE CONTRIBUTORS

Tineke A. Abma is a professor in the Department of Medical Humanities of the VU University Medical Centre and EMGO+ research institute for health and primary care research in Amsterdam. Over the past 20 years Abma has worked with many patient groups in her research, including older people, disabled people, those who suffer chronic diseases, and those who live with mental health problems. Her scholarly work focuses on the theory and practice of responsive evaluation, patient participation and empowerment, and care ethics.

Vivianne E. Baur is a researcher at the Department of Medical Humanities, VU University Medical Centre and EMGO+ research institute for health and primary care research in Amsterdam. She is involved in several responsive evaluation and participatory action research projects on client participation in long-term care institutions and in communities. Her work focuses on dialogical learning processes, partnership development, empowerment, and collective action.

Katrina L. Bledsoe is a research scientist and senior evaluation specialist at the Education Development Center, Inc. (EDC) in Washington, DC. Bledsoe received her doctoral degree in 2003 from Claremont Graduate University in psychology with a concentration in applied social psychology and specialization in evaluation. She is a trained evaluator, mixed methodologist, and social psychologist with almost twenty years of evaluation experience at the local, state, and federal government levels. Her expertise is in applied social psychology, community-based and social services program evaluation and evaluation research, and cultural contexts. She has worked in community-based settings with cultural communities, using theory-driven evaluation, culturally responsive evaluation, as well as other participatory evaluation approaches such as transformative evaluation.

Timothy J. Cash is a PhD candidate in educational psychology at the University of Illinois, Urbana-Champaign. From 2009 to 2013, he was managing editor of the *American Journal of Evaluation*.

Jill Anne Chouinard is an assistant professor in the Department of Educational Research Methodology at the University of North Carolina at Greensboro. Her main interests in evaluation are in cross-cultural approaches and the use of participatory evaluation processes as leverage for social change. She received her PhD in organizational studies and evaluation in 2010 from the University of Ottawa and continues to teach there at the Faculty of Education. She has published several articles and books on cross-cultural evaluation and participatory approaches.

J. Bradley Cousins is a professor of evaluation at the Faculty of Education, University of Ottawa, and Director of CRECS. Cousins's main interests in program evaluation include participatory and collaborative approaches, use, and capacity building. He received his PhD in educational measurement and evaluation from the University of Toronto in 1988. Throughout his career he has received several awards for his work in evaluation, including the "Contribution to Evaluation in Canada" award (CES, 1999), the Paul F. Lazarsfeld award for theory in evaluation (AEA, 2008) and the AERA Research on Evaluation "Distinguished Scholar Award" (2011). He has published many articles and books on evaluation and was editor of the *Canadian Journal of Program Evaluation* from 2002 to 2010.

George F. Grob is president, Center for Public Program Evaluation, an evaluation company focusing on evaluation, public policy, strategic planning, and communications. His work has spanned the fields of health, human development services, housing, international development, and the environment. Before forming his independent evaluation consultancy, Grob was director of planning and policy coordination and later deputy inspector general for evaluation and inspections at the US Department of Health and Human Services. Immediately before retiring from federal service, he was executive director of the Citizens' Healthcare Working Group, a congressionally established commission charged with developing options for health care reform based on citizen input. Most recently he served as deputy inspector general for evaluation at the Federal

Housing Finance Agency. He received his MA in mathematics at Georgetown University.

Stuart Hanson is research manager for the Center for Applied Local Research in Richmond, California. He has extensive policy and evaluation research experience in the fields of disability, mental health, health care finance and delivery, and social services. He is also a lecturer in the Department of Social Work at California State University East Bay, where he teaches qualitative and quantitative research methods.

Jean A. King is a distinguished teaching professor in the Department of Organizational Leadership, Policy and Development at the University of Minnesota, where she coordinates the all-university Program Evaluation minor and serves as director of the Minnesota Evaluation Studies Institute (MESI). A sought-after presenter and long-time writer on evaluation topics, she is the author of numerous articles, chapters, and reviews. She led the team that developed the Essential Competencies for Program Evaluators, and her most recent book, *Interactive Evaluation Practice* (with Laurie Stevahn), was published in 2013. King has received several awards for her work, including the Myrdal Award for Evaluation Practice and the Ingle Award for Extraordinary Service from the American Evaluation Association, three teaching awards, and three community service awards.

Norma Martínez-Rubin is a public health practitioner, independent evaluation consultant, occasional lecturer, and trainer. As an evaluator, she applies her formal training and experience from a public health career with responsibilities in program planning, design and evaluation, contract management, quality improvement, and supervision. She has been a staff member as well as external consultant for county, state, and national projects aimed at improving the quality of health and human services at the local level. Her interests include the use of evaluation findings to assist program managers and policy makers in improving quality of services for vulnerable and underserved populations. A native Californian, Martínez-Rubin is pleased that a bilingual and bicultural upbringing has heightened her professional reach.

Michael Quinn Patton is an independent evaluation consultant based in Minnesota. He is former president of the American

Evaluation Association (AEA). He has authored six evaluation books, including a fourth edition of *Utilization-Focused Evaluation* and a third edition of *Qualitative Research and Evaluation Methods*. He is recipient of the Alva and Gunnar Myrdal Award for "outstanding contributions to evaluation use and practice" and the Paul F. Lazarsfeld Award for lifetime contributions to evaluation theory, both from the AEA. The Society for Applied Sociology honored him with the Lester F. Ward Award for Outstanding Contributions to Applied Sociology. His latest book is *Developmental Evaluation: Applying Complexity Concepts to Enhance Innovation and Use*.

Sharon F. Rallis is the Dwight W. Allen Distinguished Professor of Education Policy and Reform in the College of Education of the University of Massachusetts–Amherst, where she teaches courses in inquiry, program evaluation, qualitative methods, and organizational theory. The 2005 president of the American Evaluation Association, Rallis has been involved with evaluation for over three decades. She has conducted evaluations of educational, medical, and social programs, and her research and evaluation work has taken her throughout the United States and the world, including China, Canada, Afghanistan, Palestine, and Turkey. Her eleven published books, several of which have been translated into other languages, draw on her experience as a researcher and evaluator. *Learning in the Field: An Introduction to Qualitative Research* (Sage Publications, written with Gretchen Rossman), is in its third edition and is widely used in methodology courses. Rallis has also published extensively in various evaluation journals or books and is currently editor of the *American Journal of Evaluation*.

Thomas A. Schwandt is professor of educational psychology at the University of Illinois, Urbana-Champaign. He has written widely on philosophical and methodological issues in qualitative inquiry and on its use in evaluation. He is editor emeritus of the *American Journal of Evaluation* and the author of the *Dictionary of Qualitative Inquiry* (Sage Publications).

Laurie Stevahn is professor, chair, and director of the educational leadership doctoral program in the College of Education at Seattle University. She earned her doctorate in educational psychology from the University of Minnesota and teaches graduate courses in research methods, evaluation practice, organization development, and leadership for social justice. Her research focuses on constructive cooperation, competition, and conflict resolution grounded by social interdependence theory and on identifying and validating essential competencies for program evaluators across diverse contexts. Stevahn has published on these topics in such journals as the *American Educational Research Journal*, *American Journal of Evaluation*, *Journal of Social Psychology*, and others. She also is coauthor of several books, including the most recent titled *Interactive Evaluation Practice: Mastering the Interpersonal Dynamics of Program Evaluation*. In addition to her work with organizations across the United States, Stevahn's international work includes invited presentations in Australia, Canada, Mexico, England, Greece, Italy, the Czech Republic, and the Netherlands.

ACKNOWLEDGMENTS

Without Andy Pasternack at Jossey-Bass this book never would have been started. Over breakfasts at conferences and on conference calls, Andy provided support and guidance as we developed our ideas. Just as important, Andy gave us realistic feedback when we needed to be corralled. His generosity and vision made this work possible. We are so glad to have known him, and we miss him.

Without Seth Schwartz, this book never would have been completed. A million thanks to Seth for taking over from Andy and remaining patient while we worked with the chapter authors, survived multiple rounds of edits, and asked a million questions.

Reviewers Ann Dozier, Oliver T. Massey, and Sandra Mathison provided thoughtful and constructive comments on the complete draft manuscript.

QUALITATIVE INQUIRY IN EVALUATION

1

THE INTERSECTION OF QUALITATIVE INQUIRY AND EVALUATION APPROACHES

Programs are designed by people; they are implemented by people; they affect the lives of participants and the viability of communities; and they often are supported by people who care deeply about the issues addressed by the program. Perhaps because the common denominator of any program is the human element, qualitative inquiry has been intentionally incorporated into the practice of evaluation over the past several decades. Program stakeholders, including people who financially support evaluations, often ask questions that go beyond simple assessments of program goals and objectives. Stakeholders also want answers to *how* and *why* questions. They are interested in improving the program, learning for whom and in what settings the program works best, and understanding how a particular program experience can inform policy. *How* and *why* questions require evaluation approaches that capture complexity and nuanced individual perceptions. Enter qualitative inquiry in the practice of evaluation.

A key to gaining confidence and prowess in the practice of evaluation, particularly evaluations that use qualitative inquiry, is to enter the field with a solid theoretical and methodological foundation. Part 1 of this volume begins with an overview of the origins and rationale of incorporating qualitative inquiry into the practice of evaluation. The remaining chapters focus on a few prominent evaluation approaches that provide critical direction and guideposts for the professional practice of evaluation. Although not an exhaustive examination of all the evaluation approaches that incorporate qualitative inquiry, each chapter illustrates the critical role that qualitative inquiry plays within a particular evaluation framework, including some evaluation approaches that are not necessarily associated with qualitative inquiry.

1

The Origins, Meaning, and Significance of Qualitative Inquiry in Evaluation

Thomas A. Schwandt and Timothy J. Cash

Key Ideas

- The definition of qualitative evaluation has been constantly contested. Several narrative accounts exist of the genesis of qualitative inquiry; each sets a particular framework for the introduction of qualitative inquiry and establishes its role in the development of program evaluation.

- The move to incorporate qualitative evaluation into the lexicon was, in some ways, a response to educational researchers' failures to demonstrate program effects using experimental designs and came on the heels of Cronbach's (1963) call for evaluators to "reconceptualize evaluation."

- Influenced by anthropology and sociology, qualitative evaluation brought new approaches to understanding human actions and meaning making to evaluation.

- Qualitative evaluation relies on methods used to generate qualitative data (e.g., interviewing, observation, focus groups, document review) and makes use of such reporting conventions as narratives, stories, and case studies.

■ Qualitative evaluation prioritizes value pluralism and considers both the stakeholders' values and the evaluator's values.

■ Within qualitative evaluation, an evaluation is more about social communication than about technical reporting.

This chapter sets the stage for subsequent chapters that discuss how qualitative inquiry is related to prominent evaluation approaches and how those who conduct and are committed to the practice of qualitative inquiry view several critical issues in evaluation practice. The chapter is meant as preliminary in the sense of a beginning or general orientation to key issues involved with the origins, meaning, and significance of qualitative evaluation; it is not an exhaustive examination of these issues. The chapter begins with two brief sections—the first presents a perspective on ways in which qualitative evaluation originated; the second discusses the contested definition of the term *qualitative evaluation*. The third section identifies what, in our view, are important contributions of the extensive literature in qualitative inquiry in evaluation to shaping the practice of evaluation.

THE GENESIS OF QUALITATIVE EVALUATION

Some notable narratives over the past three decades describe the advent and development of qualitative inquiry in the field of evaluation in several unique ways (e.g., Campbell, 1984; Conner, Altman, & Jackson, 1984; Guba & Lincoln, 1987; Madaus & Stufflebeam, 2000; Patton, 1975; Rossi & Wright, 1987; Scriven, 1984). Madaus, Scriven, and Stufflebeam (1983) argued that qualitative evaluation was one of many new conceptualizations of evaluation that arose in the late 1960s and early 1970s, primarily in the field of education. These developments followed on the heels of Cronbach's (1963) call for educational evaluators to "turn away from their penchant for post hoc evaluations based on comparisons of norm-referenced test scores of experimental and control groups" and to "reconceptualize evaluation—not in terms of a horse race between competing programs but as a process of gathering and reporting information that could help guide curriculum development" (cited in Madaus, Scriven, &

Stufflebeam, 1983, p. 12). Similarly, Guba (1969) pointed to what he called the failure of educational evaluation, arguing "the application of conventional experimental design to evaluation situations . . . conflicts with the principle that evaluation should facilitate the continuous improvement of a program" (p. 8).

For some scholars, the advent of qualitative inquiry in evaluation was inspired in large part by the failure of attempts to demonstrate the effects of Title I projects (funded by the Education and Secondary Education Act of 1964) using experimental designs. For Rossi and Wright (1987, p. 59), the introduction of qualitative evaluation was an "intellectual consequence . . . of [the] close-to-zero effects" of the social programs of the 1960s and 1970s. A strong critic of the national evaluation of Follow Through (an extension of the Head Start Program), begun in 1967 as a planned variation experiment, wrote:

> We will not use the antiseptic assumptions of the research laboratory to compare children receiving new program assistance with those not receiving such aid. We recognize that the comparisons have never been productive, nor have they facilitated corrective action. The overwhelming number of evaluations conducted in this way have shown no significant differences between "experimental" and "control" groups. (Provus, 1971, p. 12)

Greene (2000) claimed that constructivist, qualitative approaches to evaluation emerged against the backdrop of several intellectual and social developments in the 1970s in the United States, including the "dethroning of experimental science as the paradigm for social program evaluation" (p. 992); a decline in the authority accorded social science theory; a decline in the authority of political figures in view of the Vietnam War, Watergate, and so on; and increased interest in value pluralism.

For Guba and Lincoln (1981, 1987, 1989; Lincoln & Guba, 1985; Guba, 1978) and Patton (1975), qualitative evaluation is about the birth (or perhaps discovery) in the 1970s of a new paradigm for evaluation derived from fieldwork methods in anthropology and qualitative sociology and from a strong interest in appropriating insights of the Verstehen tradition in German sociology. Scholars in that tradition held that understanding the actions of human beings as uniquely meaning-making creatures required methods different from those used to study the behavior of nonhuman objects. Lincoln and Guba (1985) initially called this new paradigm "naturalistic inquiry" and later refined it as responsive constructivist evaluation or "fourth-generation evaluation" (Guba & Lincoln, 1989). They claimed that three prior generations of evaluation (characterized as measurement, description, and judgment) were beset by several serious problems—a tendency toward managerialism, a failure to accommodate value pluralism, and an over-commitment to a scientific paradigm of inquiry. They argued that the fourth generation addresses these problems and offers a salutary alternative.

Each of these narratives presents a different understanding of the development of program evaluation and the role qualitative inquiry has played in that story. Each employs a particular framework for shaping its account of the introduction and development of qualitative evaluation. Each provides a partial perspective on how it is that qualitative approaches arose in the broad field of evaluation. The strongest reaction to the dominance of experimental and psychometric traditions in evaluation in the 1960s and 1970s came from scholars in education who were initially trained in those traditions, including Robert Stake, Egon Guba, Lee Cronbach, and others.

The history of qualitative evaluation has often been portrayed as a struggle between different methodologies and methods or of fundamental epistemological disagreements between, for example, strong empiricists and interpretivists or post-positivists and social constructionists. These accounts are accurate to the extent that they reflect the dominance of experimental methods and the hypothetico-deductive paradigm found in texts discussing evaluation research in the late 1960s and 1970s, (e.g., Bernstein & Freeman, 1975; Reicken & Boruch, 1974; Rossi & Williams, 1972; Suchman, 1967).

Guba and Lincoln are unique in interpreting the appearance and development of qualitative evaluation as a narrative of progression or generations (although a similar idea has been advanced by Denzin and Lincoln [1994] regarding the development of qualitative research in the social sciences more generally). We are more skeptical of this way of viewing the genesis of qualitative evaluation, for there is a modernist narrative of progress implicit in the movement from one "generation" of evaluation to the next. Our thinking about evaluation may indeed develop over time—for example, an enlargement on, improvement in, rejection of, or expansion on concepts and ideas—but earlier generations of evaluation thinking are still very active and still very much in dialogue with one another. One generation has not ceased to exist or completely given way to another.

An engaging, intellectual history of the advent and development of qualitative inquiry in the field of evaluation in the United States has yet to be written. Such a history would have to account for more than the methods wars or paradigm wars characteristic of several explanations. It would trace the influence that debates both within and outside the social sciences had on how the field of evaluation took shape, developed its multiple perspectives on what constitutes legitimate approaches to evaluation, wrestled with the politics of knowledge construction, and defined the role of professional evaluation expertise in contemporary society. Developing such an account is not our purpose here. After a brief discussion of definitions of qualitative evaluation, we offer a modest version of three sets of ideas that have their origins in the work of early proponents of the importance of qualitative inquiry in evaluation. These ideas are enduring contributions affecting the way many evaluators aim to practice what is often called qualitative evaluation.

WHAT IS QUALITATIVE EVALUATION?

The term *qualitative evaluation,* as with most terms, from its advent in the language of evaluation (e.g., Fetterman, 1988) has been constantly contested terrain and not readily definable, because "the meaning one adopts for terms is heavily dependent on the social theory or theories that guide the use of those terms, even [between] those who use the same term" (Lincoln & Guba, 2004, p. 226). To illustrate this point, Lincoln and Guba (2004) offered the term *accountability* as an example of the many meanings a single word can take. Two people using the word may have in mind different standards for judging what accountability means, vastly different audiences, as well as vastly different social and political contexts (see also the two uses of the term in Biesta, 2004). Given that the evaluation field is filled with scholars from diverse disciplinary backgrounds who bring with them different social theories (as well as social locations and perspectives), no wonder the terms *qualitative evaluation* and *qualitative research* are difficult to define. Schwandt's (2007) *Dictionary of Qualitative Inquiry* is evidence of this view. He offered commentary on some 380 words and phrases that are part of the vocabulary of qualitative research generally and argued that the language constituting the aim, methods, and significance of the multiple practices of qualitative research is constantly being reinterpreted.

Testimony to the fact that qualitative evaluation is not easily definable is apparent when one considers that a popular textbook on evaluation (Fitzpatrick, Sanders, & Worthen, 2011) and a comprehensive review of twenty-six approaches to conducting evaluation (Stufflebeam & Shinkfield, 2007) do not contain an entry for the term in their respective indexes. The former book indexes the term *qualitative research* in reference to a discussion of methods for gathering qualitative data. Both books do, however, discuss two ways of thinking about evaluation that are often identified as qualitative—Stake's responsive evaluation approach (2004) and Guba and Lincoln's naturalistic, constructivist, fourth-generation approach. The former book treats both as instances of participant-oriented approaches to evaluation; the latter treats each as examples of social agenda and advocacy approaches.

In his *Evaluation Thesaurus,* Scriven (1991) construed the term *qualitative evaluation* as follows:

> A substantial part of good evaluation (of personnel and products as well as programs) is wholly or chiefly qualitative, meaning that description and interpretation make up all or most of it. . . Qualitative evaluation is not a "thing in itself" but rather a complement to quantitative methods, to be combined with them when and to the extent appropriate. (p. 293)

Taking a cue from Scriven's definition, we might consider the term *qualitative evaluation* from the point of view of method—the procedures used in a particular inquiry. In this sense, an evaluation is qualitative to the extent that it relies principally on methods used to generate qualitative data, such as unstructured interviewing, field observation, focus groups, document analysis, and so on, and analyzes and interprets those data by nonstatistical means such as analytic induction, comparative analysis, thematic analysis, taxonomies, typologies, discourse analysis, narrative analysis, qualitative content analysis, and so on. Qualitative evaluation also, generally, makes use of reporting formats particularly suited to presenting qualitative data, including narratives, stories, case studies, and in some cases, performance texts (texts that are dialogic, multivocal) and performance art (e.g., visual displays, sociodrama). For example, in his "Qualitative Evaluation Checklist," Patton (2003) noted that qualitative evaluations often derive their data from fieldwork observations to describe activities, behaviors, actions, conversations, interpersonal interactions, and organizational or community processes, as well as open-ended interviewing to generate in-depth responses on the experiences, perceptions, feelings, and knowledge of individuals involved in an evaluation. He pointed out that these kinds of methods are often used because they yield data that facilitate capturing and telling both the "program's story" and "participants' stories."

However, the use of qualitative data per se in an evaluation does not provide a definitive clue as to the type of evaluation approach being employed. Many evaluations make use of qualitative data. That is fairly commonplace. Even evaluators who strongly defend the importance of using experimental designs to evaluate social interventions argue that qualitative data are necessary (Gorard & Cook, 2007; Smith & Smith, 2009). Making use of methods to gather and analyze qualitative data may be necessary for defining an evaluation as "qualitative," but it is not sufficient. This is so because many qualitative evaluations do not rely exclusively on qualitative data. Consider, for example, this argument from Lincoln and Guba (2004):

> Please note that while some individuals think that constructivist evaluation or research is about qualitative methods or utilizes only qualitative methods, this is quite simply not true, at least as we have 'constructed' the paradigm. . . Naturalistic and constructivist evaluators utilize whatever methods best collect the data that answer one or another specific question. . . It is our contention that constructivist evaluation utilizes whatever data have authentic meaning for the question at hand, whether qualitative or quantitative. (p. 233)

Thus, method choice is clearly not the sole determinant of whatever one identifies as qualitative evaluation.

When considered from the point of view of methodology—a framework of assumptions and principles for how a particular approach to inquiry should proceed—defining qualitative evaluation becomes even more complicated. A number of approaches to evaluation are possible, including educational connoisseurship and criticism, case study evaluation, responsive evaluation, illuminative evaluation, naturalistic inquiry or fourth-generation evaluation, appreciative inquiry, feminist evaluation, culturally responsive evaluation, and variants of participatory and collaborative evaluation. Each draws heavily on the methods noted above but does not necessarily share the same methodological characteristics and assumptions about what constitutes significant evaluation knowledge and how it is to be established and warranted. The approaches differ in important ways in their assumptions about the nature of knowledge, the politics of knowledge production, and the responsibility and role of the inquirer/evaluator. This suggests that qualitative evaluation is perhaps, more or less, a family of approaches comprising relatives that do not always agree but generally are happy to share a common name.

Some of these approaches may endorse (either explicitly or tacitly) a form of social and cognitive constructionism (Greene, 2000; Guba & Lincoln, 1989). Social constructionism is the view that "the actions, artifacts, and events of everyday life depend (to some degree) for their identity, intelligibility, stability, and consequences on collective practices, conventions, and representations" (Heap, 1995, p. 52). Cognitive constructionism is the view that the identity, stability, and so on of these aspects of everyday life depend (to some degree) "on cognitive representations (plans, schemata, goals, processing rules) and processes as enabled and constrained by cognitive architecture" (p. 52). Constructionists, in brief, hold that we do not discover the meaning of actions, events, or concepts such as deviance, disability, identity, gender, race, selfhood, and so on, but rather we construct or make meaning against a backdrop of shared understandings, language, and practices. This kind of constructionism is opposed to a version of realism that assumes that our knowledge is a reflection or mirror of what is out there in the world. However, neither a necessary nor an irrevocable connection exists between the use of qualitative methods as discussed and a social constructionist way of thinking. In other words, evaluators can quite readily and reasonably make observations and conduct interviews—look, see, and record—even if they are realists and believe that they are recording the way things "really are."

Despite their differences, all members of the family called qualitative evaluation share what Stake (2004, p. 30) has called a "naturalistic disposition" or "persuasion" to value "ordinary activities in their settings." Patton (2003) similarly speaks of naturalistic inquiry as being about studying a program "as it unfolds naturally and openly, that is, without a predetermined focus or [predetermined] categories of analysis" (p. 3). This disposition can be elaborated to include:

- A concern for programs and projects being evaluated as multifaceted, complex compositions of the experiences of those individuals and groups most strongly influenced or affected by the program or project; experiences are permeated with meaning (perceptions, understandings, judgments)

- A concern with capturing the diachronic (historical or long-term) and synchronic (specific point in time) character of program and project activity

- A strong interest in grasping the views and voices of people associated with that activity via rich description and explanation of processes occurring in local contexts (Schwandt & Burgon, 2006).

ENDURING CONTRIBUTIONS

We have already identified a shared disposition among members of the family of qualitative evaluation. Here we single out prominent commitments that further shape the way in which those who subscribe to the importance of qualitative inquiry practice evaluation. The emphasis here is primarily on decisions made in practice, where practice is understood not as a site or location where theory or abstract concepts are applied but as engaged, "embodied, materially mediated arrays of human activity centrally organized around shared practical understanding" (Schatzki, 2001, p. 2). Although we do not subscribe to a sharp theory–practice divide (Schwandt, 2002, 2006), we do not concern ourselves here with an examination of philosophical or, more specifically, epistemological commitments as much as with decisions that orient the way an evaluation is crafted and conducted.

The "shared practical understanding" of many advocates of qualitative inquiry in evaluation is reflected in ways an evaluation is focused, values are understood, and an evaluation is communicated. Given the preliminary nature of this chapter, we do not tackle the considerable literature that involves extensions, commentary, and critical appraisal of these commitments.

Focusing an Evaluation

Patton (2008, p. 229) noted that the act of focusing an evaluation involves answering the question of "what's worth knowing," and he emphasized that many different answers to that question can be legitimately posed in evaluation, including, was the program effective, were objectives achieved, what intended (and unintended) outcomes occurred, how was a program implemented, were resources used appropriately, what is the relation between program costs and outcomes, and so on.

Broadly speaking, three signature responses to "what's worth knowing" occur for many who practice qualitative forms of evaluation. For those evaluators committed to forms of ethnographic evaluation guided by anthropological theory (Dorr-Bremme, 1985; Fetterman & Pittman, 1986; Hopson, 2002), "what's worth knowing" relates to understanding a program's culture. For many evaluators influenced by responsive evaluation, "what's worth knowing" are issues. Stake (2004) explained:

> Issues are regularly taken to be "conceptual organizers" for the investigation, more so than needs, objectives, hypotheses, group comparisons, and cost–benefit ratios. Issues are obstacles, organizational perplexities, and social problems, drawing attention especially to unanticipated responsibilities and side effects. With the term issues, we try to draw thinking toward the interactivity, particularity, and subjective valuing felt by persons associated with the program. (p. 209)

For evaluators more attuned to constructivist, fourth-generation evaluation, issues not only take on a somewhat different meaning from that found in Stake's responsive evaluation, but also claims and concerns become important aspects of what's worth knowing as well. Guba and Lincoln (1989) explained:

> A claim is any assertion that a stakeholder may introduce that is favorable to the evaluand, for example, that a particular mode of reading instruction will result in more than a year's gain in standard test reading scores for every year of classroom use, or that a particular mode of handling domestic disturbance calls by police will materially reduce recidivism in offenders. A concern is any assertion that a stakeholder may introduce that is unfavorable to the evaluand, for example, that instruction in the use of a computer materially reduces pupils' ability to do computations by hand . . . [and] an issue is any state of affairs about which reasonable persons may disagree, for example, the introduction of education about AIDS into elementary schools . . . Different stakeholders will harbor different claims, concerns, and issues; it is the task of the evaluator to ferret these out and to address them in the evaluation. (p. 40)

Both responsive evaluation and fourth-generation evaluation clearly welcome a plurality of stakeholder views. However, as noted later, a difference is seen in the way that plurality is addressed. Responsive evaluation regards multiple perspectives, more or less, as the conceptual structure that the evaluator uses to portray the program in question. Fourth-generation evaluation puts these perspectives into dialogue with one another in the process of conducting the evaluation.

Individuals practicing qualitative forms of evaluation employ these broadly responsive and cultural orientations in different ways. For example, Abma (2006) has incorporated Stake's idea of responsiveness with Guba and Lincoln's emphasis on a strong view of stakeholder participation and the manner in which an evaluation can (should) facilitate dialogue and action among stakeholders. She frames evaluation as "an engagement with and among all stakeholders about the meaning of their practice. Responsive evaluation focuses on stakeholder issues and engages stakeholders in dialogues about the quality of their practice. The aim is to heighten the personal and mutual understanding of stakeholders as a vehicle for practice improvement" (Abma, 2006, p. 31). (See Chapter 7 of this volume to learn how Vivianne

Baur and Tineke Abma facilitated dialogue and action to address power differences.)

Culturally responsive evaluation (Hood & Rosenstein, 2005), another form of evaluation that makes heavy use of qualitative inquiry, also is oriented in this way, although it argues that being responsive to issues, concerns, and experiences of stakeholders in cultures other than one's own is an epistemological, ethical, and political challenge.

In response to claims, concerns, and issues of stakeholders most closely associated with a program, qualitative evaluators are primarily interested in gathering the subjective perceptions of what is going on with respect to a program. In this instance, *subjective* does not mean biased or unreliable (a common use of the word). Rather, subjective is used to indicate that these perceptions come from the subject—they represent the personal view of an individual or the subject's point of view based on his or her (or their) historical, political, cultural, social, material lived experience. Typically this kind of information is gathered via qualitative methods such as interviewing and focus groups, although collecting such information via surveys and questionnaires is also possible.

Valuing in Evaluation

Grasping the multiple perspectives of key stakeholders in an evaluation inevitably involves the qualitative evaluator in understanding the values associated with those perspectives. As Stake (2004) has expressed it, "responsive evaluation recognizes multiple sources of valuing and multiple grounds" (p. 210). Qualitative evaluations are inherently concerned not simply with the facts of the matter (what happened, when, to whom, how often, and so forth). They are also concerned with values, including making the evaluator's own value commitments recognizable as well as "helping stakeholders articulate their values, considering the values inherent in the evaluation, and working to portray the program through different stakeholders' perspectives" (Fitzpatrick, Sanders, & Worthen, 2011, p. 116).

Generally speaking, qualitative evaluators adopt a stance of value pluralism (Berlin, 1990), which is a belief that genuine values are many and may, and often do, come into conflict with one another. Endorsing value pluralism means acceptance of the heterogeneity of values and ways of knowing that characterize everyday life and the practices of teaching, learning, managing, leading, providing health and human services, and the like in which we find ourselves embedded. Pluralism stands in opposition to a monist view that only one set of values or one way of knowing is correct, true, and valid; all others are incorrect, false, and invalid. It also opposes a relativist view, which holds that my values or way of knowing are mine, yours are yours, and neither of us can claim to be right.

For some evaluators, pluralism is about finding ways to orchestrate, juxtapose, and place into a coherent, engaging conversation multiple views. Just how that is to be done is the subject of considerable debate among those who endorse a qualitative view of evaluation. In their model of constructivist, fourth-generation evaluation, Guba and Lincoln (1989) argued for a process they labeled the hermeneutic dialectic circle, in which evaluators and stakeholders confront each other's constructions. They explained that

> Using what Stake called "portrayals," various aspects of the program are displayed, explained, explored from multiple perspectives, and stakeholders invited to comment or elaborate upon, correct, amend, extend, or otherwise make more accurate or precise the information, data, and interpretations. . . . The constant interaction . . . is what makes this model hermeneutic. Such interaction creates new knowledge, and permits old or taken-for-granted knowledge to be elaborated, refined, and tested. The dialectic of this evaluation model is the focus on carefully bringing to the fore the conflict inherent in value pluralism. (Lincoln & Guba, 2004, p. 235)

Lincoln and Guba (2004, p. 235) claimed that getting at "core values of participants and stakeholders" is necessary "so that when decisions are made, the value commitments that those decisions represent are clear, negotiable, and negotiated between and among stakeholders." Although not fully endorsing all of the assumptions of Lincoln and Guba's constructivist approach to evaluation, House and Howe (1999) argued similarly that value pluralism is best addressed through a process of democratic deliberation in which both facts and values are debated. House (2005, p. 220) stressed that such a process "aspires to arrive at unbiased conclusions by considering all relevant interests, values, and perspectives; by engaging in extended dialogue with major stakeholders; and by promoting extensive deliberation about the study's conclusion."

Other broadly qualitative approaches to evaluation, such as empowerment evaluation (Fetterman, Kaftarain, & Wandersman, 1996) and transformative evaluation (Mertens, 2008), argue strongly for privileging the voices of the least advantaged individuals and groups with a stake in a program being evaluated. One distinction among practitioners of qualitative evaluation (and all practitioners of evaluation, for that matter) is whether they adopt a descriptive or prescriptive approach to valuing. In a descriptive approach, an evaluator

> Describes values held by stakeholders, determines criteria they use in judging program worth, finds out if stakeholders think the program is good, and sees what they think should be done to improve it. The claim is not that these values are the best but that they are perceptions of program worth that are grist for the mill of decision making" (Shadish, Cook, & Leviton, 1991, p. 49).

A prescriptive theory of valuing argues that some value perspectives are more important than others.

Another dimension of valuing in evaluation is specifically concerned with the evaluator's own value stance. Again, broadly speaking, evaluators committed to qualitative inquiry in evaluation are highly critical of a stance of value neutrality on the part of the evaluator—the view that evaluators (and social scientists, more generally) should concentrate on improving methods for generating descriptions and explanations and leave questions of valuing to others. They freely acknowledge that the evaluator brings to an evaluation his or her own value commitments and perspectives and that evaluation itself, as a social practice, embodies particular political and moral commitments. Transformative evaluation, culturally responsive evaluation, and Greene's (2006) thinking about the relationships among evaluation, democracy, and social justice are all illustrative of this idea.

Communicating an Evaluation

Early critics of the dominance of experimental and psychometric methods in evaluation often opposed the use of these methods on the grounds that the kinds of data collected and reported were simply not useful to helping those most intimately involved with a program better understand what was happening in the program and how it might be improved. The reporting was often so technically sophisticated that the experience of what the program was actually like for those involved with it was obscured or completely lost. Although a concern with use permeates all forms of evaluation, qualitative inquiry in evaluation strongly emphasizes that an evaluation is less an act of technical reporting and more an act of social communication. This idea is clearly evident in Guba and Lincoln's view of how information is shared with stakeholders, as noted previously.

In a keynote presentation at a conference on "New Trends in Evaluation" in October 1973, at the Institute of Education at Göteborg University, Stake (1974) was highly critical of approaches to educational evaluation that he labeled "preordinate," which relied on a statement of program goals and objectives, the use of objective tests as the primary means of collecting data, on standards held by program personnel, and on research-type reports. He argued that his idea of responsive evaluation is less reliant on formal communication and more reliant on natural communication. He added:

> We need a reporting procedure for facilitating vicarious experience. And it is available. Among the better evangelists, anthropologists, and dramatists are those who have developed the art of storytelling. We need to portray complexity. We need to convey holistic impression, the mood, even the mystery of the experience. The program staff or people in the community may be 'uncertain.' The audiences should feel that uncertainty. More ambiguity rather than less may be needed in our reports. (p. 12)

The central idea here is that evaluation reporting should be a means of enhancing understandings of a program across the principal stakeholders in that program. More recently, Stake

(2004) has explained that responsive evaluation reports are "expected to be, in format and language, informative and comprehensible to the various audiences. . . Thus even at the risk of catering, different reports or presentations may be prepared for different groups. Narrative portrayals, storytelling, and verbatim testimony will be appropriate for some, data banks and regression analyses for others" (p. 213). The preference of many evaluators committed to qualitative inquiry in evaluation for case-study forms of reporting that heavily emphasize careful description and detail is consonant with this way of thinking about evaluation as a form of social communication. Consider, for example, this definition drawn from a US General Accounting Office (1990) report: "A case study is a method for learning about a complex instance, based on a comprehensive understanding of that instance obtained by extensive description and analysis of that instance taken as a whole and in its context."

CONCLUSION

This brief description of what qualitative inquiry means for the practice of evaluation is intended to be more illustrative and generative of further thought than definitive. A full explanation of the role that qualitative inquiry plays in evaluation would require examining the many evaluation approaches that make use of qualitative inquiry and investigating how these approaches address, for example, evaluation purpose and evaluator roles and responsibilities. We have endeavored to illustrate the complexity behind how qualitative inquiry came to be regarded as a significant dimension of evaluation theory and practice. Likewise, we have cautioned that no simple exercise in defining terms can capture what it means to endorse the importance of qualitative inquiry in evaluation. Much more remains to be said about how the theory and practice of qualitative inquiry in evaluation rests on important issues in the epistemology, politics, and ethics of evaluation theory and practice. Those caveats considered, we believe this chapter serves as a preliminary look at what the practice of qualitative evaluation entails. It is reasonable to believe that the family of evaluators committed to the value of qualitative evaluation does in fact share the general orientations we have identified.

KEY CONCEPTS

Constructivism

Continuous improvement

Culturally responsive
evaluation

Deliberation

Descriptive

Empiricists

Epistemology

Evaluand

Experimental designs

Fourth-generation evaluation

Interpretivists

Naturalistic inquiry

Post-positivists

Prescriptive

Qualitative evaluation

Qualitative inquiry

Responsive evaluation

Social constructionists

Subjective

Value pluralism

DISCUSSION QUESTIONS

1. The introduction of qualitative inquiry to evaluation in the
    late 1960s and early 1970s significantly informed and
    expanded the field. How have the values associated with
    qualitative inquiry influenced the field of evaluation?

2. The authors describe the importance of storytelling to
    portray the complexity of a program. Discuss various ways
    that an evaluator can write a formal report that "tells the
    story" of the program in a manner that is meaningful,
    interesting, and useful to the sponsor of an evaluation.

3. The authors discuss the concept of "what's worth knowing"
    for evaluators who practice qualitative inquiry in evaluation.
    They present the information from the perspective of the
    evaluator. How might an evaluator navigate a situation in
    which the evaluator thinks one thing is worth knowing, but
    the funder thinks something else is worth knowing?

REFERENCES

Abma, T. (2006). The practice and politics of responsive evaluation. *American Journal of Evaluation*, *27*(1), 31–43.

Berlin, I. (1990). *Four essays on liberty*. Oxford, UK: Clarendon Press.

Bernstein, I., & Freeman, H. E. (1975). *Academic and entrepreneurial research: Consequences of diversity in federal evaluation studies*. New York, NY: Russell Sage Foundation.

Biesta, G. J. J. (2004). Education, accountability, and the ethical demand: Can the democratic potential of accountability be regained? *Educational Theory*, *54*(3), 233–250.

Campbell, D. T. (1984). Can we be scientific in applied social science? In R. F. Conner, D. G. Altman, & C. Jackson (Eds.), *Evaluation studies review annual* (Vol. 9, pp. 26–48). Beverly Hills, CA: Sage.

Conner, R. F., Altman, D. G., & Jackson, C. (1984). A brave new world for evaluation? In R. F. Conner, D. C. Altman, & C. Jackson (Eds.), *Evaluation studies review annual* (Vol. 9). Beverly Hills, CA: Sage.

Cronbach, L. J. (1963). Course improvements through evaluation. *Teachers College Record*, *64*(8), 672–683.

Denzin, N. K., & Lincoln, Y. S. (Eds.). (1994). *Handbook of qualitative research*. Thousand Oaks, CA: Sage.

Dorr-Bremme, D. W. (1985). Ethnographic evaluation: A theory and method. *Educational Evaluation and Policy Analysis*, *7*(1), 65–83.

Fetterman, D. M. (1988). A qualitative shift in allegiance. In D. M. Fetterman (Ed.), *Qualitative approaches to evaluation in education* (pp. 3–19). New York, NY: Praeger.

Fetterman, D. M., Kaftarain, S., & Wandersman, A. (Eds.). (1996). *Empowerment evaluation: Knowledge and tools for self-assessment and accountability*. Thousand Oaks, CA: Sage.

Fetterman, D. M., & Pittman, M. A. (Eds.). (1986). *Educational evaluation: Ethnography in theory, practice and politics*. Newbury Park, CA: Sage.

Fitzpatrick, J. L., Sanders, J. R., & Worthen, B. R. (2011). *Program evaluation: Alternative approaches and practical guidelines* (4th ed.). Boston, MA: Pearson.

Gorard, S., & Cook, T. (2007). Where does good evidence come from? *International Journal of Research & Method in Education*, *30*(3), 307–323.

Greene, J. C. (2000). Understanding social programs through evaluation. In N. K. Denzin & Y. S. Lincoln (Eds.), *The Sage handbook of qualitative research* (2nd ed., pp. 981–1000). Thousand Oaks, CA: Sage.

Greene, J. C. (2006). Evaluation, democracy and social change. In I. F. Shaw, J. C. Greene, & M. M. Mark (Eds.), *Handbook of evaluation*. London, UK: Sage.

Guba, E. G. (1969). The failure of educational evaluation. *Educational Technology*, *9*, 29–38.

Guba, E. G. (1978). Toward a methodology of naturalistic inquiry in educational evaluation. *CSE monograph series in evaluation* (Vol. 8). Los Angeles, CA: Center for the Study of Evaluation.

Guba, E. G., & Lincoln, Y. S. (1981). *Effective evaluation.* San Francisco, CA: Jossey-Bass.

Guba, E. G., & Lincoln, Y. S. (1987). The countenances of fourth generation evaluation: Description, judgment, and negotiation. In D. S. Cordray & M. W. Lipsey (Eds.), *Evaluation studies annual review* (Vol. 11, pp. 70–88). Beverly Hills, CA: Sage.

Guba, E. G., & Lincoln, Y. S. (1989). *Fourth generation evaluation.* Newbury Park, CA: Sage.

Heap, J. L. (1995). Constructionism in the rhetoric and practice of fourth generation evaluation. *Evaluation and Program Planning*, *18*(1), 51–61.

Hood, S., & Rosenstein, B. (2005). Culturally responsive evaluation. In S. Mathison (Ed.), *Encyclopedia of evaluation.* Los Angeles, CA: Sage.

Hopson, R. M. (2002). Making (more) room at the evaluation table for ethnography. In K. E. Ryan & T. A. Schwandt (Eds.), *Exploring evaluator role and identity.* Greenwich, CT: Information Age Press.

House, E. R. (2005). Deliberative democratic evaluation. In S. Mathison (Ed.), *Encyclopedia of evaluation* (p. 220). Thousand Oaks, CA: Sage.

House, E. R., & Howe, K. R. (1999). *Values in evaluation and social research.* Thousand Oaks, CA: Sage.

Lincoln, Y. S., & Guba, E. G. (1985). *Naturalistic inquiry.* Beverly Hills, CA: Sage.

Lincoln, Y. S., & Guba, E. G. (2004). The roots of fourth generation evaluation: Theoretical and methodological origins. In M. C. Alkin (Ed.), *Evaluation roots: Tracing theorists' views and influences* (pp. 225–241). Thousand Oaks, CA: Sage.

Madaus, G. F., Scriven, M., & Stufflebeam, D. L. (Eds.). (1983). *Evaluation models: Viewpoints on educational and human services evaluation.* Boston, MA: Kluwer-Nijhoff.

Madaus, G. F., & Stufflebeam, D. L. (2000). Program evaluation: A historical overview. In D. L. Stufflebeam, G. F. Madaus, & T. Kellaghan (Eds.), *Evaluation models: Viewpoints on educational and human services evaluation* (pp. 3–18). Norwell, MA: Kluwer Academic Publishers.

Mertens, D. M. (2008). *Transformative research and evaluation.* New York, NY: Guilford Press.

Patton, M. Q. (1975). *Alternative evaluation research paradigm.* Grand Forks, ND: University of North Dakota.

Patton, M. Q. (2003). *Qualitative evaluation checklist.* Available at www.wmich.edu/evalctr/archive_checklists/index.html

Patton, M. Q. (2008). *Utilization-focused evaluation*. Thousand Oaks, CA: Sage.

Provus, M. (1971). *Discrepancy evaluation for educational program improvement and assessment*. Berkeley, CA: McCutchan.

Reicken, H. W., & Boruch, R. F. (1974). *Social experimentation: A method for planning and evaluating social intervention*. New York, NY: Academic Press.

Rossi, P. H., & Williams, W. (Eds.). (1972). *Evaluating social programs: Theory, practice and politics*. New York, NY: Seminar Press.

Rossi, P. H., & Wright, J. D. (1987). Evaluation research: An assessment. In D. S. Cordray & M. W. Lipsey (Eds.), *Evaluation studies annual review* (Vol. 11, pp. 48–69). Beverly Hills, CA: Sage.

Schatzki, T. R. (2001). Introduction: Practice theory. In T. R. Schatzki, K. K. Cetina, & E. Von Savigny (Eds.), *The practice turn in contemporary theory* (pp. 2–14). London, UK: Routledge.

Schwandt, T. A. (2002). *Evaluation practice reconsidered*. New York, NY: Peter Lang.

Schwandt, T. A. (2006, November). Initiation into the theory and practice of evaluation: A commentary on key ideas guiding our thinking. Paper presented at the annual meeting of the American Evaluation Association, Portland, OR.

Schwandt, T. A. (2007). *Dictionary of qualitative inquiry* (3rd ed.). Thousand Oaks, CA: Sage.

Schwandt, T. A., & Burgon, H. (2006). Evaluation and the study of lived experience. In I. F. Shaw, J. C. Greene, & M. M. Mark (Eds.), *Handbook of evaluation: Policies, programs and practices* (pp. 98–117). London, UK: Sage.

Scriven, M. (1984). Evaluation ideologies. In R. F. Conner, D. G. Altman, & C. Jackson (Eds.), *Evaluation studies review annual* (Vol. 9, pp. 49–80). Beverly Hills, CA: Sage.

Scriven, M. (1991). *Evaluation thesaurus*. Thousand Oaks, CA: Sage.

Shadish Jr., W. R., Cook, T. D., & Leviton, L. C. (1991). *Foundations of program evaluation: Theories of practice*. Newbury Park, CA: Sage.

Smith, M. S., & Smith, M. L. (2009). Research in the policy process. In G. Sykes, B. Schneider, & D. N. Plank (Eds.), *Handbook of education policy research* (pp. 372–397). Washington, DC: American Educational Research Association.

Stake, R. E. (1974). Program evaluation, particularly responsive evaluation. Reproduced in W. B. Dockrell & D. Hamilton (Eds.). (1980). *Rethinking educational research*. London, UK: Hodder and Stoughton.

Stake, R. (2004). Stake and responsive evaluation. In M. C. Alkin (Ed.), *Evaluation roots: Tracing theorists' views and influences* (pp. 372–397). Los Angeles, CA: Sage.

Stufflebeam, D. L., & Shinkfield, A. J. (2007). *Evaluation theory, models, and applications*. San Francisco, CA: Jossey-Bass.

Suchman, E. A. (1967). *Evaluative research: Principles and practice in public service and social action programs*. New York, NY: Russell Sage Foundation.

US General Accounting Office. (1990, November). *Case study evaluations. USGAO program evaluation and methodology division*. Washington, DC: Author.

Qualitative Inquiry in Utilization-Focused Evaluation

Michael Quinn Patton

Key Ideas

- Utilization-focused evaluation is highly personal and situational because it addresses how real people in the real world apply evaluation findings.

- The presence of an identifiable individual or group of people who personally care about the evaluation, also known as the *personal factor*, is central to conducting a utilization-focused evaluation.

- Qualitative inquiry is particularly appropriate when a utilization-focused evaluation is conducted for any of the following purposes:

    A focus on quality enhancement

    Documenting the qualitative dimension of program outcomes

    Evaluating individualized outcomes

    Process studies

    Documenting program implementation

    Comparing a program in different contexts

Utilization-focused evaluation begins with the premise that evaluations should be judged by their utility and actual use; therefore, evaluators should facilitate the evaluation process and design any evaluation with careful consideration of how everything that is done, *from beginning to end*, will affect use. Utilization-focused evaluation is concerned with how real people in the real world apply evaluation findings and experience the evaluation process. Therefore, the *focus* in utilization-focused evaluation is on intended use by intended users.

In any evaluation, there are many potential stakeholders and an array of possible uses. Utilization-focused evaluation requires moving from the general and abstract (i.e., possible audiences and potential uses) to the real and specific: actual primary intended users and their explicit commitments to concrete, specific uses. The evaluator facilitates judgment and decision-making by intended users rather than acting solely as a distant, independent judge. Because no evaluation can be value-free, utilization-focused evaluation answers the question of whose values will frame the evaluation by working with clearly identified, primary intended users who have responsibility to apply evaluation findings and implement recommendations. In essence, utilization-focused evaluation is premised on the understanding that evaluation use is too important to be merely desired or assumed. Use must be planned and facilitated.

Utilization-focused evaluation is highly personal and situational. The evaluator develops a working relationship with intended users to help them determine what kind of evaluation they need. This requires negotiation in which the evaluator offers a menu of possibilities. Utilization-focused evaluation does not depend on or advocate any particular evaluation content, model, method, theory, or even use. Rather, it is a process for helping primary intended users select the most appropriate content, model, methods, theory, and uses for their particular situation. Situational responsiveness guides the interactive process between evaluator and primary intended users. As the entries in this book demonstrate, many options are now available in the feast that has become the field of evaluation. In considering the rich and varied menu of evaluation, utilization-focused evaluation can include any evaluative purpose (formative, summative, developmental), any kind of data (quantitative, qualitative, mixed), any kind of design (e.g., naturalistic, experimental), and any kind of focus (processes, outcomes, impacts, costs, and cost–benefit, among many possibilities). Utilization-focused evaluation is a process for making decisions about these issues in collaboration with an identified group of primary users, focusing on their intended uses of evaluation.

For primary intended users to participate in methods and design deliberations and make an informed decision about priority evaluation questions and appropriate methods, the utilization-focused evaluator must be able to present the primary options, their strengths and weaknesses, and what makes them more or less appropriate for the evaluation issues at hand. This means that, first and foremost, qualitative inquiry is always on the menu, and the evaluator needs to understand and be sufficiently proficient at conducting qualitative evaluations to present it as a viable option and explain its particular niche and potential contributions. This chapter focuses on how that is done.

THE FOCUS ON EVALUATION USE AS THE PRIMARY EVALUATION OUTCOME

A psychology of use undergirds and informs utilization-focused evaluation. In essence, research on evaluation use (Patton, 2008) indicates that intended users are more likely to use evaluations if they understand and feel ownership of the evaluation process and findings; they are more likely to understand and feel ownership if they have been actively involved; and by actively involving primary intended users, the evaluator is training users in use, preparing the groundwork for use, and reinforcing the intended utility of the evaluation every step along the way. Although concern about utility drives a utilization-focused evaluation, the evaluator must also attend to the evaluation's accuracy, feasibility, and propriety (Joint Committee on Standards, 1994). Moreover, as a professional, the evaluator has a responsibility to act in accordance with the profession's adopted principles of conducting systematic, data-based inquiries; performing competently; ensuring the honesty and integrity of the entire evaluation process; respecting the people involved in and affected by the evaluation; and being sensitive to the diversity of interests and values that may be related to the general and public welfare (AEA, 2004).

BASIC DEFINITIONS

Program evaluation is the systematic collection of information about the activities, characteristics, and outcomes of programs to make judgments about the program, improve program effectiveness, or inform decisions about future programming. Utilization-focused program evaluation (as opposed to program evaluation in general) is evaluation done for and with specific intended primary users for specific, intended uses.

This general definition has three interrelated components: (1) the systematic collection of information about (2) a potentially broad range of topics (3) for a variety of possible judgments and uses. The definition of utilization-focused evaluation adds the requirement to specify intended use by intended users. This matter of defining evaluation is of considerable import, because different evaluation approaches rest on different definitions. The use-oriented definition offered here contrasts in significant ways with other approaches that define evaluation as measuring goal attainment, providing accountability, or emphasizing the application of social science methods to judge program effectiveness.

INVOLVING INTENDED USERS IN MAKING EVALUATION DECISIONS

Many decisions must be made in any evaluation. The purpose of the evaluation must be determined. Concrete evaluative criteria for judging program success usually will have to be established. Timelines and resources for evaluation must be negotiated. And, of special concern for this book, methods will have to be considered and selected, including the extent to which qualitative methods will be used. Because different methods involve different timelines and require different amounts of resources, for example, qualitative inquiry being especially labor-intensive because of the fieldwork involved, deliberation on and negotiation of these issues cannot be conducted in some simple step-by-step, linear fashion. The issues are interrelated and the negotiations iterative, circling back to consider how later options (such as methods) affect earlier issues (such as priority evaluation questions). All of these are important issues in any evaluation. The question is: Who will decide these issues? The utilization-focused answer is: primary intended users of the evaluation. Figure 2.1 displays these major evaluation issues in relation to each other and the nonlinear, iterative nature of typical design deliberations.

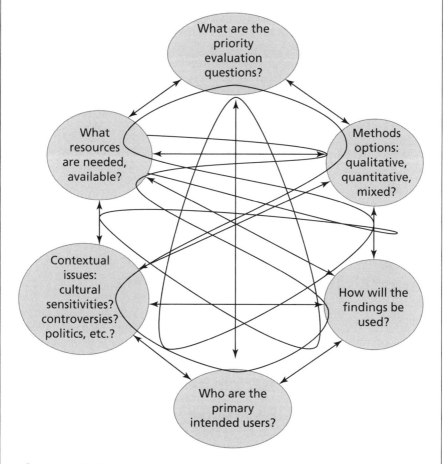

Figure 2.1 **The Iterative and Interdependent Set of Evaluation Questions that Must be Negotiated with Primary Intended Users in a Utilization-Focused Evaluation**

Clearly and explicitly identifying people who can benefit from an evaluation is so important that evaluators have adopted a special term for potential evaluation users: *stakeholders.* Evaluation stakeholders are people who have a stake—a vested interest—in evaluation findings. For any evaluation there are multiple possible stakeholders: program funders, staff, administrators, and clients or program participants. Others with a direct, or even indirect, interest in program effectiveness may be considered stakeholders, including journalists and members of the general public, or, more specifically, taxpayers, in the case of public programs. Stakeholders include anyone who makes decisions or desires information about a program. However, stakeholders typically have diverse and often competing interests. No evaluation can answer all potential questions equally well. This means that some process is necessary for narrowing the range of possible questions to focus the evaluation. In utilization-focused evaluation, this process begins by narrowing the list of potential stakeholders to a much shorter, more specific group of primary intended users. Their information needs (i.e., their intended uses) focus the evaluation.

Different people see things differently and have varying interests and needs. This can be taken as a truism. However, this truism is regularly and consistently ignored in the design of evaluation studies. To target an evaluation at the information needs of a specific person or a group of identifiable and interacting persons is quite different from what has been traditionally recommended as "identifying the audience" for an evaluation. Audiences are amorphous, anonymous entities. Nor is it sufficient to identify an agency or organization as a recipient of the evaluation report. Organizations are an impersonal collection of hierarchical positions. People, not organizations, use evaluation information—thus the importance of the personal factor.

QUALITATIVE INQUIRY INTO EVALUATION USE: EMERGENCE OF THE PERSONAL FACTOR

The personal factor is the presence of an identifiable individual or group of people who personally care about the evaluation and the findings it generates. The importance of the personal factor first emerged in a qualitative study of the use of federal evaluations (Patton, 1978) and has since been validated in numerous case studies and qualitative inquiries into factors that affect use. Reviewing briefly the findings from that early qualitative study of evaluation use is worthwhile because it illustrates one kind of finding that can emerge from qualitative evaluations generally, especially inquiry into the meaning and manifestations of a sensitizing concept, in this case: evaluation use. The notion of a sensitizing concept anticipates a particularly important contribution of qualitative inquiry in evaluation that I will discuss in greater depth later. Basically, programs and interventions of all kinds typically have some concept that is at the core of the program's theory of change. Examples are:

- *Affordable housing* for low-income people

- *Empowerment* of battered women to take control of their lives

- *Community engagement and ownership* in a community development initiative

- *Social justice* in an immigration campaign

- Enhancing *soft skills* in an employment program

- *Gender equity* in international development

- *Quality of life* in a program for senior citizens

- *Self-sufficiency* in a welfare program

In each of these examples, there is a core concept the meaning of which is central to understanding both what the program accomplished (its outcomes and impacts) and how it was conducted. A common form of qualitative inquiry in evaluation is to interview participants, program staff, administrators, and funders to find out what they mean by these core concepts. This was the approach we took when studying what it means to *use an evaluation*, which is at the heart of utilization-focused evaluation.

In the mid-1970s, as evaluation was emerging as a distinct field of professional practice, I undertook a study with colleagues and students of twenty federal health evaluations to assess how their findings had been used and to identify the factors that affected varying degrees of use. We interviewed project managers, program officers, and evaluators. That study marked the beginning of the formulation of utilization-focused evaluation presented in this chapter. Two factors emerged as consistently important in explaining utilization: (1) political considerations and (2) a factor we called "the personal factor." This latter factor was unexpected and emergent, and its clear importance to our respondents had, we believed, substantial implications for the use of program evaluation.

Time after time, when asked what factor most explained evaluation use, they responded in terms of the importance of individual people. I want to include examples of those responses in this chapter to illustrate the nature of qualitative findings and to demonstrate the way in which utilization-focused evaluation—as a framework for and approach to engaging in evaluations with focus on the personal factor and working with primary intended users—is grounded in and emerged from qualitative inquiry. Here, then, are illustrative responses to the question about what factor most explained evaluation use in their particular evaluation.

- I would rank as the most important factor this division director's interest, [his] interest in evaluation. Not all managers are that motivated toward evaluation.

- [The single most important factor that had the greatest effect on how the study got used was] the principal investigator . . . If I have to pick a single factor, I'll pick people any time.

- That it came from the Office of the Director—that's the most important factor . . . The proposal came from the Office of the Director. It had had his attention and he was interested in it, and he implemented many of the things.

- [The single most important factor was that] the people at the same level of decision making in [the new office] were not interested in making decisions of the kind that the people [in the old office] were, I think that probably had the greatest impact. The fact that there was no one at [the new office] after the transfer who was making programmatic decisions.

- Well, I think the answer there is in the qualities of the people for whom it was made. That's sort of a trite answer, but it's true. That's the single most important factor in any study now that's utilized.

- Probably the single factor that had the greatest effect on how it was used was the insistence of the person responsible for initiating the study that the Director of _____ become familiar with its findings and arrive at judgment on it.

- [The most important factor was] the real involvement of the top decision makers in the conceptualization and design of the study, and their commitment to the study.

While these comments concern the importance of interested and committed individuals in studies that were actually used, studies that were not used stand out in that there was often a clear absence of the personal factor. One evaluator remarked:

> I think that since the client wasn't terribly interested . . . and the whole issue had shifted to other topics, and since we weren't interested in doing it from a research point of view . . . nobody was interested.

Another highly experienced evaluator was particularly adamant and articulate on the theory that the major factor affecting use is the personal energy, interests, abilities, and contacts of specific individuals. When asked to identify the one factor that is most important in whether a study gets used, he summarized his viewpoint as follows:

> The most important factor is desire on the part of the managers, both the central federal managers and the site managers. I don't think there's [any doubt], you know, that evaluation should be responsive to their needs, and if they have a real desire to get on with whatever it is they're supposed to do, they'll apply it. And if the evaluations don't meet their needs, they won't. About as simple as you can get. I think the whole process is far more dependent on the skills of the people who use it than it is on the sort of peripheral issues of politics, resources. . . Institutions are tough as hell to change. You can't change an institution by coming and doing an evaluation with a halo. Institutions are changed by people, in time, with a constant plugging away at the purpose you want to accomplish. And if you don't watch out, it slides back.

Our sample included another rather adamant articulation of this premise. An evaluation of a pilot program involving four major projects was undertaken at the instigation of the program administrator. He made a special effort to make sure that his question (Were the pilot projects capable of being extended and generalized?) was answered. He guaranteed this by personally taking an active interest in all parts of the study. The administrator had been favorable to the program in principle, was uncertain what the results would be, but was hoping that the program would prove effective. The evaluation findings were, in fact, negative. The program was subsequently ended, with the evaluation carrying "considerable weight" in that decision. Why was this study used in such a dramatic way? His answer was emphatic:

> Look, we designed the project with an evaluation component in it, so we were committed to use it and we did. . . It's not just the fact that [evaluation] was built in, but the fact that we built it in on purpose. That is, the agency head and myself had broad responsibilities for this, wanted the evaluation study results, and we expected to use them. Therefore, they were used. That's my point. If someone else had built it in because they thought it was needed, and we didn't care, I'm sure the use of the study results would have been different.

Presence of the personal factor increases the likelihood of long-term follow-through, that is, persistence in getting evaluation findings used. One study in particular stood out in this regard. It was initiated by a new office director with no support internally and considerable opposition from other affected agencies. The director found an interested and committed evaluator. The two worked closely together. The findings were initially ignored because it was not a hot political issue at the time, but over the ensuing four years the director and evaluator personally worked to get the attention of key members of Congress. The evaluation eventually contributed to passing significant legislation in a new area of federal programming. From beginning to end, the story was one of personal human commitment to getting evaluation results used.

Though the specifics vary from case to case, the pattern is markedly clear: Where the personal factor emerges, where some individuals take direct, personal responsibility for getting findings to the right people, evaluations have an impact. Where the personal factor is absent, there is a marked absence of impact. Use is not simply determined by some configuration of abstract factors; it is determined in large part by real, live, caring human beings.

Qualitative inquiry has proved particularly appropriate for studying evaluation use because each evaluation is unique, and the open-ended nature of qualitative inquiry allows whatever factors are important to emerge from interviews with key informants and case studies on factors related to use. This cumulative research on use (Patton, 2008, Chapter 3) has shown that where a person or group is actively involved with and interested in an evaluation, the evaluation is more likely to be used; where the personal factor is absent, there was a correspondingly marked absence of evaluation impact.

The personal factor represents the leadership, interest, enthusiasm, determination, commitment, assertiveness, and caring of specific, individual people. These are people who actively seek information to make judgments and reduce decision uncertainties. They want to increase their ability to predict the outcomes of programmatic activity and thereby enhance their own discretion as decision makers, policy makers, consumers, program participants, funders, or whatever roles they play. These are the primary users of evaluation.

The importance of the personal factor in explaining and predicting evaluation use leads directly to the emphasis in utilization-focused evaluation on working with intended users to specify intended uses. The personal factor directs us to attend to specific people who understand, value, and care about evaluation, and further directs us to attend to their interests. This is the primary lesson the profession has learned about enhancing use, and it is wisdom now widely acknowledged by practicing evaluators (Cousins, Donohue, & Bloom, 1996; Preskill & Caracelli, 1997).

CONSIDERATIONS FOR INCORPORATING QUALITATIVE INQUIRY INTO UTILIZATION-FOCUSED EVALUATIONS

Utilization-focused evaluation begins with identification of primary intended users. These intended users are brought together or organized in some fashion, if possible (e.g., an evaluation task force of primary stakeholders), to work with the evaluator and share in making major decisions about the evaluation. Then the evaluator and intended users commit to the intended uses of the evaluation and determine the focus for the evaluation, for example, formative, summative, or knowledge generating. Prioritizing evaluation questions will often include considering the relative importance of focusing on attainment of goals, program implementation, or the program's theory of action (logic model). The menu of evaluation possibilities is vast, so many different types of evaluations may need to be discussed. The evaluator works with intended users to determine priority uses with attention to political and ethical considerations. In a style that is interactive and situationally responsive, the evaluator helps intended users answer the question: Given expected uses, is the evaluation worth doing? To what extent and in what ways are intended users committed to intended use?

This sets the stage for working with the intended users to make methods, measurement, and design decisions. This is where considerations for incorporating qualitative inquiry become primary. The evaluator must be able to present method-ological options in a way that intended users can understand the implications of methods decisions for use. Primary intended users are involved in making methods decisions so that they fully understand the strengths and weaknesses of the find-ings they will use. A variety of options may be considered: qualitative and quantitative data; naturalistic, experimental, and quasi-experimental designs; purposeful and probabilistic sampling approaches; greater and lesser emphasis on general-izations; and alternative ways of dealing with potential threats to validity, reliability, and utility. More specifically, the discussion at this stage will include attention to issues of methodological appropriateness, believability of the data, understandability, accuracy, balance, practicality, propriety, and cost. As always for utilization-focused evaluation, the overriding concern will be utility. Will results obtained from these methods be useful—and actually used? Because many intended users may not know much about qualitative inquiry and its potential contributions, a utilization-focused evaluator must be able to provide illustra-tions of what a qualitative approach would yield. Here are some examples.

PARTICULARLY APPROPRIATE USES OF QUALITATIVE EVALUATIONS

Focus on Quality

Qualitative inquiry can be especially useful in evaluating quality. It is useful to distinguish quality control from quality enhancement. Quality control efforts identify and measure minimum acceptable results, for example, minimum competency testing in schools or maximum acceptable waiting times before seeing a physician in an emergency room. Quality enhancement, in contrast, focuses on excellence, that is, levels of attainment well beyond minimums. Quality control requires clear, specific, standardized, and measurable levels of acceptable results. Excellence, however, often involves individualization and professional judgment that cannot and should not be standardized. Excellence is manifest in quality responses to special cases or especially challenging circumstances. Thus, although quality control relies on standardized statistical measures, comparisons, and benchmarks, quality enhancement relies more on nuances of judgment that are often best captured qualitatively through case studies and cross-case comparisons. One of the particular strengths of qualitative inquiry, then, is illuminating the nature and meaning of *quality* in particular contexts. This takes on added significance since *quality of life* has become a commonly used concept and is showing growing significance in economic and political terms. What this means, in particular circumstances and in context, lends itself to qualitative inquiry and illumination.

Outcomes Evaluation

Program participant stories are an important source of data to illuminate outcomes. Through these stories we discover how program staff interact with participants and with family and friends in ways that contribute to outcomes. Tracking and documenting how program participants respond to program inputs and other factors in their lives provide insight into the nature of outcomes.

Outcomes evaluation has become a central focus, if not the central focus, of both learning-oriented and accountability-driven evaluations. However, the language of "measuring outcomes" can make stakeholders think that the only way to document outcomes attainment is with numbers. Percentage increases in desired outcomes (e.g., higher achievement test scores) and percentage decreases in undesirable outcomes (reductions in rates of child abuse and neglect) are important to provide concrete evidence of overall patterns of effectiveness. What such statistics cannot do, however, is show the human faces behind the numbers. This is important to provide critical context when interpreting statistical outcomes as well as to make sure that the numbers can be understood as representing meaningful changes in the lives of real people. Thus, a utilization-focused evaluator has to be able to provide examples of how documenting the qualitative dimensions of outcomes can provide value.

In an adult literacy program, the test results showed an average increase of 2.7 grade levels over a three-month period. The people in this sample included the following:

- A Puerto Rican man who was learning to read English so that he could help his young daughter with school work

- An eighty-seven-year-old African American grandmother who, having worked hard throughout her life to make sure that her children and grandchildren completed school, was now attending to her own education so that she could personally read the Bible herself

- A manager in a local corporation who years earlier had lied on her job application about having a high school diploma and was now studying at night to attain a Graduate Equivalency Degree (GED)

In judging the effectiveness of this program and making decisions about its future, understanding the stories behind the numbers can be as important as having the statistics themselves. One can justifiably criticize the past reporting practices of many human service agencies for having been limited to successful anecdotes, with no accountability reporting on overall patterns of effectiveness. However, swinging the pendulum to the other extreme of only reporting aggregate statistics presents its own problems and limitations. Numbers are subject to selection and distortion no less than anecdotes. Well-crafted case studies can tell the stories behind the numbers, capture unintended impacts and ripple effects, and illuminate dimensions of desired outcomes that are difficult to quantify (e.g., what it means for someone to become "self-sufficient"). Such qualitative data can add significantly to statistical reporting to create a more comprehensive accountability system.

Detailed case studies can be even more important when evaluating outcomes attainment for program improvement (as opposed to external accountability reporting). To simply know that a targeted indicator has been met (or not met) provides little information for program improvement. Getting into case details better illuminates what worked and did not work along the journey to outcomes—the kind of understanding that is needed by a program to undertake improvement initiatives.

Evaluating Individualized Outcomes

Utilization-focused evaluation emphasizes working with intended users to match methods to the nature of the program and priority evaluation questions. Programs that emphasize individualized and diverse outcomes are especially good candidates for qualitative methods. Individualization means matching program services and treatments to the needs and interests of individual clients. Successful social and educational programs adapt their interventions to the needs and circumstances of specific individuals and families. Flexibility, adaptability, and individualization can be important to the effectiveness of educational and human service programs. Highly individualized programs operate under the assumption that outcomes will be different for different clients. Not only will outcomes vary along specific common dimensions, but outcomes will be qualitatively different and will involve qualitatively different dimensions for different clients. Under such conditions program staff are justifiably reluctant to generate standardized criteria and scales against which all clients are compared. They argue that their evaluation needs are for documentation of the unique outcomes of individual clients rather than for measures of outcomes standardized across all clients.

Numerous examples are available of individualized programs or treatments. Open education, for example, is partly a model of educational processes that assumes that the outcomes of education for each child are unique. Open and experiential approaches to education offer diverse activities to achieve diverse and individualized outcomes. Moreover, the outcomes of having engaged in a single activity may be quite different for different students. For example, a group of primary school students may take a field trip, followed by dictating stories to the teachers and volunteers about that field trip, and then learning to read their stories. For some students such a process may involve learning about the mechanics of language: sentence structure, parts of speech, and verb conjugation, for example. For other students the major outcome of such a process may be learning how to spell certain words. For other students the important outcome may be having generated an idea from a particular experience. For yet other students the important outcome may have been something that was learned in the exercise or experience itself, such as knowledge about the firehouse or the farm that was visited. Other students may become more articulate as a result of the dictation exercise. Still other students may have learned to read better as a result of the reading part of the exercise. The critical point is that a common activity for all students could result in drastically different outcomes for different students, depending on how they approached the experience, what their unique needs were, and which part of the activity they found most stimulating. Educators involved in individualized approaches, then, need evaluation methods that permit documentation of a variety of outcomes and they need to resist measuring the success of complex, individualized learning experiences by any limited set of standardized outcome measures (for example, improved reading scores, better spelling, or more knowledge about some specific subject). Qualitative case studies offer a method for capturing and reporting individualized outcomes.

The more a program moves beyond training in standard basic competencies to more individualized development, the more qualitative case studies will be needed to capture the range of outcomes attained. A leadership program that focuses on basic concepts of planning, budgeting, and communications skills may be able to measure outcomes with a standardized instrument. However, a leadership program that engages in helping participants think in systems terms about how to find leverage points and intervention strategies to transform their own organizations will need case studies of the actual transformation efforts undertaken by participants, for their individual endeavors are likely to vary significantly. One may be the director of a small community-based nonprofit. Another may be a middle-level government manager. Still another may be part of a large national organization. "Transformation" will mean very different things in these different settings. Under such circumstances, qualitative case study methods and design strategies can be particularly useful for evaluation of individualized participant outcomes and organization-level impacts.

Process Studies

In addition to documenting outcomes, another issue that regularly surfaces in working with intended users to clarify evaluation priorities is how to focus on documenting program processes, that is, looking at how participants engage in a program in addition to examining outputs and outcomes. Evaluations vary in their emphasis on process, in part because programs vary in their attention to process. Some therapy approaches in psychology are highly process-oriented in that they focus on the relationship between the client and therapist, how the client is approaching issues, how the client feels about the process, and the nature of the interactions that occur during therapy, rather than focusing only or primarily on behavioral outcomes. Groups, programs, even entire organizations may be characterized as highly "process-oriented" if how members and participants feel about what is happening is given as much attention as the results achieved. Some styles of community and organizational development operate on the premise: "What we do is no more important than how we do it." This statement means that actively involving people in the development process is an end in itself, not just a means to some more concrete end; the process is the point rather than simply the means of arriving at some other point. The journey, not the destination, is what matters. For example, a planning process for a community or organization may be carried out with a heavy emphasis on participation and involvement such that building relationships and mutual understandings along the way is at least as important as the focus of the actual plan produced. The process, in such a case, becomes the outcome. That is, producing a plan (the apparent intended outcome) actually becomes a means to building community (the real desired outcome).

In contrast, other interventions and programs downplay process. The emphasis is on results and outcomes. Even in these cases, however, some process is undertaken to achieve results, and understanding the process–outcomes relationship necessitates documenting and understanding processes.

Qualitative inquiry is highly appropriate for studying process because (1) depicting process requires detailed descriptions of how people engage with each other; (2) the experience of process typically varies for different people so their experiences need to be captured in their own words; (3) process is fluid and dynamic, so it cannot be fairly summarized on a single rating scale at one point in time; and (4) participants' perceptions are a key process consideration. Process evaluations aim at elucidating and understanding the internal dynamics of how a program, organization, or relationship operates. Process studies focus on the following kinds of questions: What are the things people experience that make this program what it is? How are clients brought into the program, and how do they move through the program once they are participants? How is what people do related to what they are trying to (or actually do) accomplish? What are the strengths and weaknesses of the program from the perspective of participants and staff? What is the nature of staff–client interactions?

A process evaluation requires sensitivity to both qualitative and quantitative changes in programs throughout their development, which typically means monitoring and describing the details of the program's implementation. Process evaluations not only look at formal activities and anticipated outcomes, but they also investigate informal patterns and unanticipated interactions. A variety of perspectives may be sought from people with dissimilar relationships to the program, that is, inside and outside sources.

Process data permit judgments about the extent to which the program or organization is operating the way it is supposed to be operating, revealing areas in which relationships can be improved as well as highlighting strengths of the program that should be preserved. Process descriptions are also useful in permitting people not intimately involved in a program—for example, external funders, public officials, and external agencies—to understand how a program operates. This permits such external persons to make more intelligent decisions about the program. Formative evaluations aimed at program improvement often rely heavily on process data. Finally, process evaluations are particularly useful for dissemination and replication of model interventions where a program has served as a demonstration project or is considered to be a model worthy of replication at other sites. By describing and understanding the details and dynamics of program processes, it is possible to isolate critical elements that have contributed to program successes and failures.

A good example of what can emerge from a process study comes from an evaluation of the efforts of outreach workers at a prenatal clinic in a low-income neighborhood. The outreach workers were going door to door identifying women, especially teenagers, in need of prenatal care to get them into the community prenatal clinic. Instead of primarily doing recruiting, however, the process evaluation found that the outreach workers were spending a great deal of time responding to immediate problems they were encountering: need for rat control; need for English-as-a-second-language classes; and protection from neglect, abuse, or violence (Philliber, 1989). The actual interactions that resulted from the door-to-door contacts turned out to be significantly different from the way the door-to-door process was designed and conceptualized. These findings, which emerged from interviews and observations, had important implications for staff recruitment and training, and for how much time needed to be allocated to cover a neighborhood.

Implementation Evaluation

Intended users often want to know the extent to which a program is effective after it is fully implemented; to answer that question, however, one must know the extent to which the program was actually implemented. If primary intended users have to choose between implementation information and outcomes information because of limited evaluation resources, in many instances implementation information will prove of greater value, especially early in the life of a program. A decision maker can use implementation information to make sure that a policy is being put into operation according to design, or to test the very feasibility of the policy. Unless one knows that a program is operating according to design, there may be little reason to expect it to produce the desired outcomes. Furthermore, until the program is implemented and a "treatment" is believed to be in operation, there may be little reason even to bother evaluating outcomes. When outcomes are evaluated without knowledge of implementation, the results seldom provide a direction for action because the decision maker lacks information about what produced the observed outcomes (or lack of outcomes). Pure pre-post outcomes evaluation is the "black box" approach to evaluation.

One important way of studying program implementation is to gather detailed, descriptive information about what the program is doing. Implementation evaluations answer the following kinds of questions: What do clients in the program experience? What services are provided to clients? What does staff do? What is it like to be in the program? How is the program organized? As these questions indicate, implementation evaluation includes attention to inputs, activities, processes, and structures.

Implementation evaluations tell decision makers what is going on in the program, how the program has developed, and how and why programs deviate from initial plans and expectations. A process of ongoing adaptation to local conditions characterizes much program implementation. The methods used to study implementation need to be open-ended, discovery-oriented, and capable of describing developmental processes and program changes. Qualitative methods are ideally suited to the task of describing such program implementation.

Comparing Programs: Focus on Diversity

Programs differ from place to place because places differ. In evaluating statewide, national, and international programs with many different sites, primary intended users often want to compare sites and understand variations from place to place. Differences among sites emerge as programs adapt to local community needs and circumstances, as discussed earlier in the implementation evaluation section of this chapter. Although some basic framework of how programs should function may originate in Washington, DC, Ottawa, Brussels, or Canberra, or some state or provincial capital, program implementation at the local level seldom follows exactly the proposed design.

When an evaluation requires gathering data from several local sites, quantitative measures may be appropriate for comparing local programs along standardized dimensions, but qualitative descriptions are necessary to capture the unique diversities and contrasts that inevitably emerge as local programs are adapted to local needs and circumstances. Local sites that are part of national or even international programs show considerable variation in implementation and outcomes. These variations are not such that they can be fully captured and measured along standardized scales; they are differences in kind—differences in content, in process, in goals, in implementation, in politics, in context, in outcomes, and in program quality. To understand these differences, a holistic picture of each unique site is needed. Thus, qualitative data are necessary to give a complete evaluation picture of local variations within national programs, a picture that is necessarily incomplete so long as the only data available are aggregated and standardized statistics about these diverse programs.

Documenting Development over Time and Investigating System Changes

The very language of evaluating "the" program connotes a static, fixed image of a program. Interacting with primary intended users about how they perceive the program and the likelihood of changes over time opens up the utility and potential appropriateness of using qualitative methods to follow and document development changes. This returns us to the value of qualitative inquiry for process studies, discussed earlier in this chapter, for development is best understood as a process. Organizational development, community development, human development, leadership development, and professional development—these are process-oriented approaches to facilitating change. Pre- and posttests do not do justice to dynamic development processes. Pre and post measures imply a kind of linear, ever upward, less-to-more image of growth and development. In reality, development usually occurs in fits and starts, some upward or forward progress, then backsliding or consolidation. Pre- and posttesting tells you where you started and where you ended up, but not what happened along the way. Quantitative measures can parsimoniously capture snapshots of pre and post states, even some interim steps, but qualitative methods are more appropriate for capturing evolutionary and transformational developmental dynamics. For example, I worked with a new and innovative employment-training program that was constantly reorganizing staff and participant teams, realigning courses, trying new mixes of activities, and restructuring as growth occurred. We found that even quarterly reflective practice sessions were insufficient to capture all the changes occurring. To study this highly dynamic program required ongoing fieldwork framed against a chaos theory metaphor, because the program development really was like walking through a maze whose walls rearrange themselves with every step you take—and it was a major challenge to develop a data collection process that could capture those rearrangements, but that is what primary intended users wanted and needed, so that is what we did.

The utilization-focused evaluator works with primary intended users to consider options and match methods with priority questions, illustrating what kinds of data are particularly appropriate for different questions and issues. They develop an appreciation for the value of incorporating qualitative approaches and thus participate in making informed decisions about methods.

VALUE OF INCORPORATING QUALITATIVE APPROACHES

During interactions with primary intended users aimed at facilitating methods choices, the value of various methods—their strengths, benefits, weaknesses, and limitations—need to be illuminated in ways that are understandable and concrete. Because this book focuses on qualitative methods, we pay particular attention here to the distinct contributions that qualitative approaches offer, with examples.

- Purposeful sampling is valuable for getting in-depth understanding of information-rich cases (e.g., finding out what is going on with dropouts, examining successes in depth, and learning from variation). For example, an employment training program aimed at chronically unemployed men of color was experiencing a high dropout rate. Dropouts are hard to locate, but their feedback about their experiences can be critical for program improvement. Setting up a system for identifying dropouts immediately and following up quickly revealed that many were intimidated by the program's formal contracting approach, emphasis on following rules, and probation for what they considered minor lapses. In essence, they experienced the program culture as punitive in a way that brought back bad memories from negative high school experiences (which had led them to drop out of high school). This feedback led to a major reorientation and redesign of the program culture and staff-participant relationships. The sample was relatively small (n = 15) but carefully selected (purposeful sampling) to yield critical and timely insights.

■ The open and emergent nature of qualitative inquiry facilitates discovery of unanticipated consequences and side effects of programs, which can only be detected through fieldwork. For example, an adult literacy program began using computers for students to practice reading exercises. The purpose of the computer instruction was to allow students to progress at their own pace with a software program that provided quick feedback about errors without embarrassment. An unexpected outcome, however, was that many participants had the opportunity to use computers for the first time, and that experience led them into employment training for jobs that required keyboarding skills, something they would never have considered, and it was not an intended outcome of the literacy program. This finding emerged from open-ended follow-up interviews with graduates.

■ Qualitative inquiry can humanize and personalize evaluation through the capturing and telling of stories. An evaluation of an inner city community development initiative included collecting stories from the recent immigrant population. The immigrants appreciated the chance to tell their stories in their own words (in contrast to the endless and intimidating forms they had to fill out). Word spread in the community that being interviewed for the evaluation was a good experience.

■ Qualitative evaluations can capture how *context matters* with details about how programs adapt to their environments.

Appreciating context and taking it into account in evaluation has become a matter of increasing sensitivity in evaluation (AEA, 2009). An inner-city housing program added Internet access as a standard feature in subsidized housing because Internet access had become so important for job searches and kids doing homework. The information age context of technological innovation creates a growing gap between the poor without Internet access and those better off who have access. Acknowledging this gap and its effects emerged from open-ended needs assessment interviews with the residents in the subsidized housing about their priority concerns. Before those interviews, the housing program had not considered Internet access something that could be a housing issue for low-income residents.

■ Qualitative inquiry allows moving beyond the simple summative question of, *Did the program work?* to the more nuanced, and often more enlightening and useful question, *What worked for whom in what ways with what consequences? And why?* This involves digging into the details of causal mechanisms. For example, an evaluation of an early childhood parent education program found that the mothers who formed friendships with each other were more likely to follow-through on parenting suggestions because the friendships became a mechanism of reinforcing and going more deeply into the things they learned in class. As a result, the program started building in more time to facilitate formation of friendships and offered ways for friends to engage with class material outside of class together.

■ Qualitative inquiry can support *systems thinking* through systems-oriented case studies, including attention to system complexities and dynamics. In an evaluation of the child protection system in a major city, mothers whose children were victims of child sexual abuse had to deal with the following systems: police, social welfare, courts, human services agencies, school counselors, probation officers, health services, and mental health services. The mothers reported in interviews that these various parts of the system were completely uncoordinated, confusing, intimidating, and kept asking for the same information over and over, giving contradictory messages, and imposing conflicting requirements. The frustration, pain, and sense of re-victimization in their interviews made a powerful impression on local policy makers. The qualitative findings about the dysfunctional child protection system led the county to undertake a major systems change and coordination initiative. (For an in-depth discussion of systems thinking and complexity concepts, and their implications for evaluation, including qualitative examples, see Patton, 2010).

CHALLENGES ASSOCIATED WITH QUALITATIVE INQUIRY IN UTILIZATION-FOCUSED EVALUATIONS

- *Mixed-methods evaluations.* When offered the option of mixed-methods designs, primary intended users often find this attractive, both for the more comprehensive data that will be collected and because it also removes the need to choose between qualitative and quantitative approaches. Utilization-focused evaluations often involve mixed methods. The challenge is to understand the contributions of each method and to design the evaluation so that the quantitative and qualitative data are in genuine dialogue with each other, not just separate and unconnected sections of the final report.

- *Working with primary intended users to interpret qualitative data.* Once data have been collected and organized for analysis in a utilization-focused evaluation, intended users are actively and directly involved in interpreting findings, making judgments based on the data, and generating recommendations. Specific strategies for use can then be formalized in light of actual findings, and the evaluator can facilitate following through on actual use. This means that the intended users participate in identifying the themes in qualitative analysis or case studies. For example, when we involved program staff and some participants in analyzing interviews with mothers in an early childhood parent education program, those involved learned from the feedback in the interviews but also brought additional insights into what participants meant by some of their responses.

■ *Length of qualitative reports.* In-depth data yield in-depth reports, which tend toward being long. Today's policy makers often have short attention spans. They want Twitter-length reports. Qualitative data do not come in Twitter-sized packages. The good news about the Internet is that qualitative report summaries can be a gateway to longer, more complete qualitative reports that are posted on the web and accessible to those interested in the more in-depth case data and findings.

■ *Negotiating evaluations to fit specific situations.* Utilization-focused evaluation involves negotiations between the evaluator and intended users throughout the evaluation process. This is most obvious, perhaps, at the design stage. The design of a particular evaluation depends on the people involved and their situation: *situational evaluation.*

The standards and principles of evaluation provide overall direction, a foundation of ethical guidance, and a commitment to professional competence and integrity, but there are no absolute rules an evaluator can follow to know exactly what to do with specific users in a particular situation. This means negotiating the evaluation's intended and expected uses.

Every evaluation situation is unique. A successful evaluation (one that is useful, practical, ethical, and accurate) emerges from the special characteristics and conditions of a particular situation—a mixture of people, politics, history, context, resources, constraints, values, needs, interests, and chance. However, once stakeholders become involved and start to feel some responsibility for the evaluation, even ownership, they can worry a great deal about whether an evaluation is being done "right." Indeed, one common objection stakeholders make to getting actively involved in designing an evaluation is that they lack the knowledge to do it right. The notion that there is one right way to do things dies hard. The right way, from a utilization-focused perspective, is the way that will be meaningful and useful to the specific evaluators and intended users involved, and finding that way requires interaction, negotiation, and situational analysis. The challenge of situational matching is exacerbated with qualitative methods, because there is also no one right way to undertake a qualitative inquiry. Quantitative methods offer sample size formulas and statistical significance tests. Qualitative methods involve more judgment and adaptation. This creates an added challenge in helping intended users understand options and feel confident about the decisions they make about the evaluation.

▪ *Process use.* Most discussions about evaluation use focus on use of findings. However, being engaged in the processes of evaluation can be useful quite apart from the findings that may emerge from those processes. If, as a result of being involved in an evaluation, primary intended users learn to reason like an evaluator and operate in accordance with evaluation's values, then the evaluation has generated more than findings. It has been useful beyond the findings in that it has increased the participants' capacity to use evaluative logic and reasoning. "Process use," then, refers to using the logic, employing the reasoning, and being guided by the values that undergird the evaluation profession. Qualitative inquiry deepens and enhances process use precisely because the judgments and interpretations required are not formulaic. Intended users have to really engage with qualitative findings for them to be useful, and that deep engagement increases process use. Learning to see the world as an evaluator sees it often has a lasting impact on those who participate in an evaluation—an impact that can be greater and last longer than the findings that result from that same evaluation. Helping primary intended users understand and value process use is one of the challenges of conducting a utilization-focused evaluation. (For an in-depth discussion of process use, see Cousins, 2007; Patton, 2008, Chapter 5.)

▪ *Utilization-focused evaluators need special skills.* To nurture evaluation use and keep an evaluation from getting caught up in destructive group processes or power politics, a utilization-focused evaluator needs to be politically savvy, skillful in group facilitation, able to decipher relevant internal organizational dynamics, and a user-friendly communicator. This makes explicit that utilization-focused evaluators need not only technical and methodological skills, but also group process skills and political astuteness—what are sometimes called "people skills" for evaluators. In addition, and perhaps most important for the focus of this book, evaluators need competence in multiple methods and must be able to work with and guide primary intended users in making astute and meaningful methods choices that will result in credible and useful findings.

■ *Avoiding evaluation misuse.* Utilization-focused evaluation strives to facilitate appropriate use of evaluation findings and processes, so utilization-focused evaluators must also be concerned about misuse. Evaluation processes and findings can be misrepresented and misused in the search for political advantage or simply out of enthusiasm to call attention to what those involved consider important findings. This happens most often in qualitative evaluations when the primary intended users yield to the temptation to over-generalize and over-prescribe from the relatively small number of case studies conducted.

■ *Ethical challenges.* Because of their engagement with the evaluation design and interpretation of findings, primary intended users may have access to what would otherwise be confidential information about program staff and participants. Especially in situations of local program evaluation where primary intended users may personally know some of the staff, and even program participants, the detailed data that emerge from qualitative inquiry have to be handled with special sensitivity and attention to safeguarding confidentiality.

CONCLUSION

Utilization-focused evaluation aims to achieve intended use by intended users. The evaluator works with primary intended users to identify priority evaluation questions and facilitate consideration of what kind of data will be credible and useful in answering those questions. To facilitate these negotiations, utilization-focused evaluators must be able to present intended users with methodological options and explain the strengths and weaknesses of various methods, with concrete examples to illustrate the differences. I find over and over again, and have for thirty-five years, that when primary intended users are offered examples of what qualitative data can yield and the insights it can offer, they choose to include qualitative inquiry as a central design element of the evaluation.

KEY CONCEPTS

Case studies

Formative evaluation

Implementation evaluation

Individualization

Intended users

Intended uses

Local community needs and circumstances

Methodological appropriateness

Methods decision

Outcomes evaluation

Personal factor

Prioritizing evaluation questions

Process data

Process studies

Program evaluation

Psychology of use

Quality control

Quality enhancement

Sensitizing concept

Stakeholders

Utilization-focused evaluation

DISCUSSION QUESTIONS

1. Brainstorm ways to discuss the inclusion of qualitative inquiry in evaluations when key stakeholders perceive evaluation as a narrow measure of program outcomes.

2. Individual stakeholders may intend to use the evaluation findings for very different purposes. How might an evaluator address discrepancies in intended uses by different stakeholders of the same evaluation? For example, the funders are concerned with whether they should offer continued support, but the program staff want to inform program improvement.

3. Imagine discovering that the results of your evaluation will not be used by anyone, yet you are bound by the ethics of practice as established by the American Evaluation Association. Would you conduct the evaluation? Justify your answer.

4. How can someone new to the field of evaluation use qualitative inquiry to gain the insights needed about the context, the stakeholders, and the program to conduct a utilization-focused evaluation?

REFERENCES

AEA (American Evaluation Association). (2004). *Guiding principles for evaluators*. Available at http://www.eval.org/Publications/Guiding Principles.asp

AEA (American Evaluation Association). (2009). *Context and evaluation, theme of the 2009 annual conference of the American Evaluation Association*. Available at http://www.eval.org/eval2009/09cfp.htm

Cousins, J. B. (Ed.). (2007). Process use in theory, research, and practice. *New directions for evaluation* (No. 116). San Francisco, CA: Jossey-Bass.

Cousins, J. B., Donohue, J. J., & Bloom, G. A. (1996). Collaborative evaluation in North America: Evaluators' self-reported opinions, practices and consequences. *Evaluation Practice*, *17*(3), 207–225.

Joint Committee on Standards for Educational Evaluation. (1994). *The program evaluation standards*. Thousand Oaks, CA: Sage. Available at http://www.wmich.edu/evalctr/jc/

Patton, M. Q. (1978). *Utilization-focused evaluation*. Beverly Hills, CA: Sage.

Patton, M. Q. (2008). *Utilization-focused evaluation* (4th ed.). Thousand Oaks, CA: Sage.

Patton, M. Q. (2010). *Developmental evaluation: Applying complexity concepts to enhance innovation and use*. New York, NY: Guilford Press.

Philliber, S. (1989). *Workshop on evaluating adolescent pregnancy prevention programs*. Children's Defense Fund Conference (March 10). Washington, DC: Children's Defense Fund.

Preskill, H., & Caracelli, V. (1997). Current and developing conceptions of use: Evaluation use TIG survey results. *American Journal of Evaluation*, *18*(3), 209–226.

3

Qualitative Inquiry for Policy Makers

George F. Grob

Key Ideas

- Evaluators who want to influence policy making need to include not just policy makers in their target audiences, but people who influence policy makers, including reporters, editors, and correspondents, and leaders in major issue organizations.

- Policy makers are voracious readers and have staff who brief them on complex issues. They like to meet people, and they tend to start with questions rather than answers.

- Policy makers need multiple perspectives on issues and problems, and they are oriented toward solutions. They look toward consensus to solve problems, but listen to a broad range of constituents with issues and ideas.

- Qualitative analyses, with deep probes of personal attitudes and experiences, can help policy makers understand the needs and aspirations of people in ways that quantitative analysis, even public opinion polls, often cannot.

- Ensuring that policy makers find evaluation studies useful entails:

    Providing both qualitative and quantitative data

    Balancing breadth and depth in the data collected and presented

Observing programs in action

Connecting with common citizens and including their perspectives

Considering carefully whether and how to use quotes

Avoiding strongly worded advocacy

Managing policy makers' expectations

Putting yourself in policy makers' shoes

My intention with this chapter is to offer some practical advice to the purveyors of qualitative analysis whose products are or may be of interest to policy makers and their influencers. I base it on my experience and consultations with other evaluators who, like myself, have spent major portions of their careers supplying evaluations and policy analyses to those who pass laws, write regulations, prepare government budgets, and engage in other forms of policy making. In our discussions we have found much similarity in how policy makers carry out their responsibilities at federal, state, and local government levels.

I have spent some forty years in the halls and chambers of policy makers, on both the executive and legislative sides of the federal government, where, unbeknownst to them, I deliberately and somewhat systematically observed how they behaved, especially the most successful among them. My secret goal was to figure out how they succeeded when they did, and why they failed. I wish I had had the time to be as systematic in my search and analysis as those of you who are reading this book. I did keep notes about which policy proposals were adopted, and wrote down my musings of the practices and characters of key players. However, the long tenure of my lucky positions sped by too fast for more than a loose and on-the-fly reflection of what I witnessed. With this cautious confession, I offer here my reflections for what they are worth, and no more. With all of the above in mind, I single out certain principles for consideration by evaluators who are exploring the use of qualitative analysis for policy makers. But first, it will be helpful to understand just who these policy makers are.

WHO ARE THE POLICY MAKERS AND HOW DO THEY OPERATE?

It is useful to set the stage for advice about qualitative methods for policy makers by describing who policy makers are, how they work, and how evaluators can influence them. I and others have written about this in other places (Chelimsky, 2009; Grob, 1992, 2003; Jonas, 1999; Mohan & Sullivan, 2006; Zajano & Lochtefeld, 1999), so here I offer only a brief summary.

By policy makers I mean people who hold high-level positions in which they are required to make major decisions that affect a substantial portion of an agency's activities. Policy decisions typically involve a lot of financial and other resources, span multiple years, and establish new program directions, whereas operational or managerial decisions are narrower in scope. At the national level, policy makers include the president, secretaries of federal departments, heads of agencies, assistant secretaries, administrators or directors of major programs, their senior staff members, members of Congress, chairs of congressional committees and subcommittees, their professional staff, the Director of the Office of Management and Budget (OMB), and senior OMB staff. At a state level, it would include state counterparts to the federal officials (e.g., the governor, state legislators, agency heads, all their senior staff, and the like). At the local level this would include mayors, chief executives of counties, city and county councils, planning commissioners, and so forth. Among foundations and nonprofit organizations, it would include the president, CEO, board of trustees, and program directors.

Others who are not policy makers are in strong positions to influence them. This includes editors, leading reporters, and correspondents of the national, state, local, and trade press and other news media, as well as leaders of major stakeholder organizations. Evaluators who want policy makers to heed their findings and recommendations also need to influence these influencers.

The policy making world is simultaneously systematic and chaotic, glacially slow and lightning fast. On the federal level, legislative proposals usually eke their way through numerous procedural steps and are held up until congressional leaders detect that enough votes are aligned to ensure passage.

(For further discussion on federal policy-making processes, see Grob, 1992, 2003, 2006; see Zajano and Lochtefeld, 1999, regarding state-level policy-making processes.) Often this process is extended through two or more sessions of Congress and, for really big issues, several presidential terms.

However, when the time is right, the situation becomes intense, with mad rushes to push legislation through the same procedural steps that were previously causing it to languish. Tides ebb and flow in a matter of months, weeks, or days, and information to tip policy in one direction or another has to be available precisely when needed. Evaluators wishing to influence the outcomes need to have their reports already on the table and be able to serve up quick analyses to answer the rapid-fire questions that seem to come from all directions.

Policy makers work long hours, often on weekends and holidays, and they seldom can predict in the morning when they will go home each day. As Zajano and Lochtefeld (1999) noted, "It is difficult for those outside the legislative arena to appreciate the demands on legislators' time . . . They receive stacks of mail each day, as well as frequent visits by lobbyists, constituents, agency personnel, and others" (p. 86). Their overloaded schedules allow little time for reading and reflection, yet legislators need to be well informed on a wide array of policy issues.

In my experience in the federal arena, the successful policy makers are quite intelligent and very fast learners. They have been at their trade for a good many years and are generally well informed with the scientific and political literature of the issues that interest them. Initially they speed read, limiting their attention to executive summaries. But they will also settle in to read entire reports that are key to the issues with which they are dealing. For example, they have probably read every significant report of the Government Accountability Office, Congressional Research Service, and the Institute of Medicine (or parallel institutes in other fields); major research articles; and seminal books on the topics they encounter in their jobs. They are prolific readers. They also have hard-working staff who can brief them on complex issues. They like to meet people and personally know many of the thought leaders in their field. Despite this, they do not think of themselves as know-it-alls. In fact, they are far more acutely aware of what they do not know than what they do. They work on issues for a living and usually start with the questions rather than the answers. Of course, some policy makers are extremely doctrinaire. I remind you that I am talking about the successful ones.

WHY QUALITATIVE ANALYSIS IS IMPORTANT TO POLICY MAKERS

Qualitative analysis is very important to policy makers because of their need to get all points of view and to understand the ramifications of policies for all who might be affected by them. For most policy makers, their native instincts and professional imperatives are to solve problems through as much consensus as possible. There are two reasons for this. The first has to do with the balance of powers. Laws, regulations, budgets, and other policies are seldom enacted in the United States (whether at the federal, state, or local level) until extensive efforts have been made to consult all major stakeholders, including common citizens, and to reach agreement on the proposed policies or agree to disagree. Even for policy makers who lack the tendency to seek or the ability to develop consensus, the realities of the balance of powers built into our governments ultimately force them to (1) reach agreement, (2) succumb to overwhelming opposing political powers, or (3) accept failure. Furthermore, our leaders are subject to popular elections. Citizens and stakeholders can rise up to change the enacted policies and punish the policy makers by withdrawing support. In essence, we are fundamentally a people governed by consensus, whenever possible, or at least by public input to decision making.

The second reason for seeking consensus has to do with the fact that policy makers, like evaluators, only work on problems that the best minds of the country (or their state or locality) have not been able to solve. If solutions were obvious or easy, they would have been adopted long before. But difficult problems can be solved only if many informed and creative people work on them and share their ideas in a practical way. We therefore need a government system that requires and supplies many industrious individuals to work out solutions by listening to a broad range of people with interests and ideas.

Thus, for the sake of both consensus and efficacy, policy makers simply have to get input from many people. They cannot possibly be successful if they do not. Evaluators can help policy makers do this through qualitative analysis: listening to and observing all kinds of people, analyzing and understanding what they say and do, and explaining it to those who can do something about it.

Policy makers are particularly interested in the opinions, experiences, and insights of common citizens and program beneficiaries. They are very interested in the "human side" of things. They want to understand how their policies will impact a broad array of citizens. This is not just about catering to their constituencies to get reelected. Certainly that tendency exists, and it is strongly exhibited by some. However, in the vast majority of policy makers one can recognize a sincere desire to better the lives of those they represent. Qualitative analyses, with deep probes of personal attitudes and experiences, can help policy makers understand the needs and aspirations of people in ways that quantitative analysis, even public opinion polls, often cannot.

PRINCIPLES FOR INFLUENCING POLICY MAKERS

Here are a few broad guidelines, based on my experience, which qualitative evaluators may find helpful to consider if they want their studies to be used by policy makers.

1. **Provide qualitative and quantitative analyses when appropriate and feasible.** Although qualitative analysis is useful for policy makers, not all of them prefer it to quantitative analysis. The question of which approach is better reminds me of my first formal debate. It occurred in eighth grade. The assigned topic was: Which is more important, coal or steel? Having chosen coal, I lost that debate. However, no matter what we young debaters had to say, the correct answer, of course, was that both are important. The answer to the question about the analytical preferences (qualitative or quantitative) of policy makers is the same: both.

This somewhat simplistic observation—that policy makers want both qualitative and quantitative analyses—is perhaps the most important answer I will give here. Policy makers *as a whole* want both, but, *taken one at a time,* while still wanting both, they tend to prefer one or the other. Most people do. My own experience of many years supplying policy makers with evaluation reports is that if I offered them only quantitative analysis, about half reacted with "Well, you can get numbers to say anything," or "Numbers always lie." If I gave them a purely qualitative analysis, the other half said, "Well, what did you think they would say? I could have told you that. You could have skipped the report."

However, when I gave them a study with both approaches, I did not get a neutral answer. I received an extremely positive response: "We love your work because you don't just give us numbers; you talk to real people and tell it like it is." Or, "This is great; you didn't just tell me what other people said, you gave me facts to back it up." So strong was this positive reaction that the office where I worked made it a practice to always mix the two approaches. Our reports were geared for policy makers. We wanted them to read our reports and take action on them, so we gave them what they wanted. We did not want to lose the opportunity to make a difference.

My introduction to this issue was something of a long windup for my pitch about mixing methods. However, it may be the most important pitch I will make. That is why I put it first. I would give the same advice to those interested in quantitative analysis. Do not give policy makers the methods you like; give them what they need and want. Put qualitative and quantitative methods together, and you will greatly increase the odds that policy makers will take you seriously.

2. **Balance the breadth and depth of the data collected.** Semi-structured interviews and focus groups may sometimes give you greater insight and better understanding than larger, structured surveys. But they generally have small ns, which may make policy makers skeptical of their representativeness. Some policy makers believe that only large, randomly selected samples yield "scientific" results. Trying to persuade them that they may be wrong is pointless, so do not dive into a lecture on methodology. Instead, give them both insights and representativeness. Even if logistics demand that you use a purposive rather than random sample, a larger n of the survey will lend greater credence

to the package of insights and representativeness that they will get when you deliver the results of both in-depth interviews and broadly based surveys.

Note that this is not the same as the first principle about mixing qualitative and quantitative methods. This advice is useful even if the broader surveys yield only qualitative results. Even if the sample is purposive rather than random, the larger ns are very important to well informed readers such as policy makers. Not all policy makers believe that only surveys that use random samples are scientific. However, their instincts, whether refined by formal study, absorbed in the course of their work, or innate, are fundamentally correct. Although they will appreciate the deeper insights you can draw from smaller but more intense and adaptive semi-structured interviews, they do not want to hear from just a few people; they want to hear from many, and they want the sample to be representative.

One technique is to combine purposive and random samples. You can do this even if you have to limit the universe from which you choose the random sample. For example, in the work of our office, we found it convincing to limit a study to, say, four or five states with the largest number of Medicare beneficiaries, but to draw a random sample of beneficiaries within these states. Other examples included drawing random samples from purposive samples of states that used centralized administrative systems and others that delegated administration to their counties; states with the highest known incidence of a problem we were studying; or areas with a higher proportion of target populations or socioeconomic characteristics that were germane to the issue at hand. Policy makers seemed to understand the logistical constraints preventing the use of the entire universe of beneficiaries or service providers from which to draw a random sample. But the fact that we used a random sample even from the limited universes added credibility to our work.

Even more broadly, you can combine various methods to develop samples that are as representative as is practical. One of the best examples of this approach in which I was involved was directing staff work for the Citizens Health Care Working Group. This group was commissioned by federal statute to conduct town hall meetings across the country to find out what average citizens thought about their health care system and what they would recommend to improve it. The group conducted or sponsored one hundred town hall meetings across the country. The sites were purposively, not randomly, chosen. The statute authorizing our study specifically required us to select meeting sites from both urban and rural areas and a broad span of geographic coverage across the country. Attendees were invited to attend through various public announcements and were not randomly selected. In addition to the meetings, a web-based survey was used to poll Americans on questions similar to those explored during the town hall meetings. The survey yielded responses from some twenty thousand Americans. Of course, it was not representative of all Americans. Instead, it reflected what those who were intensely interested in health care reform thought about it. The respondents covered the spectrum of those in favor and those against government reform. While probably biased somewhat on the "pro" side, such biases were obvious, as were those of the respondents passionately against government involvement in health care. Readers of our report understood all of these limitations. One reason was that we stated them explicitly. The combination of the methods involving both structured, but adaptive, in-person meetings and a broad-based survey gave credence to the results, which were for all practical purposes identical under both approaches. The report by the Citizens Health Care Working Group was widely disseminated and made available to members of Congress and executive branch policy makers while the recent health care reform legislation was under consideration.

3. **"Hit the pavement" to observe programs in operation.** As noted in the introduction, policy makers want to know what all of the stakeholders think about an issue. However, they are particularly interested in what average citizens, beneficiaries, and service providers think. That is why, for example, congressional hearings often feature the dramatic testimony of a victimized or heroic citizen. By having these "common citizens" testify, they learn about, and make it possible for others to also learn about, the circumstances and attitudes of people who will be directly affected by the policies under review. In fact, it may be said that these "common citizen" testimonies put "everyman" on the same level as the high-ranking and expert witnesses who usually dominate congressional hearings. The citizen testimony is, in

essence, a form of qualitative data that is highly regarded by policy makers. As anyone who watches the annual presidential state of the union addresses knows, President Reagan and all of his successors have singled out in the House gallery selected private citizens who have met and overcome adversity.

I found this strong interest in issues that affect average citizens the source of many of the requests for the studies we did at the Department of Health and Human Services (HHS), where I worked. For example, two HHS Secretaries wanted to know firsthand what local communities were doing to enforce laws against the sale of cigarettes to minors, and how makers of wine coolers were labeling and placing their products in venues frequented by children. I distinctly remember being ridiculed by my professional colleagues for working on these kinds of studies. One of them taunted me, saying, "I hear you are working on a study to prevent eighteen-year-old Marines from smoking." But the Secretaries who requested these studies had good instincts and used the results of our fieldwork. For example, we were able to report back that the use of mystery shopper "stings" to determine whether stores were requiring youthful cigarette buyers to show proof of age were emerging as an effective enforcement tool to reduce the sale of cigarettes to minors. Today the practice of "carding" young shoppers buying cigarettes is almost universal in our country (HHS, 1990b). We found that wine coolers were being placed next to popular fruit juice bottles in convenience stores near schools; the fact and amount of their alcoholic content was displayed only in very small print colored nearly identically to the label background and in locations and orientations unlikely to be noticed (HHS, 1991). The Secretary who requested this study understood completely that wine coolers were becoming a gateway to alcohol for young students and used our study to focus attention on this problem.

We did not need secretarial or congressional requests to trigger a study focusing on common citizens and beneficiaries. We had our own internal planning process to identify the studies that we performed. Examples of studies initiated by our office include essentially qualitative studies of the following:

- Public cholesterol screenings that were dangerous because of drawing blood in unsanitary conditions and providing inappropriate advice to those having their blood tested. Results were obtained by visiting the public screening locations and observing the conditions first hand (HHS, 1990a).

■ Ineffective implementation of human subject research protections resulting from overwhelming workloads of institutional review boards (IRBs). Results were obtained through federal records and reports, site visits to academic health centers, scientific literature, accompanying Food and Drug Administration (FDA) inspectors, attendance at IRB meetings, and systematic gathering of data from seventy-five IRBs of varying sizes and auspices (HHS, 2008).

■ Tactics for recruiting and training foster parents. The studies revealed that the most effective route to recruiting foster parents was through networks of current foster parents, and that supportive services to help foster parents through difficult conditions and to provide sources for medical care were essential to retaining them. Results were obtained through mail surveys and in-person focus groups with foster parents and case workers (HHS, 2002a, 2002b).

All of these studies involved leaving the office to observe programs in action and interact in person with those affected by policies. "Hitting the pavement" enabled us to observe encounters between program staff and intended beneficiaries. All of these studies revealed and explained problems not fully appreciated before they were started.

Such "on the spot," "real life" encounters provided an important and quintessentially qualitative method of data collection, for several reasons. Studies such as those described remind us that qualitative methods involve not only listening to people but also observing them. The observations made during these kinds of studies provided some of our greatest payoffs from using qualitative methods. Our evaluators saw things that would never have occurred to them had they used telephone, mail, or Internet data collection methods.

For example, in the case mentioned above about IRBs, our evaluators observed boxes containing large numbers of applications for approval of research involving human subjects that had not yet been scheduled for review. This observation was offered as evidence of how overwhelmed the review system was. In the case of public cholesterol screening, our evaluators saw so-called (but poorly) "trained" health clinicians drawing blood in public venues without sterile gloves, handling money before drawing blood, and counseling clients not to worry too much about cholesterol levels over 200. They found that youths interviewed in the wine cooler study were unable to distinguish alcoholic from non-alcoholic fruit drinks even when handed the bottles and given all the time they wanted to read the labels. Foster care parents told our evaluators that they were recruited by other foster parents rather than by any of the public commercials being used unsuccessfully by foster care agencies to meet demands for enrolling new foster parents. They volunteered that one of the impediments to becoming foster parents was the unfavorable depiction of foster parents in movies and TV programs. These insights about what was really happening "out there" were largely unknown or unappreciated by policy makers at the time the studies were conducted but now are more broadly understood.

Another phenomenon we discovered was that some of our best ideas for planning future studies came from unexpected observations or comments while making field visits on earlier studies. Initially, our planning process for deciding what studies to do every year involved fairly conventional methods—scanning emerging research and policy documents, identifying troubling or promising trends in health care data, interviewing policy staff in the department and in congressional oversight committees, and the like. However, we gradually realized that through our fieldwork associated with ongoing studies we were finding things that were unknown to policy makers and their staff and unstudied by researchers, but that held promise for improving health and human services. The examples in the previous paragraphs illustrate this. Here are a couple more:

- A law was passed to promote enrollment in child health programs by simplifying the eligibility forms. To see how this was working, we sent out teams to talk to eligibility workers and potential enrollees. We found that there were other (possibly more compelling) impediments to enrollment, including fear of investigation of family members who were undocumented.

▪ In a study on ways to improve paternity establishment in child support cases, our evaluators found that the child's father would proudly celebrate the birth of his child while visiting the mother at the hospital on the day of birth but deny it afterwards (HHS, 1997b). Hospital nurses found they could improve paternity establishment if they secured a signed acknowledgment of paternity in the hospital on the day of the birth.

Perhaps these insights from qualitative observations are well known now; some might even say they were well known when our field teams "discovered" them. However, at the time, these were not topics that were being prominently discussed in policy circles, even though they were highly policy relevant. We were able to make this information known to program administrators who could then adopt and adapt them as appropriate.

The bottom line about "being there" is threefold. Qualitative data gained on-site about what happens at the point where services are delivered is of high interest to policy makers; being on-site provides the benefits of qualitative observations in addition to listening; it provides rich and otherwise unknown insights and understandings that can greatly enhance policy making.

4. **Include the perspectives of all major stakeholder groups.** Although policy makers are especially interested in connecting with common citizens, to be successful, all major stakeholder groups on any given issue must be engaged. That is one reason that stakeholder organizations are so influential. By stakeholders I mean not only the federal, state, and local government offices responsible for implementing the programs, but also the private sector groups that look out for the interests of their clients. Examples related to health care policy include national associations of home health providers, medical equipment suppliers, physicians, hospitals, nursing homes, nurses, and the like; and advocacy groups for program beneficiaries such as persons with disabilities, children in foster care, persons needing community-based care, and the elderly. Each stakeholder group is prepared to rapidly, professionally, and impressively weigh in on any pending policy matter germane to their constituency. Therefore, to the extent possible, qualitative analysts also need

to gather information from as many relevant stakeholder groups as possible.

Whereas evaluators are naturally concerned about the quality of their own methods and analysis, policy makers will generally not challenge them on their methods, at least not initially. They assume that the experts—the evaluators—did their jobs in accordance with professional standards. But failure to connect with, or at least acknowledge the need to consult with, relevant stakeholders is one shortcoming they will not easily tolerate. I vividly remember testifying before a congressional committee on Medicare home health benefits. Our auditors had completed a study that showed that as much as 40 percent of Medicare claims were made in error (HHS, 1997a). The effect of this error rate was as much as $7 billion in potential waste. Our auditors had done a really thorough job in reaching this conclusion, and our evaluations shed light on why this was happening. One of the first questions I got from one of the congressional panelists was, "Did you talk to the doctors who authorized the services?" Fortunately, I was able to say, "Yes we did," and to tell him how many physicians our auditors had interviewed. That really helped make our case. If I said "No" or "I don't know," our findings would have been completely undermined.

Of course, interviewing representative samples of all stakeholders is not always possible. An upfront acknowledgment of the limitations of the sample is an effective way to deal with this problem. This is much better than "admitting" it when challenged. Another tactic is to point to other studies that reflect the stands of organized stakeholder groups and hold out the evaluator's study as filling the gaps represented by those studies.

As discussed in the Introduction, there is another powerful reason for engaging relevant stakeholders. It is one of the best ways to solve problems. It brings buy-in to the evaluation findings and recommendations. But even more importantly, it provides a method for coming up with practical solutions. This can be illustrated by the emergence several years ago of significant problems with human tissue used for surgeries. A newspaper reporter discovered a patient who received a bone graft that led to a severe infection in his leg. On investigation, the graft was found not to have been harvested, tested, or processed in accordance with generally accepted practices. Other problems of unsatisfactory processing and storage of human tissues—skin, bones, tendons, and the like—from international sources came to the fore. This included problems with how the tissues were harvested. Families of dying and recently deceased patients were approached by human tissue bank personnel asking for permission to harvest the tissues of dying relatives immediately after death. They said that the tissues were needed to treat burns and other emergencies. In some cases, however, the tissue was being used for cosmetic surgery unrelated to medical emergencies. Although such use is legitimate, the tissue in these cases had been harvested under false representations. The donating families, approached as they were during the trying moments surrounding the death of a loved one, were extremely upset to discover how the tissue had been used.

Our office was asked to quickly discover the extent of both kinds of problems—quality control and misrepresentation in the process of tissue donation. In conducting our studies we interviewed families of tissue donors and representatives of the tissue bank industry (HHS, 2001a, 2001b). At one time we had representatives of both groups in the office simultaneously, during a briefing of senior departmental officials dealing with the problem. At the end of that meeting, the representatives of the industry asked if they, the donor families, and our evaluation team could remain after the meeting. During the course of an hour-long discussion that followed, the families and the tissue bank representative came up with the outline of a new policy to govern the process of harvesting tissue. The revised policy was publically issued shortly thereafter to the mutual satisfaction of the two groups involved. I do not think we would have achieved this result without interviewing both groups and having them both in the room when the findings were discussed. Certainly, it was to their mutual advantage to solve this problem. The qualitative evaluation set the stage for solving a difficult problem in an efficient way.

5. **Carefully consider the use of quotes.** A question often arises as to whether evaluators should use quotations from interviewees in their evaluation reports. (See Grob, 1992, 2010a, 2010b, for a broader discussion on writing for impact.) It may seem strange to give this issue such prominence in this chapter. However, it comes up frequently and is a very

important matter. No reliable answer to this question exists, except to advise that evaluators consult with the commissioners of the evaluation about whether to include quotes. Even though qualitative evaluators use systematic methods to collect their data, policy makers may view excerpts from the qualitative data (quotes and examples) as merely anecdotes; thus the caution. Here are some pros and cons to using quotes.

On the pro side, some people believe that such quotations are powerful mechanisms to drive home the important findings of the evaluation. They believe that systematically collected quotes and examples humanize and bring life to otherwise boring disserta-tions, make the thrust of interviews clear to readers, leave lasting impressions about the relevance and reality of what was found, and promote action on the report's recommendations. More ana-lytically, they believe that quotes and anecdotes are an essential part of the evidence supporting the findings, and that failure to include them is actually an analytical flaw.

On the con side, some readers believe that using quotes and examples adds a non-analytic feature to the evaluation report. They interpret what the interviewees are saying as self-serving rhetoric. They hold the viewpoint expressed earlier in this chapter: "They always say that. What did you expect? I already thought that's what they would say." Perhaps more importantly, they simply are not persuaded by this kind of "evidence." The more colorful and flamboyant quotes sound like emotional outbursts. They believe that the evaluator is becoming an advocate instead of remaining an independent analyst.

Two of my recent evaluations included interviewee quotes because the sponsors of the evaluations explicitly requested that they be included. In both cases they argued strongly that they were needed to analytically prove the findings of the report. Con-versely, I had previously worked in an office that established a policy to seldom use such quotes because they believed they were analytically unbecoming.

I cannot explain why the mere use or nonuse of interviewee quotes is itself such a strong issue with readers. I only know that it is. All I can say is that it is a very big deal with significant consequences for your work. There is not a "correct" position on this matter. It is all in the eye of the beholder, and reasonable, well-informed people feel strongly on both sides of this issue. So here is the advice I offer:

First, consult with the commissioners of the evaluation in advance and honor their preference—not about which quotes to use (that is your prerogative as an independent evaluator) but simply whether quotes will be used. Second, if you use interviewees' quotes, try to find quotes that *explain* rather than simply describe. For example,

- "The program staff were extremely considerate and polite. This made it easier for us to understand and negotiate the complex eligibility rules."

- "The program office helped resolve differences among the grantees. As a result we were able to come up with practical plans."

- "The policy is not followed just because it is written. Our office had already developed a culture to proceed in that way."

Third, be careful about "One person said, '...'" quotes. Make sure you indicate whether the quote reflects a prevailing or exceptional viewpoint, and if prevailing, that it is representative. For example, do not just quote someone as saying, "We were afraid to ask." Instead, say: typical of a majority of our interviewees, one person said, "We were afraid to ask."

If interviewees were promised confidentiality, take extreme care in describing the source of your quotes without revealing the speaker. You can do this by saying something along the following lines: "We have followed these procedures for more than 10 years" (senior program administrator).

6. **Avoid strongly worded advocacy.** The starting point of policy makers is one of respect for our professionalism. Policy makers will trust you if you exhibit professionalism at all times. So will stakeholders and reporters. They can get biased opinions whenever they want. They highly value your independence. It is yours to lose. The way to preserve your independence is to *be* independent. A strong advocacy tone, especially an emotional one, will undermine the independence of the evaluator and thereby the "cause" for which the evaluator wants to take a stand.

Although evaluators should stand by their recommendations, they should not come across as strongly representing a particular set of clients or program beneficiaries or appearing to have agendas of their own. Evaluators should stick to their facts and analysis. Policy makers do not need another advocate in evaluator's clothing. They are all hoping you will bring facts, insights, and hints of possible solutions to the seemingly intractable problems they are working to resolve.

7. **Manage policy makers' expectations.** If you are doing an evaluation at the request of a policy maker who needs results to meet a very tight deadline, such as a few weeks or a couple months, you need to make sure that what you can deliver will be credible to your client and to others. Your client will not have much trouble agreeing to limit the scope of your study. The limitations can surround such things as the evaluation questions to be addressed and the methods to be used. However, you must be explicit and public about such limitations to maintain your credibility with the broader audience for the findings. Here are some important things to consider under such circumstances:

- After (better yet, during) negotiations, get a written request for the study, including the questions to be addressed and the schedule of deliverables. You may be able to facilitate both the negotiations and the availability of a written request by taking a first stab at the letter yourself and then going back and forth with the requester and his or her staff on expectations.

- Include the letter in your report.

- Include a section in your report on the limitations of scope and method, referring again to the letter.

- Aim to fill a gap in what is generally known on the topic to be evaluated. Briefly explain in your report what is already known on the topic, the relevance and importance of the evaluation questions, and why you and the policy maker have chosen the limited questions, scope, schedule, and methods.

- Do not agree to do the study unless you are comfortable with what you have negotiated.

- Make it clear to the policy maker that while the scope, questions, and the schedule are negotiable, the methods and the results are not. Some policy makers requesting studies may try to influence the outcomes of the study by specifying what methods are to be used and hinting at what they think the findings should be.

One reason to get and publish an acceptable request letter is that things can change during the course of your evaluation. The most common one is a change of key personnel. The person who requested the study may have moved on to another job before the study is completed; without the letter, the incoming official who is replacing the original requestor may deny that any request was made. Without the letter, you will have difficulty explaining why your evaluation is limited in scope and may therefore have the appearance of incompleteness. You do not need to worry about the limited scope and methods if you have the letter of request, as policy makers and those who work with them understand the exigencies of getting analytic information in time to support decision making.

I have found it helpful to use the following approach when dealing with requestors of studies. Somewhere near the beginning of the engagement I say to them something like this: "As you probably know, professional evaluators like myself have to remain independent in conducting our studies. We will gladly perform a study to address the issues you have raised. However, we will have to decide the methods and results. That having been said, we would greatly appreciate and benefit from your input into the study." Then, when the meeting is over, I say something such as: "Thanks again for your input and advice. We will get back to you shortly with our study design." My clients generally accept this approach.

CONCLUSION

Perhaps the best way to guide the selection of methods to support policy makers in making hard choices is to put yourself in their shoes. As a policy maker you would want to make sure that you fully understand the technical aspects of the issues you are dealing with. For that purpose you will want both quantitative and qualitative information. But you would also probably care a lot about meeting the needs of all the stakeholders you represent. And you will want to understand them in a very human way.

Qualitative evaluations are particularly well suited to bringing the human side of things to bear in policy making, but it is important to present such information from all legitimate sides of the issue.

KEY CONCEPTS

Advocacy	Mixing methods
Anecdotes	Observation
Breadth of analysis	Policy influencers
Consensus	Policy makers
Credibility	Purposive samples
Depth of analysis	Quality control
Government	Random samples
Independence	Stakeholder organizations

DISCUSSION QUESTIONS

1. The policy-oriented evaluations described in this chapter affect real people and real organizations on a very large scale; if the evaluations are used as planned, governmental policies are influenced as a result. The author states, "Qualitative analysis is very important to policy makers because of their need to get all points of view and to understand the ramifications of policies for all who might be affected by them." Identify a federal, state, or local public policy issue about which you are passionate. Who are the "real people" affected by the issue? Whose points of view should be gathered to inform policy deliberations on this topic (major stakeholder groups, relevant policy makers, and other leading influencers), and what methods might you use to do so?

2. Imagine that you are meeting with a group of policy makers to discuss plans for an upcoming evaluation. You are proposing a study that includes qualitative and quantitative methods. One policy maker clearly favors quantitative

methods and asserts that qualitative approaches are not scientific and should be omitted from the study design. How might you respond to such a blanket assertion?

3. The author emphasizes the paradoxical nature of the policy-making world, characterizing it as "simultaneously systematic and chaotic, glacially slow and lightning fast." He describes the "mad rush" that occurs "when the time is right" and stresses that "evaluators wishing to influence the outcomes need to have their reports already on the table and be able to serve up quick analyses to answer the rapid-fire questions that seem to come from all directions." What are some ways evaluators can prepare for these situations? What tradeoffs might present themselves?

4. The author puts forward some principles for increasing the likelihood that policy makers will use qualitative findings. What aspects of these principles align with the guidance for evaluators, particularly those incorporating qualitative inquiry, to "stay true to the data"?

REFERENCES

Chelimsky, E. (2009). Integrating evaluation units into the political environment of government: The role of evaluation policy. In W. M. K. Trochim, M. Mark, & L. Cooksy (Eds.), *Evaluation policy and evaluation practice: New directions for evaluation* (Vol. 123, pp. 51–66). San Francisco, CA: Jossey-Bass.

Grob, G. F. (1992). How policy is made and how evaluators can affect it. *Evaluation Practice, 13*, 175–183.

Grob, G. F. (2003). A truly useful bat is one found in the hands of a slugger. *American Journal of Evaluation, 24*, 499–505.

Grob, G. F. (2006). The evaluator's role in policy development. In R. Mohan & K. Sullivan (Eds.), *Promoting the use of government evaluations in policymaking: New directions for evaluation* (Vol. 112, pp. 99–108). San Francisco, CA: Jossey-Bass.

Grob, G. F. (2010a). Providing recommendations, suggestions, and options for improvement. In J. Wholey, H. Hatry, & K. Newcomer (Eds.), *Handbook of practical program evaluation* (3rd ed., pp. 581–593). San Francisco, CA: Jossey-Bass.

Grob, G. F. (2010b). Writing for impact. In J. Wholey, H. Hatry, & K. New-comer (Eds.), *Handbook of practical program evaluation* (3rd ed., pp. 594–619). San Francisco, CA: Jossey-Bass.

Jonas, R. K. (1999). Against the whim: State legislatures' use of program evaluation. In R. K. Jonas (Ed.), *Legislative evaluation: Utilization-driven research for decision makers; New directions for program evaluation* (Vol. 81, pp. 3–10). San Francisco, CA: Jossey-Bass.

Mohan, R., & Sullivan, K., eds. (2006). *Promoting the use of government evaluations in policymaking: New directions for evaluation* (Vol. 112, pp. 7–23). San Francisco, CA: Jossey-Bass.

US Department of Health and Human Services (HHS), Office of Inspector General. (1990a). *Public cholesterol screening.* Washington, DC: Author.

US Department of Health and Human Services (HHS), Office of Inspector General. (1990b). *Youth access to cigarettes.* Washington, DC: Author.

US Department of Health and Human Services (HHS), Office of Inspector General. (1991). *Youth and alcohol: A national survey: Do they know what they are drinking?* Washington, DC: Author.

US Department of Health and Human Services (HHS), Office of Inspector General. (1997a). *Audit of Medicare home health services in California, Illinois, New York and Texas.* Washington, DC: Author.

US Department of Health and Human Services (HHS), Office of Inspector General. (1997b). *In-hospital voluntary paternity acknowledgement program: Effective practices in hospital staff training.* Washington, DC: HHS.

US Department of Health and Human Services (HHS), Office of Inspector General. (2001a). *Informed consent in tissue donation: Expectations and realities.* Washington, DC: Author.

US Department of Health and Human Services (HHS), Office of Inspector General. (2001b). *Oversight of tissue banking.* Washington, DC: Author.

US Department of Health and Human Services (HHS), Office of Inspector General. (2002a). *Recruiting foster parents.* Washington, DC: Author.

US Department of Health and Human Services (HHS), Office of Inspector General. (2002b). *Retaining foster parents.* Washington, DC: Author.

US Department of Health and Human Services (HHS), Office of Inspector General. (2008). *Institutional review boards: A time for reform.* Washington, DC: Author.

Zajano, N. C., & Lochtefeld, S. S. (1999). The nature of knowledge and language in the legislative arena. In R. K. Jonas (Ed.), *Legislative evaluation: Utilization-driven research for decision makers; New directions for program evaluation* (Vol. 81, pp. 85–94). San Francisco, CA: Jossey-Bass.

Qualitative Inquiry within Theory-driven Evaluation

Perspectives and Future Directions

Katrina L. Bledsoe

Key Ideas

- Theory-driven evaluation is employed when there is a desire to understand and explain the difference between what program designers intended to happen and what actually happened.

- Theory-driven evaluation includes two key features—norms and causes—and one key component—logic models.

- The evolution of theory-driven evaluation has been shaped by how to best capture and illustrate norms and causes.

- Qualitative inquiry is essential to ensure effective implementation of theory-driven evaluation.

When originally asked to write a chapter on the use of qualitative inquiry within the theory-driven evaluation (TDE) approach, I responded with a confident and resounding, "Yes!" because I knew that qualitative inquiry is an important aspect of TDE. I also knew that although many evaluation practitioners employ elements of TDE in their work (logic models, for example), many are not familiar with TDE's historical and theoretical grounding and how these concepts have shaped evaluation practice. In the field of evaluation, I come from a practitioner perspective that advocates using multiple approaches (Bledsoe & Graham, 2005) and mixed methodologies and methods (Bledsoe & Hopson, 2009; Mertens, Bledsoe, Sullivan, & Wilson, 2010); therefore, in addition to a strong understanding of TDE itself, I have an intimate understanding of how, in my own practice, qualitative inquiry is woven throughout TDE. But early attempts to draft this chapter proved that actually describing the use of qualitative inquiry in TDE is challenging. Even though qualitative inquiry is now considered a critical component of TDE (at least from the evaluation practitioner perspective), for many years, quantitative characteristics were the primary focus of TDE evaluators and theorists.

Theory-driven evaluation has evolved over time. Although the key elements of TDE have remained relatively constant, the TDE approach has been shaped by prominent theorists and practitioners alike. Indeed, because many people have contributed to the development of TDE, there are different perspectives on the approach. Furthermore, some of the key elements are regularly used in other evaluation approaches, often without explicit reference to TDE. This can cause some confusion because practitioners may use some of the elements and think "I understand TDE," but they have only adopted a piece of TDE without thoroughly grounding themselves and their work in the approach as a whole. My goal in this chapter is to make sense of the multi-faceted properties associated with TDE, but more specifically to describe the importance of using qualitative inquiry to ensure the effective implementation of TDE.

Before getting into the details, let me begin by describing a big picture of TDE. A theory-driven evaluation assesses the difference between the hypothesis of the program and the reality of the program. In other words, people who design programs often want to accomplish something fairly specific; they can describe in detail the issue the program is attempting to address, as well as the processes used to accomplish the goals of the effort. However, reality sometimes interferes with the best-laid plans! The difference between what the designers intend and what actually happens—and why—is at the heart of TDE.

Evaluators who employ a TDE approach seek to understand and explain the disconnect between what is supposed to happen in a program and what actually happens.

If this general description sounds familiar, but you are not well versed in TDE as an evaluation approach, it may be because various theorists and practitioners have coined different terms to reflect the practice of TDE. The most common terms associated with TDE include theory of change, theory-based evaluation, and program theory, which is also known as stakeholder theory (Gargani, 2003). Despite these different terms, they are all variations of TDE and originate from the same basic foundation: a focus on the link between the theory (e.g., particular social science theory, program theory, or stakeholder theory), the processes by which programs operate to generate the intended outcome, and the impact of the program. Indeed, these variations on the theme of TDE illustrate how the approach has been shaped and thus evolved over time.

A *theory of change* seeks to explain the central changes that would be required to bring about a long-term goal or impact. In many cases, a theory of change includes antecedents to the perceived problem as well as the program's intended outcomes. These are often noted in a pathway, map of change, or a change framework. These maps indicate the change that is desired and the pathway by which the program is intended to achieve that change (Gargani, 2003).

In a *theory-based* evaluation, the focus is not necessarily on the causal pathway or exact theoretical tenets per se; in fact, there may not be a need to understand the factors that cause change at all. What is more important in theory-based evaluation is to identify the quality of inputs needed to increase (or decrease) a causal link. For example, my colleagues from Education Development Center and I worked with a teacher professional development program in North Carolina. They had hypothesized that using strategies that are effective when teaching gifted and talented students (e.g., critical thinking and exploration) could have the same positive effect with students in regular or mainstream classrooms, where teaching strategies such as lecture and memorization are more commonly practiced (Gayle & Hargett, 2003, as cited in Project Tomorrow, 2003). Thus, strategies that were considered a "higher quality" input were presumed to increase the strength of the causal link of teaching strategies to student performance.

Program theory is a term used by evaluators and increasingly by program staff. Program theory is sometimes called *stakeholder theory,* because it represents the general idea that program staff and associated stakeholders have in their minds about how a program or intervention should work. Program theory may or may not be buttressed by a scholarly foundation; nonetheless, it provides a general mapping of the intervention, including how it is intended to generate change or improve the identified problem or situation. Similar to theory-based evaluation, program theory is often driven by values and perceived expectations of how the program *should* function (Chen, 2005; Donaldson, 2007).

This strong focus on intended impact derived from the program theory means that TDE tends to be associated with outcomes: the extent to which a program meets its goals as outlined in the intent of the program. Because of this, much of what we *hear* about TDE contains an emphasis on positivistic paradigm study designs (e.g., randomized controlled trials [RCTs]) that specifically investigate cause-and-effect relationships. Even the most accepted definitions of TDE include such terminology. Yet, TDE theorists such as Carol Weiss (1997), and more recently, Patricia Rogers (e.g., Funnell & Rogers, 2011), have advocated for the inclusion of qualitative inquiry and methods in the implementation of TDE. For example, Rogers advocates that evaluators develop a program theory (to inform the evaluation) in concert with stakeholders and program staff. Such collaboration leads to an examination of values, perspectives, processes, and subjectivities that may drive the program design and implementation as well as frame the evaluation. Moreover, evaluation practitioners who articulate how they actually conduct an evaluation using a TDE approach consistently describe a process that incorporates qualitative inquiry (e.g., Bledsoe & Donaldson, forthcoming 2014; Fitzpatrick, Christie, & Mark, 2009).

My goal in this chapter is to describe how qualitative inquiry is integral to the application of TDE. To accomplish this, I have divided the chapter into four sections. The first presents a brief history of TDE. The second section discusses the three key elements of TDE—causes, norms, and logic models—and how qualitative inquiry is commonly used in each element. In the third section, I argue that qualitative inquiry is not only a strategy used in TDE, but is actually imperative for effective TDE implementation. I conclude with some thoughts about the future of TDE.

THEORY-DRIVEN EVALUATION: A BRIEF HISTORY

Although TDE has been employed since the time of Ralph Tyler, a 1930s education theorist (Gargani, 2003), the approach did not become widely discussed in evaluation circles until the late 1960s and beyond. At this time, evaluators such as Carol Weiss, Peter Rossi, and Lee Cronbach engaged in conversations that pushed the boundaries of evaluation by positing that theories—in particular, social science theories—could buttress evaluations conducted at federal, state, and local levels of government (Shadish, Cook, & Leviton, 1991; see also Schwandt and Cash, Chapter 1 in this volume, for a discussion of how qualitative inquiry in evaluation was developing at the same time). The idea was that linking specific social science theories to evaluations could provide information that could be used in policy making. Discussions within TDE circles focused on theories and models borrowed from traditional social science fields, such as experimental and social psychology, as well as education (e.g., see Coryn, Noakes, Westine, & Schröter, 2011; Donaldson, Christie, & Mark, 2011, for comments on historical perspectives).

Weiss, Rossi, and Cronbach (Shadish et al., 1991) encouraged evaluators to go beyond the prevailing *black-box* approach (Patton, 1987; Weiss, 1998). Michael Scriven (1991) defined the black-box approach to evaluation as one in which the focus is on measuring the results of a programmatic intervention, without emphasis on why and how results were (or were not) achieved. Indeed, for Scriven, it was not always necessary to understand how outcomes were generated, especially with limited time and financial resources. In contrast, Chen and Rossi (1983,1987) proposed that the black box *should* be opened through an effective evaluation. They argued that understanding how a program works is especially important in trying to determine the extent to which the intent or theory of the program was predictive of the outcomes the program did or did not achieve. They also contended that knowledge of the inner workings of a program would be useful when trying to replicate a successful program.

It was during these discussions that the use of qualitative inquiry in TDE began to creep into the conversation. Chen (1990), while highlighting the importance of quantitative data to determine outcomes, also underscored the importance of the perspectives held by program stakeholders. These stakeholder perspectives were acknowledged to form the foundation for the conceptual models on which more causative designs were based; what is noteworthy was the recognition by Chen that such perspectives are best elicited through qualitative inquiry. Likewise, Weiss's writings on theory-driven approaches in evaluation evolved over time (Shadish et al., 1991). Her early writings focused on the use of experimental methods; later, she advocated for the use of mixed methods (e.g., Weiss, 1997), including the incorporation of qualitative inquiry, because it would generate wider understanding about the theoretical underpinnings of the program and encourage the use of evaluation results by various stakeholders.

In the twenty-first century, additional demands have been placed on professionals to design programs and evaluations that are more culturally sensitive and reflect the increasing diversity of voices needed to effectively address complex social, economic, and environmental issues. Theorists such as Frierson, Hood, and Hughes (2010) noted the dynamic nature of the social contexts in which evaluations are conducted. To respond to these changes, evaluators, including those who practice TDE, increasingly embrace a broader set of methods and methodologies in their work. Nontraditional data sources, collection, and analytic methods (e.g., video diaries and visual facilitation) have become acceptable.

Even more recently, Patricia Rogers and her colleague Sue Funnell (Funnell & Rogers, 2011) have articulated how qualitative inquiry can be used in developing theories of change. They have noted that evaluators are increasingly included at the formative and conceptual stages of program development to help align the program components and expected outcomes to their theoretical foundations. As is evident from this brief history, the lack of a specific definition of TDE arises from the need for this approach to continually evolve to keep pace with the demands of the ever-changing field of evaluation, along with the broader society and social norms.

KEY ELEMENTS IN THEORY-DRIVEN EVALUATION (TDE)

Two key features and one key component are commonly associated with TDE. The two key features are norms and causes; the key component is a logic model (Chen, 2005). Norms include the values held by stakeholders that drive the goals and objectives of a particular program. Causes are the factors that contribute to the impacts or consequences of the program. Logic models provide a graphic representation of the pathway by which the program is designed to reach specific goals.

Qualitative inquiry is best suited for gathering information to understand the norms and values held by stakeholders to construct a logic model. Causes are often determined using quantitative inquiry and analysis. Note, however, that both quantitative and qualitative approaches to inquiry live side-by-side in a TDE framework. For clarification, let us consider the three elements (norms, causes, and logic models) separately.

Norms

Norms provide guidance concerning what values and goals should be prioritized for a program to be effective in an *ideal* world and setting (Chen, 1990, emphasis added). For instance, a drug prevention program might be guided by the societal norm that engaging in drug use as an adolescent is a poor choice. Thus, a program strategy might be to provide life skills training to adolescents to help them make appropriate life choices. This feature of TDE relies on a particular theory (e.g., social science theory, a program's theory) and contextualizing the norms of the key stakeholders within the situation; without programmatic norms, there could be no TDE approach to the evaluation. Indeed, a TDE approach to evaluation does not center on a particular program or strategy per se; rather, the focus is on developing a plausible explanation about the complexity of the context and the factors that might influence it, but all of this is based on accepted norms of the program. In other words: "Based on our values and norms, what do we expect to happen as a result of this program?" To be an effective TDE evaluator, one must understand the norms constituted and implemented by the stakeholders and the context in which the program is conducted.

Chen (2005) tacitly acknowledged that understanding various contextual factors (e.g., political landscape, community environment) is primarily a qualitative endeavor. Indeed, comparing what is desired with what is perceived to be reality is characteristically a qualitative process. How a community interprets the alignment of its perceived values and goals has much more to do with the understanding of factors such as history, experiences, and self-reflection (Kirkhart, 2013); these complex factors and norms are more appropriately understood through the lens of qualitative inquiry than trying to reduce the factors to a set of simple, quantifiable measurements.

When an evaluator begins a theory-driven evaluation, qualitative inquiry is frequently the first line of the data collection process because norms must be determined early in the evaluation (e.g., Chen, 1990). The evaluator often starts with informal approaches, such as meeting with select stakeholders to learn about the program and gain an understanding of the purpose(s) of the evaluation. This entrance into the evaluative setting is intended to begin the process of "opening the black box" and identifying the norms that might ultimately inform meaningful data collection and analysis. Once the direction of the evaluation plan has been formulated, a more systematic process of collecting data to ascertain the various values and beliefs that stakeholders hold about the program and context is undertaken. Data collection may include focus groups, individual interviews, or observations. This step is critical. Often, one of the purposes of a theory-driven evaluation is to make relevant changes to the program; without understanding how the program is envisioned and experienced by many different stakeholder groups, improvements may not be properly grounded in the context in which the program is conducted (e.g., Bledsoe, 2005; Chen, 2005).

Theorists and practitioners of the TDE approach (e.g., Funnell & Rogers, 2011) have put more emphasis on qualitative inquiry to provide credible information for program development and improvement. For instance, my colleague James Graham and I (Bledsoe & Graham, 2005) made use of qualitative interviews conducted with staff and parent participants in a family literacy program to provide feedback on aspects of the program they found most effective. Our findings, which included the importance of family bonding time, had not surfaced through other methods of data collection, such as surveys and quantitative observational protocols, commonly known as *checklists*. Similarly, Fredericks, Deegan, and Carman (2008) conducted an evaluation of a disability program and used interviews to help capture how the individualized services provided to people with disabilities led to an improved quality of life. These interviews informed subsequent measurement, using path analysis, by identifying and articulating the key constructs for survey item development. My work with an obesity prevention program aimed at urban high school students in Trenton, New Jersey (Bledsoe, 2005) used qualitative discussions with staff and students to guide decision-making concerning the types of questions to be asked in the evaluation as well as articulating the venue in which measures should be applied. Likewise, Donaldson (2007) used interviews and focus groups in the *Work and Health Initiative* to discern the opinions, perspectives, and linkages of unemployed workers who were learning new skills in employment seeking. Those perspectives and opinions helped the evaluation team understand how each of the program components might work, under what circumstances the components might work, and with which populations the components might be effective.

Donaldson's (2007) more recent work on TDE articulated a three-step process: (1) formulating evaluation questions about the program; (2) prioritizing the evaluation questions; and (3) answering the questions. Formulating and prioritizing questions, as well as collecting the necessary data to answer the questions, is rooted in all evaluation approaches. However, at the minimum, qualitative inquiry facilitates the formulation and prioritization of the questions. For instance, he noted that engaging stakeholders, specifically getting the opinions of those affected by the program, is key to the process of formulating questions to develop the backstory of a logic model. In prioritizing questions, he emphasized describing the norms, needs, and values espoused by the stakeholders. Because the first two steps of his three-step process are buoyed by qualitative inquiry, Donaldson ultimately advocated for the use of logic models that may be multi-level, complex, and value-laden. In advocating for the use of such logic models, he suggested that qualitative methods and designs might, depending on the questions asked, be the most appropriate and credible methods to use in conducting the evaluation.

Donaldson has stated repeatedly (e.g., Donaldson, Gooler, & Weiss, 1998; Donaldson in Fitzpatrick, Christie, & Mark, 2009) that understanding and measuring program processes and effectiveness are rooted in stakeholders' personal perspectives. These perspectives are surfaced through facilitated conversations and thus are rooted in qualitative inquiry. In essence, the personal values of program participants and other stakeholders matter. As a result, Donaldson ultimately advocates for the use of logic models that can accommodate complexity and incorporate the values articulated by program stakeholders.

Causes

Evaluations that use the TDE approach tend to focus on the impact of a program. This includes accounting for intended and unintended outcomes. The general idea behind TDE is to sufficiently understand the program so that it can be implemented or generalized beyond a particular context. In essence, the key to the TDE approach is to understand the factors that might be directly associated with achieving (or failing to achieve) outcomes. Understanding unintended outcomes further increases the likelihood that positive outcomes may be achieved when the program is implemented in another setting. Indeed, an overarching goal of TDE is program generalizability.

Although generalizability may be a goal of TDE, Chen (2005) acknowledged that attaining positive outcomes with the same program in a different setting is difficult because each context consists of unique variables that will affect program implementation and outcomes. The context informs the program implementation; thus, initial discussions with stakeholders are recommended to build a logic or conceptual model based on important contextual factors (see prior discussion of qualitative inquiry's role in uncovering these contextual issues and developing program theory). Unique contexts must be explored, because no two settings are assumed to be alike. When the same program is implemented in different settings, one must examine the similarities and differences between them to assess the potential impact the context may have on implementation (Chen, 2005).

Logic Models

Although norms and causes are features or characteristics of TDE, a logic model is the most commonly identifiable component of TDE. Logic models provide a causal sketch of a program's intended effectiveness while also considering contextual factors and incorporating norms and causes (Chen, 2005). The logic model graphically presents the hypothetical change that is to occur as a result of the program, as well as the pathway by which the program is designed to accomplish the desired changes or goals. For instance, in the development of the American Evaluation Association's public statement on cultural competence in evaluation, visual facilitation was used to delineate a "logical" pathway for (1) the dissemination of the statement to the association's membership; and (2) the effect the statement was expected to have on the membership's practice of evaluation. This, in effect, is a logic model.

Although logic modeling primarily has been presented as a linear activity within TDE, this perspective is not necessarily prescribed; instead, a logic model developed in tandem with stakeholders can take on many forms. Logic models have become more complex and systems-level focused, allowing for a more interactive and multilevel understanding of the environment in which the program is situated. Thus, logic models are increasingly multifaceted, circular, and often embedded within other models.

Qualitative inquiry could be considered the cornerstone of logic model development. Chen's (2012) recent work suggested a more systemic and multilevel perspective than previous recommendations; he presented the importance of considering aspects such as environmental, historical, and political contexts. For example, his framework attempts to situate a program within a systems perspective, underscoring the particular and often chaotic environment in which a program and participants exist. He divides a program logic model into two interconnected levels, with level 1 focusing on an action model and level 2 focusing on a change model. The action model includes considerations such as who the implementers are and the ecological context in which the program is being implemented. The change model outlines the theoretical perspective or hypothesis (either lay or scholarly) that serves as the foundation for the program. Chen showed how this two-level logic model addresses the complexity and inherent "messiness" of broader systems, such as an organization or community, while acknowledging how feedback on the program might be generated at different levels.

In acknowledging the use of a subjective perspective in the development of a logic model, evaluation questions must be grounded in the norms and context of the program rather than what is found in a review of the theoretical literature. This places great value in a grounded, bottom-up perspective (Chen, 2005), thereby focusing on the values, goals, and by extension, what the stakeholders want to know from the evaluation. This shifts the focus to the quality, credibility, and meaning of the evaluation questions, rather than simply how the questions will be operationalized, measured, and quantified. The aim of the evaluation questions is to expound on and represent the values and goals defined by the stakeholders, grounded by the programmatic context.

As a concrete example of the development of a logic model using qualitative inquiry, I was asked recently to assist a university-sponsored community group in defining a theory about how to increase parental engagement in low-income, predominately African American community schools. Using a passing knowledge of academic achievement in the scholarly literature, the hypothesis was that an increase in parental engagement would lead to an increase in student performance in school classrooms (e.g., Broderick, O'Connor, Mulcahy, Heffernan, & Heffernan, 2011; Warren, Hong, Rubin, & Uy, 2009). Based on the literature, the goal of the project was to examine parental engagement in the community under study. Although parental engagement was the specific variable of interest for the community group, I took a constructivist approach to gaining knowledge by asking a series of broad-based questions concerning the community (context); political/historical factors, including school closings (moderating variables); fiscal issues (resources); and school performance (outcomes). These questions were designed to ascertain the norms and values that undergirded the goal of increasing parental engagement.

As a result of my approach, stakeholders were engaged in a larger discussion of: (1) community values; (2) culture and cultural competence; and (3) other extenuating variables and circumstances, such as teacher expectations of students of color in general. The conversation started with questions that encouraged stakeholders to provide context and background; questions were intentionally asked to link their understanding of the scholarly and academic literature with what they perceived as the problem or story at hand. Only after a discussion of the background and context of the community (e.g., issues of desegregation and re-segregation of schools) did we work toward gaining an understanding of the issue of parental engagement as originally conceived in the program goals. Moderating variables, intended as well as unintended, also were considered. The conversation began to unveil community hurt, neglect, and anger about overarching issues such as re-gentrification, stereotypes about African Americans, and community members from African nations and the West Indies. Finally, a telling discussion of values took place, leading to the development of a logic model that addressed many of the variables that actually shaped the issue of parental engagement.

Although much of the development of a "theory" behind parental engagement started with formal literature, it was greatly informed and ultimately fashioned by these discussions. The information we gained was used to further develop questions related to the actual creation of the logic model. The logic model included not only the norms and values (articulated as goals), it also modeled antecedents to the program (causes that would ultimately undergird the theory).

QUALITATIVE INQUIRY: AN IMPERATIVE TO THEORY-DRIVEN EVALUATION

At the beginning of this chapter, I mentioned that the elements of TDE are somewhat ubiquitous throughout evaluation practice, as evidenced by the use of program/stakeholder (and sometimes scholarly) theories, logic models, and the like. I find this is particularly true when working in community-based settings.

Before an evaluation can begin in a community-based setting, the appropriate stakeholders must be identified and invited to the table (Frierson, Hood, & Hughes, 2010; Mertens, 2009). Bringing constituents to the table is not always easy; many people who are key to the discussion are hard to reach. However, their conceptualizations of the context, patterns of living, cultural mores, and anecdotal information are essential to guiding the evaluation. Chen (2005) noted that the difficulty in developing a good program theory is that the material that informs it must (1) be generated from the bottom up and (2) be grounded within the values, perceptions, and experiences of the stakeholders. I have often said that this level of engagement can sometimes resemble a therapy session; it can be messy and emotional, and it requires skillful facilitation (Bledsoe, 2009; see Stevahn and King, Chapter 6 of this volume, for more discussion of competencies for facilitating qualitative inquiry).

Most of this chapter has described how effective implementation of TDE is inherently based on a qualitative approach to data collection and analysis. Nevertheless, before a decision is made of the type of methods applied or types of analyses conducted, one must consider (1) the values and ethics on which the program is based; (2) the perceptions on which these values are based; and (3) the set of "truths" or perspectives that can and should be addressed. To measure these, one can use quantitative methods in the evaluation, of course; however, the manner by which TDE evaluators seek to understand a specific program and the stakeholders associated with the program is decidedly a qualitative activity. Meeting with stakeholders to construct relevant evaluation questions involves dialogue, meaning making, and arriving at a common understanding of program goals (Mertens & Wilson, 2012). These activities may be accomplished only through qualitative inquiry.

Frequently, qualitative methods are used to prepare for quantitative methods in an evaluation. Indeed, some evaluators consider qualitative inquiry as a precursor to quantitative inquiry; the argument is that quantitative data will provide "rigorous" evidence (Coryn et al., 2011). However, comparing the value of qualitative and quantitative data is mixing apples and oranges.

The evaluation questions posed (and in TDE, these are based on understandings of stakeholder and program norms, values, and perceptions) determine the type of data needed and manner of its collection. Randomized controlled trials (RCT) that use quantitative data are often considered the "gold standard" because cause and effect are examined as if they are beyond the effects of human interaction and contextual factors. Although "testing" the applicability of social science theory in real world settings can be conducted in a variety of ways, a simplistic "yes" or "no" to the question is generally insufficient for program and community stakeholders. Community members and stakeholders are often interested in questions that are contextual in nature. However, the answers to these questions often require additional questions and answers, especially, *"Why did a program or intervention work or not work?"* Qualitative inquiry appropriately illuminates the *why* element of this question and reflects the complexity and nuances of real people living in real communities.

Increasingly, the field of evaluation recognizes that unique program contexts need to be explored, because no two settings are entirely alike. This has implications for the TDE concept of program generalizability. Initial discussions with stakeholders result in the building of logic and other types of conceptual models based on important contextual factors. When a given program is implemented in different settings, one must examine the similarities and differences between the original and new settings to assess the potential impact the contexts may have on implementation (Chen, 2005). This alters the concept of "generalizability" in TDE, challenging the ideal of being able to *replicate* an effort in another setting. Instead, TDE evaluations seek to sufficiently understand how a program works in one setting. Through careful examination of additional settings, evaluators and program stakeholders can consider how the original program logic model might be adapted to other contexts.

Previously, I suggested that TDE is inherently predisposed to be culturally responsive because the theoretical underpinning of this evaluation approach takes into consideration culture, context, historical perspectives, and other factors related to values and norms (Bledsoe, 2005). For example, authors Mercier, Piat, Peladeau, and Dagenais (2001) used graphing techniques to identify the best hours to host and staff a drop-in youth center.

Mercier et al. discovered that the cultural context in which urban drop-in centers were established greatly influenced how much the centers were used and, by extension, how effective they were. Graphing techniques allowed Mercier et al. to develop a logic model that was most representative of the functioning of the centers, thereby ensuring a more accurate measurement of their effectiveness.

Rodney Hopson and I (Bledsoe & Hopson, 2009) noted that to consider the ethical treatment of underserved communities and foster cultural responsiveness in evaluation, determining what might be a significant outcome *for* the community must be at the forefront of evaluation planning. Conducting culturally responsive TDE assumes that evaluators are willing to explore diverse methodologies and ways of interpreting information. Qualitative inquiry is integral to achieving this more nuanced and refined approach to TDE. For instance, in our upcoming article (Bledsoe & Donaldson, forthcoming 2014), we posit that a culturally responsive approach to TDE includes considering the types of questions asked, understanding historical perspectives held by key stakeholders, and having iterative conversations about the culture and cultural context of the community and program.

CONCLUSION

Although qualitative inquiry is not often highlighted in the literature on TDE, it provides an essential means of understanding norms and causes, and for developing appropriate, situated, and contextually representative logic models. It also increases the robustness of program theories and subsequent evaluations. For instance, in my work with community-based stakeholders in the state capital of New Jersey (Bledsoe, 2005), qualitative inquiry drove the process of developing program theory. Meetings, listening sessions, and discussion groups were used to (1) provide data; (2) continue to refine evaluation questions; and (3) continue to address issues of social justice or cultural responsiveness (or lack thereof) in the development of a prenatal program aimed at reducing infant mortality among African American women. The trend of accentuating the role that qualitative inquiry plays in the effective implementation of TDE will likely continue, and possibly even accelerate.

In the field of evaluation, developing a logic model and identifying the program or stakeholder theory that underlies and guides the program or services is now standard practice. Logic models also attempt to describe the norms of a program and how they might cause change. Theorists and practitioners in TDE (e.g., Bledsoe, 2005; Chen 2005; Donaldson, 2007; Funnell & Rogers, 2011) have begun to frame TDE as a much broader and more inclusive approach than its previous focus on experimental and quasi-experimental designs (Chen, 2005, 2012; Funnell & Rogers, 2011). The approach benefits from the use of both quantitative and qualitative methods. Rather than focusing on the use of quantitative methods, increasingly the focus is on understanding the underlying values and judgments as well as exploring perspectives. Proponents of TDE (e.g., Bledsoe & Graham, 2005; Chen, 2005; Hopson, Kirkhart, & Bledsoe, 2012; Mertens, 2009) have cautioned evaluators against the reliance on a singular approach, instead advocating for the use of mixed methods, and using qualitative designs when appropriate. The program norms, stakeholders' perspectives and priorities, and contextual realities drive decisions about the appropriate evaluation approach and methods. In fact, the decision may be that a qualitative evaluation is the most appropriate way to answer the evaluation questions.

Said another way, in the future, TDE practitioners will approach evaluations with the knowledge that evaluation designs are contingent on the factors that frame the program theory; this includes all the relevant perspectives, norms, values, and contextual understanding that go into developing that theory. With this in mind, the evaluation must match the values and culture of the people and the setting in which the program operates. Donaldson, Chen, Rogers, and I have written about the development of a "contingency model" of TDE evaluation, advocating that stakeholders ultimately lead in establishing what is considered credible evidence to determine the effectiveness or impact of a particular program. Thus, in the coming decades, TDE theorists and practitioners might embrace new ways of thinking about TDE evaluation and move toward more of a mixed-methods approach, with an explicit qualitative core to the approach. Furthermore, evaluation approaches such as empowerment, democratic, culturally responsive, and transformative evaluation (e.g., Bledsoe & Donaldson, forthcoming 2014; Fetterman & Wandersman, 2005; Greene, 2011; Mertens, 2009) can be successfully incorporated into TDE.

In summary, TDE as an evaluation approach is a work in progress. TDE could be described as having consistent elements (norms, causes, and logic models) and an unwavering commitment to ensuring that the values held by stakeholders and community norms serve as the foundation for program development, implementation, and evaluation. Likewise, examining and understanding the causes associated with program outcomes is another consistent aspect of the TDE approach. Although TDE as an approach has roots, it is evolving, through the development of related evaluation theories and through the knowledge gained from practice.

The evolution of TDE has been shaped by explorations in how to best capture and illustrate norms and causes. The use of logic models continues to dominate TDE, but the actual logic models have become less linear and more nuanced and complex. They incorporate changes in cultural norms and expectations. Additionally, the concept of generalizability has shifted from the idea that a successful program can be replicated anywhere to the recognition that context matters and for a program to be successful, appropriate adaptation to context is required.

These shifts suggest that the use of qualitative inquiry will assume a greater role in the TDE approach in the future so as to better reflect norms and causes and inform sophisticated logic models. Those of us who wish to inform future TDE evaluations must consider and publically embrace the use of qualitative methods and paradigms such as ethnography, because this would broaden TDE's appeal, making evaluation processes and findings more relevant to more stakeholders and enhancing utilization of evaluation results.

KEY CONCEPTS

Black-box approach	Contextual factors
Cause-and-effect relationships	Contingency model
Causes	Generalizability

Intended and unintended outcomes

Logic models

Mixed methods

Norms

Program theory

Stakeholder personal perspectives

Theory-driven evaluation

Theory of change

DISCUSSION QUESTIONS

1. TDE involves an examination of the norms and values that underpin the program to be evaluated. This requires that the evaluator be deeply engaged in the program setting. However, the author notes that "this level of engagement can sometimes resemble a therapy session; it can be messy and emotional, and it requires skillful facilitation." Discuss how one can maintain appropriate boundaries for a professional evaluation, yet uncover and manage the emotions often associated with norms and values.

2. It is not uncommon for various stakeholders associated with the same program to have divergent values. If you were to conduct a TDE, how might you write a report that reflects such divergent values?

3. One of the goals of TDE is the scalability of a program; however, TDE theorists acknowledge that different contexts must be considered when replicating a program. How might an evaluator use qualitative methods to recommend adaptations to a program so that it reflects a context different from the original program setting?

REFERENCES

Bledsoe, K. L. (2005). Using theory-driven evaluation with underserved communities: Promoting program development and program sustainability. In S. Hood, R. H. Hopson, & H. T. Frierson (Eds.), *The role of culture and cultural context: A mandate for inclusion, the discovery of truth and understanding in evaluative theory and practice. Evaluation and Society Series* (pp. 175–196). Greenwich, CT: Information Age Publishing.

Bledsoe, K. L. (2009). Evaluation of the Fun with Books Program: An interview with Katrina Bledsoe. In J. Fitzpatrick, T. Christie, & M. Mark (Eds.), *Evaluation in action: Interviews with the experts.* (pp. 299–323). Thousand Oaks, CA: Sage.

Bledsoe, K. L., & Donaldson, S. I. (forthcoming 2014). Culturally responsive theory-driven evaluation. In S. Hood, R. Hopson, K. Obeidat, & H. Frierson (Eds.), *Continuing the journey to reposition culture and cultural context in evaluation theory and practice.* Chicago, IL: Information Age Publishing.

Bledsoe, K. L., & Graham, J. A. (2005). Using multiple evaluation approaches in program evaluation. *American Journal of Evaluation, 26,* 302–319.

Bledsoe, K. L., & Hopson, R. H. (2009). Conducting ethical research in underserved communities. In D. M. Mertens & P. Ginsberg (Eds.), *Handbook of ethics for research in the social sciences* (pp. 391–406). Thousand Oaks, CA: Sage.

Broderick, Z., O'Connor, C., Mulcahy, C., Heffernan, N., & Heffernan, C. (2011). Increasing parent engagement in student earning using an intelligent tutoring system. *Journal of Interactive Learning Research, 22,* 523–550.

Chen, H. T. (1990). *Theory-driven evaluations.* Thousand Oaks, CA: Sage.

Chen, H. T. (2005). *Practical program evaluation: Assessing and improving planning, implementation, and effectiveness.* Thousand Oaks, CA: Sage.

Chen, H. T. (2012). The roots and growth of theory-driven evaluation: Assessing viability, effectuality, and transferability. In M. Alkin (Ed.), *Evaluation roots* (pp. 113–129). Thousand Oak, CA: Sage.

Chen, H. T., & Rossi, P. H. (1983). Evaluating with sense: The theory-driven approach. *Evaluation Review, 7*(3), 283–302.

Chen, H. T., & Rossi, P. H. (1987). The theory-driven approach to validity. *Evaluation and Program Planning, 10,* 95–103.

Coryn, C., Noakes, L., Westine, C., & Schröter, D. (2011). A systematic review of theory-driven evaluation practice from 1990 to 2009. *American Journal of Evaluation, 32,* 199–226.

Donaldson, S., Christie, D., & Mark, M. (Eds.). (2011). *What counts as credible evidence in applied research and evaluation practice?* Los Angeles, CA: Sage.

Donaldson, S. I. (2007). *Program theory driven science.* Mahwah, NJ: Lawrence Erlbaum and Associates.

Donaldson, S. I. (2009). Evaluation of the Work and Health Initiative with a focus on winning new jobs: An interview with Stewart I. Donaldson. In J. Fitzpatrick, T. Christie, & M. Mark (Eds.), *Evaluation in action: Interviews with the experts.* (pp. 211–247). Thousand Oaks, CA: Sage.

Donaldson, S. I., Gooler, L. E., & Weiss, R. (1998). Promoting health and well-being through work: science and practice. In X. B. Arriaga & S. Oskamp (Eds.), *Addressing community problems: Psychological research and intervention* (pp. 160–194). Newbury Park, CA: Sage.

Fetterman, D., & Wandersman, A. (2005). *Empowerment evaluation principles in action*. New York, NY: Guilford Press.

Fitzpatrick, J., Christie, C., & Mark, M. (Eds.). (2009). *evaluation in action: Interviews with the experts*. Thousand Oaks, CA: Sage.

Fredericks, K. A., Deegan, M., & Carman, J. C. (2008). Using system dynamics as an evaluation tool: An experience from a demonstration program. *American Journal of Evaluation, 29*, 251–267.

Frierson, H. T., Hood, S., & Hughes, G. B. (2010). A guide to conducting culturally-responsive evaluations. In J. Frechtling (Ed.), *The 2010 user-friendly handbook for project evaluation* (pp. 75–96). Arlington, VA: National Science Foundation. Available at http://www.westat.com/westat/pdf/news/ufhb.pdf.

Funnell, S., & Rogers, P. (2011). *Purposeful program theory: Effective use of theories of change and logic models*. San Francisco, CA: Jossey-Bass.

Gargani, J. (2003). *A historical review of theory-based evaluation*. Unpublished manuscript. University of California, Berkeley.

Greene, J. (2011). The construct(ion) of validity as argument. In H. T. Chen, S. I. Donaldson, & M. M. Mark (Eds.), *Advancing validity in outcome evaluation: Theory and practice: New Directions for Evaluation* (pp. 81–130). San Francisco, CA: Jossey-Bass.

Hopson, R. K., Kirkhart, K., & Bledsoe, K. L. (2012). Decolonizing evaluation in a developing world: Implications and admonitions for equity-focused evaluation (EFE). *How to design and manage equity-focused evaluations*. New York, NY: UNICEF.

Kirkhart, K. E. (2013). Advancing considerations of culture and validity: Honoring the key evaluation checklist. In S. I. Donaldson (Ed.), *The future of evaluation in society: A tribute to Michael Scriven* (pp. 129–160). Charlotte, NC: Information Age Publishing.

Mercier, C., Piat, M., Peladeau, N., & Dagenais, C. (2001). An application of theory-driven evaluation to a drop-in in youth center. *Evaluation Review, 24*, 73–91.

Mertens, D. M., Bledsoe, K. L., Sullivan, M., & Wilson, A. (2010). Utilization of mixed methods for transformative purposes. In C. Teddlie & A. Tashakkori (Eds.), *Handbook of mixed methods research* (2nd ed., pp. 193–214). Thousand Oaks, CA: Sage.

Mertens, D. M. (2009). *Transformative research and evaluation*. New York, NY: Guilford Press.

Mertens, D. M., & Wilson, A. (2012). *Program evaluation theory and practices: A comprehensive guide*. New York, NY: Guilford Press.

Project Tomorrow. (2003). *Student Success in the 21st Century, 8*(1).

Patton, M. Q. (1987). *How to use qualitative methods in evaluation.* Thousand Oaks, CA: Sage.

Scriven, M. S. (1991). *Evaluation thesaurus* (4th ed.). Thousand Oaks, CA: Sage.

Shadish, W. R., Cook, T. D., & Leviton, L. C. (1991). *Foundations of program evaluation: Theories of practice.* Thousand Oaks, CA: Sage.

Warren, M., Hong, S., Rubin, C., & Uy, P. (2009). Beyond the bake-sale: A community-based approach to parent engagement in schools. *Teachers College Record, 111,* 2209–2254.

Weiss, C. H. (1997). How can theory-based evaluation make greater headway? *Evaluation Review, 21,* 501–524.

Weiss, C. H. (1998). *Evaluation* (2nd ed.). Upper Saddle River, NJ: Prentice Hall.

Conceptual and Practical Intersections between Participatory Evaluation and Qualitative Inquiry

Jill Anne Chouinard and J. Bradley Cousins

Key Ideas

- Participatory evaluation is distinguished by its relational and dialogic nature, active involvement of program participants, and relationships forged between evaluators and stakeholders.

- Qualitative inquiry supports participatory evaluation's focus on reflexivity at the point of practice.

- Participatory evaluation comprises two distinct forms: practical participatory evaluation (P-PE) and transformational participatory evaluation (T-PE).

  Practical participatory evaluation is based on observations that evaluation findings are more likely to be used for program improvement if stakeholders are involved in the evaluation process.

  Transformational participatory evaluation evolved from the fields of community and international development and is positioned closer to critical theory.

- Three essential and enduring characteristics of qualitative inquiry:

  It is based in a social constructivist epistemology, in which knowledge is co-constructed.

  It was founded in philosophical hermeneutics with a focus on understanding and listening.

  Local context informs understanding.

- Four distinct issues intersect participatory evaluation and qualitative inquiry:

  Relationships between evaluator and participants

  Evaluator positionality

  Values

  Cultural context

A participatory approach to evaluation can be used to address numerous program and organizational needs, and can be adapted for use in diverse program contexts. Although no specific technique or method explicitly sets it apart from other evaluation approaches, participatory evaluation can be distinguished by its relational and dialogic nature, the active involvement and training of program participants in the evaluation process, and the relationships that are forged between evaluators and stakeholders. We offer the following three scenarios to illustrate a participatory approach to evaluation:

- **Scenario 1:** A community-based reproductive health program in Tanzania aims to improve the quality of reproductive services in over 100 public district hospital sites. In an effort to build local capacity and ownership of the quality improvement process, evaluators from an international reproductive health organization collaborated with local program stakeholders in a long-term participatory monitoring and evaluation process. Emphasis was placed on joint discussions about what quality meant and how it could be improved over time. Supervisors and site staff used a self-assessment technique called COPE (a participatory decision-making process that encourages large group participation, inclusiveness, self-assessment, problem identification, and so forth) as a way to raise questions, generate debate, and identify issues to be resolved. Evaluators acted as change agents, emphasizing partnerships with site staff as a way to empower them to gain skills, insight, and understanding, to enable them to define what changes are required (Bradley, Mayfield, Mehta, & Rukonge, 2002).

■ **Scenario 2:** Phoenix Rising, an HIV, hepatitis, and substance abuse prevention program targeting homeless young adults (eighteen to twenty-four years of age) works to reduce substance abuse and prevent HIV and hepatitis C infection by developing healthy coping strategies. The primary purpose of the evaluation was to determine whether desired outcomes were achieved and to assess program effectiveness and the quality of service delivery. A participatory approach was selected to ensure that the federally mandated evaluation would be useful to program partners and to ensure that the information would be used on an ongoing basis for program assessment and improvement. Data also were intended to inform program development and improvements when possible. Program staff were provided with evaluation training and an orientation to data collection and analysis to ensure their involvement in designing evaluation questions and identifying the strengths and limitations of evaluation tools and instruments (Dryden, Hyde, Livny, & Tula, 2010).

■ **Scenario 3:** WIN, a wildlife conservation education program designed for students in early childhood education classes up to fifth grade, seeks to raise children's awareness and understanding of the natural world. Most schools participating in the program are located in ethnically and culturally diverse urban communities. The purpose of this participatory evaluation was to determine program effectiveness, develop a shared understanding of the program, increase buy-in and ownership, increase use and usability of evaluation findings, and increase internal evaluation capacity. Stakeholders participated as members of an advisory panel that included primary program sponsors, program managers, program providers, and program participants. Students also were involved in identifying evaluation questions and reviewing relevant data. Advisory members were involved in evaluation training, developing questions, reviewing information and data needs, identifying data sources and types of data collection instruments, and the presentation of results (Somers, 2005).

As these three brief descriptions illustrate, a participatory approach to evaluation can be used to address numerous program and organizational needs and can be adapted for use in diverse program contexts. Given that participatory evaluation takes a social constructivist approach to the creation of knowledge and focuses on the interaction of evaluators and other stakeholders, the use of qualitative methods plays a central, although not exclusive, role. Decisions concerning the choice of methods come from participants and from the exigencies of the program and community context, rather than from any a priori philosophical or methodological positioning (Hall, 1992). The issue in participatory evaluation is not which methods to use, but whose voices to include, how to include them, and determining who will speak for whom (Greene, 2000). From a participatory perspective, the decision to use a qualitative or quantitative approach (or both) is advanced broadly as a way to enhance program understanding, value multiple and diverse ways of knowing, and actively engage with difference (Greene, 2007).

Despite the fact that participatory evaluation embraces methodological diversity, it is still very much attuned to the fundamental principles of qualitative inquiry, in terms of both its social constructivist orientation to meaning making and its focus on understanding framed within a local community and program context. In this chapter, we explore these connections further, paying particular attention to the theoretical and practical intersections between participatory evaluation and qualitative inquiry. Although we note significant areas of congruence between these spheres of inquiry, we also note areas of tension, particularly in terms of philosophical and methodological principles and assumptions. We also explore the intersections of qualitative inquiry and participatory approaches from a practice perspective, noting potential benefits and ongoing challenges.

The chapter is organized in four parts. We begin with a discussion of participatory evaluation: what it is, what its interests are, and what it looks like in practice. We then provide an overview of key characteristics that span the many different varieties of and approaches to qualitative inquiry. Next, we describe the intersections between participatory evaluation and qualitative inquiry, focusing on connections at the levels of epistemology, methodology, and method. The remainder of the chapter explores the intersection of qualitative inquiry and participatory evaluation in practice, followed by a discussion of benefits and challenges.

PARTICIPATORY EVALUATION: CONCEPTS AND PRINCIPLES OF PRACTICE

As a descriptive term that includes multiple methods and approaches, participatory evaluation has become somewhat of a "catch-all concept" that is prone to persistent conceptual and methodological blurring (Cornwall & Jewkes, 1995). This can make discerning whether an inquiry is in fact participatory a challenge. In a review of the empirical literature (Cousins & Chouinard, 2010), we found that a number of studies that self-identified as participatory merely involved non-evaluator stakeholders as data sources, rather than as true collaborators or participants. Like others (e.g., King, 2005), we have always maintained that what distinguishes participatory evaluation from other types of evaluation is having evaluators working in partnership or in collaboration with members of the program community, broadly defined (i.e., program developers, managers, implementers, funders, intended beneficiaries, or other relevant stakeholder groups) (Cousins & Earl, 1992, 1995). Many such individuals do not have prior experience with evaluation or applied social science research methodologies, and collectively, they are likely to have quite diverse interests regarding the program being evaluated. An essential consideration is the collaborative partnership between participating stakeholders and evaluators, as each brings a specific focus and value to the inquiry relationship. Generally, evaluators bring knowledge of evaluative logic and methods and standards of professional practice, while community-based stakeholders bring their knowledge of the community context within which the program exists, as well as an in-depth knowledge of the program or intervention. In fact, it is the relationship that emerges among these stakeholder groups, as well as the conversations that ensue, that help to define the parameters of participatory practice and the knowledge that is ultimately co-constructed as a result of these practices (Abma & Widdershoven, 2008). As Cornwall and Jewkes (1995) concluded, participatory research can be distinguished from other approaches based on "who defines the research problems and who generates, analyses, represents, owns and acts on the information which is sought" (p. 1668).

Approaches

Several forms of participatory evaluation and collaborative inquiry have emerged over the past two decades, each type distinguishable by the level and nature of stakeholder involvement, justification or rationale for the approach, and ideological predispositions. Based on consideration of goals and intents, Cousins and Whitmore (1998) identified two principle streams of participatory evaluation, the first being practical participatory evaluation (P-PE), with principal interests in program problem solving and enhanced evaluation use (Ayers, 1987; Cousins & Earl, 1992, 1995). Related approaches include developmental evaluation (Patton, 1994, 2011), stakeholder-based evaluation (Bryk, 1983; Mark & Shotland, 1985), and utilization-focused evaluation (Patton, 1997, 2008). Transformative participatory evaluation (T-PE), however, derives from emancipatory and political rationales where the inquiry process itself is used as leverage for social change. Related approaches include democratic evaluation (McTaggart, 1991), fourth generation evaluation (Guba & Lincoln, 1989), deliberative democratic evaluation (House & Howe, 2000), and empowerment evaluation (Fetterman, 2001; Fetterman & Wandersman, 2005).

Interests and Justifications

Although in practice one would expect to see overlap between these two participatory streams, they have significant differences in terms of their historical roots, rationales, and interests in involving stakeholders in the evaluation process. Cousins and Whitmore (1998) credited Levin (1993) with the identification of three distinct justifications or interests for collaborative inquiry. P-PE essentially emerged from evaluation practice and is based on empirical observations that evaluation findings are more likely to be used if stakeholders are involved in the evaluation process (Cousins & Earl, 1992; Patton, 1997). Stakeholder participation is thus a pragmatic response intended to enhance the relevance, ownership, and utilization of evaluation processes and results (Cousins & Whitmore, 1998). Within the P-PE stream, stakeholders are most likely to be those who are closely associated with the program, and who will likely be involved in decision making around the use of findings. These stakeholders might be called 'primary users' (Patton, 1997), those with a significant and vested interest in the program and its evaluation.

Conversely, T-PE evolved from the fields of community and international development, in large part from the pioneering work of Paolo Freire, Karl Marx, Antonio Gramsci, and Jurgen Habermas (Brisolera, 1998; Cousins & Whitmore, 1998). Within this stream, participation is viewed from a political perspective, as a way to promote social justice and empower those who have traditionally been left out of the process of social change. Stakeholder participation is thus seen as an emancipatory and liberatory process that deeply challenges the status quo in defining who creates and controls the production and use of knowledge (Cousins & Whitmore, 1998; Mertens, 2008). Given the political and emancipatory orientation of this stream, greater emphasis is placed on including intended program beneficiaries, as well as a broad range of other legitimate program stakeholders, as a way to promote social and political change. Whereas P-PE and T-PE are distinguishable based on evaluation purpose, intended outcomes, history, and ideological roots, nonetheless considerable overlap is seen, and the two are not mutually exclusive (Cousins & Whitmore, 1998).

First, although the interests of P-PE are predominantly practical in orientation, research has shown that participation in evaluation can be motivating and a worthwhile professional development experience (Amo & Cousins, 2007). Such experiences can be transformative (e.g., teachers contributing to district level decision making, organizational units developing capacity to do and use evaluation), even though such consequences were not envisioned from the outset. Similarly, T-PE processes intended, for example, to mobilize social action and community reform might also lead to improved program delivery and more efficient use of program resources as almost a side benefit. We can see from these examples that although P-PE and T-PE have distinct predilections, pragmatic and political interests are not mutually exclusive. Furthermore, Levin (1993) pointed to an additional justification for collaborative inquiry, one that is shared by both streams of participatory evaluation and that may, in the end, prove to be most central to our present purposes.

Levin's justification was *philosophical*. In the case of participatory evaluation, inquiry seeks to enhance meaning through involving members of the program community who are intimately familiar with the intervention and the context within which it is implemented. Shared meaning and understanding develop through exchange and dialogue, leading to more penetrating analysis and insight than would be the case in conventional, noncollaborative evaluation. One can easily imagine collaborative approaches lightening the burden on evaluators to bring content (program) expertise to the inquiry in P-PE or relaxing the need for evaluators to be "insiders" in community-based evaluations with social action agendas (T-PE). Although each stream of participatory evaluation is predisposed toward a particular intent, they both draw from an epistemological justification motivated by social constructivist notions concerning the importance of context and the inclusion of multiple participants in the co-construction of knowledge.

Dimensions of Process

Participatory approaches can be further distinguished from each other and from other evaluation approaches based on the level and extent of stakeholder involvement (depth of participation), the diversity among stakeholders, and the balance evaluators seek between a consultative approach and one that is driven by stakeholders (Cousins & Whitmore, 1998). *Depth of participation* refers to the extent to which stakeholders are actually involved in the inquiry process, ranging from a consultative role to deep participation in all phases of the evaluation, including planning, data collection, processing and analysis, and reporting and disseminating results. *Diversity* among stakeholders can be limited to primary users of evaluation findings (such as program managers, staff, and funders) or can extend to include all other legitimate groups (including intended program beneficiaries) with a stake in the program and in its evaluation. *Control of the evaluation process,* specifically in relation to technical decision making, can range from more direct evaluator control over the

Table 5.1 **A Summary of Differences and Similarities between P-PE and T-PE**

	P-PE	T-PE
Historical roots	Canada and US: Pragmatic evaluation practice with focus on enhancing relevance, use of results, ownership	Mostly developing world (India, Latin America, Africa)—community and international development, participatory research
Purpose	Evaluation use, program and organizational decision making, problem solving, organizational learning and change	Empowerment, emancipation, social and political change
Stakeholder inclusion	Primary users of the evaluation processes and findings: stakeholders who are involved in program decision making, such as program managers, staff, and funders	Diverse stakeholders, including program beneficiaries and primary users
Epistemology	Mutual co-construction/constructivist	Mutual co-construction/constructivist
Evaluator role	Primary facilitator, technical expert, trainer, and inquirer	Co-facilitator, empowerment resource, educator, co-inquirer, cultural broker, critic
Related approaches	Developmental evaluation, stakeholder-based evaluation, utilization-focused evaluation, school-based evaluation	Democratic evaluation, fourth generation evaluation, deliberative democratic evaluation, participatory action research

process to more power and decision-making leadership in the hands of stakeholders. We acknowledge that any participatory evaluation may reflect significant variation in these dimensions of process over time. However, at a gross level these process dimensions can be useful for distinguishing among the many approaches to participatory evaluation and helping differentiate participatory evaluation from other types of evaluation. Table 5.1 provides a brief summary of the primary differences between P-PE and T-PE.

QUALITATIVE INQUIRY: A BRIEF OVERVIEW OF KEY CHARACTERISTICS

In qualitative inquiry, the construction of knowledge is envisioned as dynamic, unfolding, and ongoing, shaping the interaction between researchers and participants. At the same time knowledge is shaped by these same encounters (Villarreal, 1992). Given the many variations of qualitative inquiry currently practiced, any attempt at providing a satisfactory description can prove daunting, as influences come from a variety of disciplines and philosophical traditions. As Preissle (2006) described, "the domain [of qualitative inquiry] is a rich fabric or tapestry of practice for which we use this umbrella term" (p. 688), a term that encompasses a broad range of philosophical, methodological, political, and ethical domains (Schwandt, 2000). Consider the varied theoretical and philosophical approaches and research foci from this partial list: ethnography focuses on cultural understanding (Geertz, 1973); social constructivism is about the social construction of the world/knowledge (Lincoln & Guba, 2000); phenomenology is concerned with understanding the essence and perceptions of lived experience (Van Maanen, 1988); hermeneutics considers understanding as interpretation within a specific context and in terms of specific perspectives (Gadamer, 1989); and narrative inquiry derives understanding and experience through stories or narratives (Clandinin & Connelly, 2000). These qualitative streams can be further combined and approached, for example, from either feminist, critical theory, cultural studies (and so forth) perspectives, leading to different research interests and contributions.

Regardless of the approach selected, essential and enduring characteristics help provide a sense of what it means and what is involved in practicing qualitative research. We understand qualitative inquiry as a relational construct, a space where both researchers and participants are considered active co-constructors who together create the social and ethnographic text (Long, 1992). We can further identify three essential and component features of this qualitative encounter: First, it is based in a social constructivist epistemology, where the knowledge that is created is considered a product of the interaction between researchers and inquiry participants founded in philosophical hermeneutics, as interactions between researchers and participants shift to a focus on understanding, listening, and interpreting within the context of social inquiry (Klemm, 1986). Within hermeneutics, understanding is conceptualized dialogically and reflexively, requiring an openness not only to

Table 5.2 **A Summary Description of Key Qualitative Features**

Social constructivist epistemology	Knowledge co-constructed, dynamic
Philosophical hermeneutics	Focus on understanding and listening
Influence of local context	Informs understanding of relationships and of broader society

what others have to say, but to an engagement with ourselves and our own biases and prejudices (Klemm, 1986). Third, the local ecology informs understanding of the complexity and patterns of human relations and embeds understanding within a larger, fundamentally interconnected social system. Within a qualitative frame, understanding is contextual (Patton, 2002). These three key components (Table 5.2) underscore the essential nature of qualitative inquiry as an interactive and dialogical process that, as Schwandt (2000) explained, "is built on a profound concern with understanding what other human beings are doing or saying" (p. 200). We now turn to a discussion of the theoretical and practical interconnections between participatory and qualitative approaches to social inquiry.

LOCATING PARTICIPATORY EVALUATION AND QUALITATIVE INQUIRY: CONCEPTUAL INTERSECTIONS

As "active social agents" (Long, 1992, p. ix), we must understand the underlying and interconnected philosophical and ethical assumptions that guide our practice. In this section, we discuss the dynamic intersections that cut across approaches to participatory evaluation and qualitative research, because these influence the parameters, the process, the relationships, and the knowledge that is ultimately created. To help make sense of the many interconnections between these two types of inquiry, we draw on Carter and Little's (2007) framework for understanding qualitative research, because it enables us to apprehend the dynamic theoretical and practical locations where participatory and qualitative inquiry intersect.

In their framework, Carter and Little (2007) offered three interconnected, yet conceptually discrete, areas that capture the issues that are relevant to an understanding of social inquiry:

■ Epistemology encompasses the philosophical assumptions that directly influence and guide our research practices, including our choice of methodologies and method selection. Schwandt (2007) defined it as "the study of the nature of knowledge and justification" (p. 87). Epistemological stances or positions thus contain either tacit or implicit assumptions about knowledge and its construction in the practice of social research (Carter & Little, 2007).

■ Methodology refers to the "assumptions, principles, and procedures" (Schwandt, 2007) that describe, explain, and justify method selection in social inquiry (Carter & Little, 2007). As Greene (2006) noted, methodology "structures the inquirer's gaze" (p. 93).

■ Method can be described as the "how to" of social inquiry (Greene, 2006), the specific tools and techniques designed to collect, analyze, and interpret data. As Carter and Little (2007) observed, "it is through methods that methodology and epistemology become visible" (p. 1325).

These three levels of abstraction, while conceptually distinct, are nonetheless interconnected, because each sheds light on a constituent aspect of the research and evaluation process. As Carter and Little (2007) explained, "methodology justifies method, which produces data and analysis. Knowledge is created from data and analysis. Epistemology modifies methodology and justifies the knowledge produced" (p. 1317). Within the broader field of social inquiry, and even within participatory and qualitative approaches, these three domains can have different theoretical and material expressions, thus leading to quite different and diverse research practices.

EPISTEMOLOGICAL INTERSECTIONS

In reaction to positivism, post-positivism has taught us that there is no disinterested social inquiry, "no neutral research" (Lather, 1991), no universal social rules (Geertz, 1993), no culture-free epistemology (Scheurich & Young, 2002), and no unbiased "truths." Thus, within the field of social inquiry, numerous competing epistemological positions justify methodological selection and the choice of methods. According to Carter and Little (2007), epistemology influences research at five distinct, yet interrelated locations: (1) at the relational level, between researchers and participants; (2) in terms of research quality; (3) in terms of researcher positionality; (4) at the level of evaluator values; and (5) in terms of the cultural context. In what follows, we locate the intersections of participatory evaluation and qualitative research along these five dimensions of influence.

Relationships in the Field

While participatory and qualitative approaches are both interactive and relational constructs, they can nonetheless be differentiated based on the nature of the interaction between and among evaluators and participants. From a participatory perspective, evaluators and stakeholders are not separate, but rather inextricably linked as active co-constructors in the evaluation process. The key point is that in participatory evaluation, stakeholders play an active decision-making role throughout the process of evaluation, moving well beyond the role of data provider, to become active partners and collaborators in producing evaluation knowledge. To illustrate, Arnstein's (1969) ladder of participation in the field of community planning depicts eight different types and levels of participation across a broad spectrum, from nonparticipation and manipulation all the way up to citizen power and control (Table 5.3).

Table 5.3 **Ladder of Participation**

8. Citizen control	Citizen power
7. Delegated power	
6. Partnership	
5. Placation	Tokenism
4. Consultation	
3. Informing	
2. Therapy	Nonparticipation
1. Manipulation	

Source: Arnstein (1969).

A participatory approach to evaluation would be located among the top rungs of the ladder, because decision making, power, and control are shared (to varying degrees) among evaluators and stakeholders. It is at the top rungs of the ladder where evaluator positionality and role changes to accommodate enhanced stakeholder involvement and participation in project decision making, with control balanced more equitably between evaluators and other project stakeholders. Despite myriad influences on evaluators, the culture of diverse stakeholders and their level of evaluation knowledge and skills have a significant impact on the roles evaluators ultimately play during the evaluation and on the relationships that are created in the process (Cousins & Chouinard, 2010).

Although qualitative inquiry can occupy the top rungs of Arnstein's ladder of participation, it is also likely to locate in the middle rungs of the ladder, where participant inclusion would be limited to providing data to predetermined questions. Thus, although qualitative inquiry must be understood as a fundamentally relational and interactive process, the essential difference is that participation and involvement can be limited to providing input into the study and corroborating findings, with decision making and power remaining firmly in the hands of the researcher (Heron & Reason, 1997).

Evaluator Positionality

A key feature of both qualitative and participatory approaches is the move away from objectivity and neutrality to an understanding of subjectivity as a key part of the research process (Peshkin, 1988). The centrality of subjectivity thus requires a heightened and "critical subjectivity" (Reason, 1999, p. 207) not only of self as researcher, but also of the epistemological and ontological assumptions and biases that guide the research. As Lather (1993) pointed out, "it is not a matter of looking harder or more closely, but of seeing what frames our seeing" (p. 675). Reflexivity thus requires that we look inward to critically examine our own personal beliefs, potential biases, and assumptions (Schwandt, 2007), enabling us to better engage the ethical complexities involved in our relationships with stakeholders within the evaluation context. Symonette (2004) referred to this as "multilateral self awareness," awareness of ourselves as cultural beings within a sociopolitical context and awareness of what this means within a particular evaluative setting. The concept of reflexivity thus helps to position the evaluator or researcher as a key part of the setting and research context, thus enabling a further reflection on practice and on the research methodologies that are applied in the field. Qualitative inquiry and participatory evaluation appear to be on common ground here.

However, an interesting and distinguishing question remains as to when and on what grounding such a perspective is developed. Participatory evaluation fosters such reflexivity at the point of practice and for particular purposes, practical or transformative. Qualitative inquiry, on the other hand, is grounded in the epistemological imperative of reflexivity. As a result, qualitative inquiry supports participatory evaluation's focus on reflexivity at the point of practice.

Values

Qualitative and participatory approaches both acknowledge the role of values in the social inquiry process. By values we mean whose questions and whose voices will be included or excluded, which methodology and methods will be selected, and what conclusions or recommendations will be advanced. As fundamentally relational constructs, both forms of inquiry privilege the "ethical space" (Schwandt, 2000) where the encounter between evaluator and participant serves to define the research problem and choice of research methodology and methods. Motivated by egalitarian notions, T-PE is thought to promote empowerment through engagement in the evaluative and decision making process (Weiss, 1998). In fact, the integration of qualitative and quantitative methodologies helps to promote pluralistic views and participant perspectives, while at the same time providing an opportunity for the inclusion of stakeholders who may have been previously excluded, thus challenging power dynamics in the creation and use of knowledge (Jackson & Kassam, 1998). The aim of transformative participatory research (T-PE) is thus action-orientated, transformative, and political, positioning it much closer to critical theory (Heron & Reason, 1997). In P-PE we would argue, values pluralism is less an issue or concern for most stakeholders, because its focus remains on program improvement and decision making.

Similar to T-PE, values pluralism plays a formative role in qualitative inquiry (Guba & Lincoln, 1989), because it is embedded in the very dimensions of practice, beginning with the identification of the research problem, the definition of research questions, and the choices surrounding process and selection of methods. As Guba and Lincoln (1989) pointed out, values are "a part of the basic foundational philosophical dimensions [of qualitative inquiry]" (p. 169). Thus, for both participatory and qualitative approaches, the initial ethical moment resides precisely in the rationale for inquiry choice, for inclusion of participants in the research, and for the promotion of plurality in the inquiry process. The difference lies in the political motivation, especially for T-PE.

Context

Participatory evaluation and qualitative inquiry also must be understood from macro- and micro-contextual perspectives that include the broader historical sociopolitical context as well as the local perspective that is descriptive of the program and community research setting. From the macro-contextual perspective, participatory and qualitative approaches to social inquiry were both strongly influenced by the dynamic and turbulent sociopolitical context of the United States in the 1960s and 1970s, a period that was defined in part by Martin Luther King Jr., and the civil rights movement, mass protests against the Vietnam war and calls for freedom, and a feminist critique of the power structures and demands for equality (Greene, 2000; Heron, 1996; House, 1993). This mass political dissent and discontent was further reflected in the social sciences (notably in the fields of sociology and anthropology), as positivist social science inquiry methods were attacked for their failure to provide answers to pressing social questions and for their failure to represent the multiple competing voices that were clamoring to be heard (Page, 2000). Qualitative researchers thus shifted their focus to developing knowledge from a local, pluralistic, interpretive, and open-ended perspective (Denzin & Lincoln, 1998).

Following the lead of qualitative inquirers, program evaluators also began to question orthodox social science and its positivist assumptions (Guba & Lincoln, 1989; Stake, 1975), focusing their critique on the overly scientific basis of evaluation and the over-privileging of managers and decisions makers relative to other program stakeholders (House, 1993). Discussions thus centered on the benefits of involving stakeholders, both as a way to increase the use of evaluation findings (Ayers, 1987; Cousins & Earl, 1992; Patton, 1997) and as a way to include the social justice perspective that had been missing up to that point (House, 1993). As Page (2000) pointed out, they were seeking more "candid representations" than those offered by more conventional social science. What was then termed the "crisis of representation" led to questions about the role of the researcher as historically detached and neutral, and to the search for social science methods that would more accurately represent the people and their social contexts (Page, 2000), while giving voice to those who had historically been excluded (Rossman & Rallis, 2003). Researchers and evaluators thus began to question how to include participants/stakeholders, who to include/exclude, who should/can speak on their behalf and on whose authority, and what role researchers and evaluators should play in the field.

From a micro-contextual perspective, there is an explicit focus on the context within which the research or evaluation takes place, as it is considered essential to understanding the community or program background, and ultimately, the construction of knowledge that is created in the field (Schwandt, 2007). The participatory approach is focused on the program and community context, because all communities are considered to have a local ecology (Kelly, 2006) that necessarily informs an understanding of the complexity and patterns of human relations between and among program community members (e.g., implementers, managers, developers, intended beneficiaries). Participatory evaluation is thus context-rich and context-specific, because it is grounded in the concerns, interests, and problems of the program community (Burke, 1998). All of this helps to shape the contours of the evaluation process and outcomes. Context is also considered a complex phenomenon in evaluation, because programs often take place in multiple sites and with different local stakeholders (Greene, 2005). Thus, although participatory evaluation does occur in a naturalistic setting, a key difference from qualitative inquiry is that, for T-PE, the setting itself is considered a site for action, experience, and political change (Burke, 1998).

Qualitative inquiry similarly takes place in a "naturalistic setting" (Lincoln & Guba, 1985), because understanding is mediated by the political, social, cultural, economic, and historic parameters of the research context. As Metz (2000) described, "[qualitative] research illumines how the social reality in a location is connected to, even partially forged by, the social structures and different cultural understandings that surround it" (p. 63). Meaning, in a qualitative study, is contextual. Table 5.4 provides a summary of the epistemological intersections between participatory evaluation and qualitative inquiry.

Table 5.4   A Summary of Epistemological Intersections

	Participatory evaluation	Qualitative inquiry
Relationships	■ Evaluators and participants actively co-construct evaluation knowledge ■ Decision making and control over process shared	■ Can assume a participatory approach between researcher and participants ■ Participants may be included as data sources, with decision making and control residing with researcher
Evaluator/researcher positionality	■ Evaluators embrace subjectivity ■ Reflexivity developed as a result of evaluation process	■ Embraces subjectivity ■ Reflexivity paramount initially and throughout process
Values	■ Role of values acknowledged in both P-PE and T-PE ■ T-PE has transformative/political agenda motivated by social justice concerns	■ Role of values acknowledged ■ Focus on values pluralism but generally no explicit political agenda
Context	■ Understanding context paramount to process ■ Developed through 1960s and 70s period of sociopolitical change ■ Context in T-PE considered a site for political and social change	■ Context key part of inquiry process ■ Influenced by sociopolitical demands of the 1960s and 70s ■ Naturalistic setting key part of understanding

METHODOLOGICAL LINKAGES

Methodologies carry philosophical assumptions about how an inquiry process should proceed, offering ways of thinking that help to shape the evaluation or research objectives, questions, and design (Carter & Little, 2007). Schwandt (2007) described methodologies as a "middle ground" between the epistemologies that guide our research and the methods that we select to gather our research findings. In a participatory evaluation, evaluators and stakeholders actively collaborate in multiple phases of the evaluation, from the initial planning stages all the way through to the dissemination of results. Given the conceptual and practical differences that define the two primary streams of participatory evaluation, each carries specific methodological implications and principles. P-PE is associated with a pragmatic methodology that is linked to program decision making and problem solving, and the use of evaluation findings and processes (Cousins & Whitmore, 1998). T-PE, however, is associated with a political methodology that is focused on empowerment, social equity, and emancipation (Cousins & Whitmore, 1998). Regardless of whether the methodology is pragmatic or political, in a participatory evaluation, the selection of methods is the result of collaborative decisions made by evaluators and stakeholders and is informed by community circumstances, funder requirements, and other contextual realities.

Qualitative inquiry is concerned with the social construction of knowledge and with understanding people's localized constructions, perceptions, and experiences. As such, it is associated with a hermeneutic and dialectic methodology that is focused on "developing improved joint constructions. . .[and in] the juxtaposition of conflicting ideas, forcing reconsideration of previous positions" (Guba & Lincoln, 1989, p. 90). Within the genre of qualitative inquiry, the focus on the social construction and reconstruction of research knowledge points to very specific methods that focus on a relational and interactive research ethic between researchers and participants. In a qualitative inquiry, methodological selection is based on the purpose of the study and the questions guiding the inquiry. For example, an ethnographic study would likely focus on cultural behavior and the development of cultural themes and analysis; a phenomenological study would focus on describing the experiences of participants and understanding the meaning and essence of the experience itself; a grounded theory approach would be tied to developing a theory or hypothesis to explain an action or phenomenon. The selected methodology would thus lead to the use of specific methods to guide the inquiry.

METHODS

Methods in social inquiry are considered "research in action" (Carter & Little, 2007, p. 1318). They share a "synergetic relationship" (Schwandt, 2007, p. 193) with methodology, because methods are translated into specific inquiry processes and procedures for data collection and analysis based on methodological assumptions. Qualitative methods are thus related to understanding people's constructions and listening to their experiences in some depth. As Lofland (1971, cited in Patton, 2002) explained:

> It is of necessity a process of learning what is happening. Since a major part of what is happening is provided by people in their own terms, one must find out about those terms rather than impose upon them a preconceived or outsider's scheme of what they are about. It is the observer's task to find out what is fundamental or central to the people or world under observation. (p. 28)

Within qualitative inquiry, data collection methods usually consist of in-depth interviewing, participant observation, and the analysis of textual data and relevant extant information. Methods are chosen according to the research problem and guiding questions. A key feature of selection also entails ensuring that methods and instruments are culturally and contextually congruent with the population and with the program setting.

Method choice and selection in participatory evaluation are made based on the contextual program and community circumstances, stakeholder and evaluator interests and strengths, and funder requirements (Hall, 1992; Jackson & Kassam, 1998). In a T-PE, the primary question is not about method selection, but about whose voices are heard, whose questions are addressed, and which values are advanced. In P-PE, method selection is shaped by problem-solving demands and exigencies (Cousins & Earl, 1995). In some contexts, a mixed-methods approach is preferred, because it can act as "a means of including diverse, often silenced, voices in the evaluation setting" (Brisolera, 1998, p. 32). Mixed methods can also enable triangulation and corroboration of findings in a practical participatory context.

While quantitative methods are by no means eschewed in participatory approaches to evaluation, some have warned that their use can be quite problematic in culturally diverse communities, particularly if they have been imposed on the community by the program funder (LaFrance, 2004; Small, Tiwari, & Huser, 2006). Yet as Chambers (2003) has so eloquently argued, numbers matter. The use of rapid rural appraisal and participatory development approaches to evaluation have led to a wide array of simple and contextually relevant methods to quantify complex phenomena of interest in ways that can be managed and understood by indigenous community members (Chambers, Samaranayake, & Zaveri, 2010).

PRACTICAL INTERSECTIONS

As we have argued, participatory and qualitative approaches to social inquiry intersect in myriad ways, leading to distinct conceptual and practical implications in the evaluation of social programs. In fact, the move toward an interpretive approach to social inquiry (Schwandt, 2000) underscores the fact that qualitative research is more than a set of methods and techniques used to collect data in the field (Weiss, 1998). It also brings a focus on understanding people's perspectives, perceptions, and experiences within a localized setting. To this juncture, we have explored conceptual interconnections between the two modes of inquiry. The following discussion centers on participatory evaluation practice and its intersection with qualitative inquiry. We provide an overview of the key phases involved in implementing a participatory process, focusing on the points at which qualitative inquiry is likely to enter into the participatory context. In laying out a framework for participatory practice, we are not advocating a stepwise prescription for engaging with this type of inquiry. Rather, we draw from our own practical experience and give comprehensive treatment to the full range of practical activities associated with any systematic inquiry process, participatory or not. Specifically, after some preliminary ground-laying activities, we turn to the usual practical challenges of evaluation planning and framing, instrument development and validation, data collection, data processing, analysis and interpretation, and dissemination and follow-up. We understand these processes to be relatively temporal in sequence yet fluid enough to permit nonlinear iterations. Specifically, we will describe the phases often involved in conducting a participatory evaluation: the creation of an evaluation steering committee, identifying a focus for the evaluation, negotiating stakeholder involvement, planning the evaluation and training stakeholders in evaluation processes, implementing the evaluation, and analyzing and interpreting findings.

Creating an Evaluation Steering Committee and Establishing Group Processes

In a participatory evaluation context, the creation of an evaluation steering committee enables frequent group discussion and provides evaluators and involved program and community stakeholders with the opportunity to communicate on a regular basis. Although an evaluation steering committee may not necessarily assume responsibility for actually implementing the evaluation project, it might productively play a strong role in determining the focus for the evaluation and for negotiating participation on the evaluation inquiry team that conducts the project. Weiss (1998) noted that committees can serve a methodological function by providing feedback on design, analysis, and technical issues, or a political function by assisting the evaluator in understanding community issues, interests, and concerns, and ensuring a more culturally responsive evaluation and process. Evaluators and community and program stakeholders each bring their own knowledge of evaluation processes and community context and work together as a team, sharing responsibility and authority for decisions about the evaluation process and implementation direction. The focus is on the relationships that emerge and on the dialogue and conversations that ensue between members of the steering committee, as they help to define the parameters of practice and the knowledge that is ultimately created. DeLuca, Poth, and Searle (2009) noted the need to develop trust as a precursor to learning, an especially critical consideration given potential power imbalances between evaluators and stakeholders and among different stakeholder groups themselves. As Torres et al. (2000) noted, the evaluator needs to create an atmosphere of communication that can "surface multiple points of view that need to be addressed and negotiated, help make individual and hidden agendas visible, contribute to building a sense of community and connection, enable sensitive topics to surface and be addressed, and facilitate individual, team, and organizational learning" (p. 28).

Identifying Evaluation Focus

The purpose of this early phase is to enable the evaluator to learn as much as possible about the program, the funding organizations, potential stakeholders, and the program context, and to define the parameters and scope of the evaluation (funding, resources, and timelines). Initial meetings with the evaluation sponsors provide the opportunity to build commitment and garner support for the evaluation process and help manage expectations about what participatory evaluation can and cannot accomplish. Support at this stage is essential to ensure the future success of the evaluation process (Cousins & Earl, 1992; Torres et al., 2000). Evaluators also may conduct informal interviews with program staff and other relevant community stakeholders to learn more about the intervention and program community and to identify potential community participants who also may be interested in participating on the evaluation team. Program documents, other relevant program materials, available published research, and professional literature are also collected and read during this initial phase. The product of these diverse activities is agreement on and identification of a coherent set of important and relevant questions to guide the evaluation. In theory, such a list would be informed by different value perspectives and stakeholder interests.

Negotiating Stakeholder Participation

In a participatory evaluation, whether P-PE or T-PE, the focus on active stakeholder involvement in the process is considered paramount, because it is considered a way to promote the political agenda of empowerment, promote the use of evaluation findings, or support learning. An important focus for the evaluation steering committee is on identifying relevant program and community stakeholders who might be interested in actively participating in the evaluation. As we have mentioned, stakeholders can include program sponsors, managers, developers, implementers, members of special interest groups, and intended program beneficiaries. The decision of who to include is often made based on evaluation rationale (Cousins & Whitmore, 1998). For instance, in a P-PE context (Cousins & Earl, 1992), stakeholders are generally those closest to the program (e.g., program managers and implementers); whereas in a T-PE context, program beneficiaries (and other relevant stakeholders) are more likely to be involved as a way to further social justice.

Level of involvement can also vary throughout the evaluation process (Brison, 2007). Evaluators often negotiate between the deep involvement of a few versus the less active involvement of a broader range of stakeholders (Taut, 2008). In other instances, a large number of stakeholders may be involved at the beginning and at the end of the evaluation, with key stakeholders involved extensively throughout the process (King & Ehlert, 2008). Although the inclusion of multiple perspectives can contribute to mutual learning and relationship building (MacLellan-Wright, Patten, de la Cruz, & Flaherty, 2007), greater diversity can also lead to increased conflict among stakeholders (J. E. King & Ehlert, 2008) and contribute to the blurring of roles (Sharkey & Sharples, 2008).

Evaluation Planning and Training

During this phase, the evaluator(s) and stakeholders involved as evaluation team members work together to build a common understanding about participatory evaluation, develop consensus about the evaluation plan (approach, design, evaluation questions, indicators, participants, and so forth), clarify roles, establish the schedule, deal with any other logistical issues, and prepare data collection instruments and tools. Data collection instruments and techniques can include qualitative, quantitative, or mixed methods. Decisions regarding methods are made based on consideration of evaluation purpose; stakeholder interests, experiences, and strengths; funder requirements; and contextual conditions. Once the methods have been selected, they must be used in a manner that is culturally appropriate and adapted to stakeholders' level of expertise (Burke, 1998).

In our experience, training of non-evaluator stakeholders at this stage occurs on-the-job and is designed to build evaluation capacity, enable them to actively participate in data collection processes and data analysis, and develop confidence in their evaluation capabilities (Feuerstein, 1998). Thus, although training enables more meaningful stakeholder participation, it also fosters relationship building and overall buy-in for the evaluation process itself (Rogers, Ahmed, Hamdallah, & Little, 2010). Whether practical or transformative in intent, participatory evaluation—as an inclusive, active, and engaged process—thus alters the traditional roles of evaluators and stakeholders. Evaluators must constantly adapt their evaluative practice to local conditions and accommodate the diverse needs of the stakeholder population. The adaptation frequently involves skills such as mediation, facilitation, or serving as a critical friend, coach, or organization developer, which extend beyond the scope of traditional evaluation training (Mercier, 1997). Evaluators can thus change from distant experts to collaborators and committed learners (Diaz-Puente, Yague, & Afonso, 2008). As Feuerstein (1998) noted, "the 'teacher' in a participatory evaluation process is both a 'learner' and a 'researcher'" (p. 23). For their part, stakeholders become active co-researchers involved in evaluation processes and practices that are typically found within the purview of evaluators. This new role can thus lead to new attitudes toward evaluation and capacity building (Diaz-Puente et al., 2008). It also can create a change in the relationship between evaluators and stakeholders, from one of expert and learner to that of partners in the evaluation process.

Evaluation Plan Implementation

Although some of this has already occurred during the early planning stages of the evaluation, one of the first issues in conducting the evaluation is negotiating entry into the organization or community and gaining access to program sites and to the people who possess relevant program and community knowledge. In some instances, going directly into a community is impossible without a cultural or community guide, someone who is trusted by the community and who can help navigate entry. In a participatory evaluation, this person can also be involved in the evaluation, helping to facilitate the data collection process and translate cultural and community norms. It is important to recognize that there may be an important role for the evaluation steering committee in this respect.

In a participatory evaluation, the data collection processes tend to emerge out of the local context and the community and program circumstances. Although data collection methods in a participatory evaluation are not different from the multiple methods used in other evaluation approaches (Garaway, 1995), a number of considerations must be taken into account (Burke, 1998; Garaway, 1995): the appropriateness to underlying assumptions and questions being asked in the evaluation; the technical difficulty and adaptability to a particular level of expertise; the practicality given the context or local conditions; cultural appropriateness; facilitation of learning; and potential barriers to participation.

Although a mixed-method approach is often selected, the key consideration is to provide participants with options so that they can choose which methods best suit their circumstances. As Tandon (1981) explained, enabling participants to select from a diversity of methods is important, because "some constituencies may feel more comfortable using stories, drawings, role-plays, theatre, puppetry, and similar other forms of data collection and analysis, while others may feel more familiar and comfortable with questionnaires, in-depth interviews, surveys and the like" (p. 10, as cited in Jackson & Kassam, 1998). Although the choice of method is based on a number of contextual and program-related circumstances, in a participatory evaluation, qualitative methods (interviews, observation, and document analysis) are often selected, because they can provide a contextualized understanding of the program from the perspective of the people who are most involved in and affected by the program. Yet, as we acknowledged previously from Chambers et al. (2010), the prospect of using culturally and contextually appropriate methods for quantification ought also to be given serious consideration.

Another important point to consider in terms of data collection is that control over the process between evaluators and stakeholders also can change throughout the evaluation, because stakeholders become more knowledgeable about the process as the evaluation unfolds. The task of the evaluator is thus not to produce knowledge herself or himself, but to facilitate the construction of knowledge by the stakeholder community. In reference to mostly T-PE interests, Brunner and Guzman (1989) explained, "in the beginning, the facilitators and the professional staff have to coach the team extensively, but as the project matures, the evaluator team becomes increasingly knowledgeable, efficient, and independent" (p. 11). Regardless of which methods are used to collect data, Crishna (2006) made an important observation that it is "the attitude and values projected that transform the evaluation from just an exercise in finding out whether the project works or not, to an empowering experience for all concerned" (p. 222). Regardless of whether the primary intent is practical or transformative, in a participatory evaluation, method selection becomes secondary to the process of stakeholder inclusion and participation.

Data Analysis and Interpretation

In qualitative inquiry, data analysis is most often emergent, beginning during data collection and continuing well after all of the data have been collected. This may or may not be the case with participatory evaluation, depending on the co-developed evaluation plan and approach. Whether the data come from interviews, observation, documents, or culturally appropriate quantitative methods, it is often productive to involve stakeholders directly in the analysis, interpretation of findings, and generation of conclusions and recommendations. Over the course of the evaluation, working group members meet on a regular basis to discuss findings and create shared meaning about what the findings indicate (King, 1998). In participatory evaluation, preliminary results are often shared with a wider stakeholder group (such as those who may have participated as interviewees), and who have a definite stake in the program (Brunner & Guzman, 1989). Feedback is recorded and used to refine and revise original interpretations. This process of dialogue and negotiation in the co-construction of knowledge among all involved stakeholders underscores the fundamentally relational, interactive, and learning features that serve to differentiate participatory evaluation from other evaluation approaches.

Critics of participatory and collaborative evaluation approaches have sometimes pointed to the potential for stakeholders' self-serving biases to intrude on the process (e.g., Scriven, 1997). In our experience, data analyses and interpretation processes represent the juncture at which such threats are most pronounced and there is an essential role for evaluators to ensure professional standards of practice. We are not suggesting that the evaluator strive to ensure that, for example, acceptable levels of 'objectivity' are maintained. Indeed, given participatory evaluation's inherent relational character, data quality assurance and trustworthiness of conclusions are to be framed much as they are with qualitative inquiry. The issue is credibility and a resonance of findings and conclusions with the lived experience of program community members. Regardless, an essential responsibility for the evaluator, whether in a P-PE or T-PE context, would be to ensure that all conclusions are warranted by the presenting evaluation evidence and that they do not derive from stakeholder wish lists.

Summary of Practical Intersections

In sum, participatory evaluation can be described as a social process, more than a specific set of data collection methods or techniques (Gaventa, Creed, & Morrissey, 1998). The relational, dialogical focus is considered paramount throughout, as evaluators and stakeholders together define the parameters of practice and the knowledge that is ultimately created throughout the evaluative process. In qualitative inquiry, the evaluator is also focused on involving and engaging participants relationally, as a way to develop a deeper understanding of participant views and beliefs, capture what people are saying, gather a detailed picture of the people and research setting, and collect direct quotations from participants (Patton, 2002). As such, the philosophical and practical aspects of qualitative inquiry must be seen as interwoven throughout the practice of participatory evaluation, far beyond the selection of methods made during data collection. Consider the following key qualitative aspects derived from the participatory process descriptions:

- The focus on relationships in the co-construction of knowledge

- The interactive and dialogic nature of the evaluation process

- The role of values woven throughout the process

- The focus on localized context and local community participation

- The role of the evaluator as engaged facilitator throughout the process

- The use of informal interviews and ongoing dialogue with the stakeholder community as a way to more fully understand the local perspective, culture, and context of the program

- The creation and use of an evaluation committee composed of interested stakeholders, which provides continuing opportunities for joint knowledge construction and ongoing learning as the inquiry process proceeds

- Data collection seen as emergent (based on the local context and community and program circumstances) rather than as prescriptive

- A holistic understanding of program and community context

- Opportunities provided for reflection/self-reflection and learning throughout

- The evaluation seen as discovery rather than prefigured

- Data analysis as interpretive and emergent

- The focus on understanding and learning

Although we do not mean to conflate all qualitative and participatory approaches (given the variety and variability found within each) as fundamentally relational and contextually grounded practices, connections between the two are deeply rooted at both philosophical and practical levels. As such, qualitative inquiry can be seen as an organic part of the participatory approach, weaving itself throughout the evaluation process from beginning to end, well beyond the collection and analysis of qualitative data. Qualitative methods are thus central in both practical and transformative participatory evaluation approaches, because they provide more in-depth understanding of the community from the perspective of those closest to the program being evaluated. In what follows, we focus on the key benefits and subsequent challenges involved in thinking about intersections among qualitative and participatory approaches.

KEY BENEFITS

The interconnections of qualitative and participatory approaches bring the focus to the relational, dialogic, contextual, and learning components of evaluation, as stakeholders and evaluators work together to build practical and conceptual knowledge. One of the key benefits of the process is thus the learning that takes place at a practical level—concerning the program, the organization, the context, and the evaluation itself—and at a conceptual level, concerning relationships to self and others. We thus can conceive of evaluation as a pedagogical and relational undertaking (Schwandt, 2003), leading to what Patton (1997) has termed the "process use" of evaluation, defined as "individual changes in thinking, attitudes, and behavior, and program or organizational changes in procedures and culture that occur among those involved in evaluation as a result of the learning that occurs during the evaluation process" (p. 155). Process use has been linked to participatory forms of inquiry (Amo & Cousins, 2007; Cousins & Earl, 1992), because collaboration has been found to foster organizational learning systems that ultimately enhance reflection, lead to changes in action or behavior, prompt changes in relationships, and yield other relevant organizational learning outcomes.

Conceptually, the focus shifts to an understanding of self and others within the evaluative context, to a hermeneutic conception of understanding, listening, and interpreting within the context of social inquiry (Klemm, 1986), and to how we interact and make meaning together. Within hermeneutics, listening and understanding are conceptualized dialogically and reflexively, requiring that we open ourselves not only to what others have to say, but to ourselves, and our own biases and prejudices (Klemm, 1986). This understanding, conceptualized as an active dialogic process, a "constructive performance" (Klemm, 1986), thus requires that we engage with our pre-judgments and biases so that we may grow. Dialogue, the point where we come together and are open to understanding self and others, is precisely the hermeneutic tension that creates the opportunity to produce new knowledge and understanding (Kimball & Garrison, 1996).

POTENTIAL CHALLENGES

As a fundamentally relational approach, the participatory process also has the potential to surface underlying issues of power and privilege between stakeholders and evaluators—and among stakeholders—that might not otherwise find expression during an evaluation. As Lennie (2005) noted, "evaluation methodologies which explicitly aim to be participatory raise many complex, theoretical and ethical issues, as power, and privilege can be brought to the fore" (p. 29). We observe macro- and micro-power issues, as relationships are defined within a broad sociopolitical landscape (Rebien, 1996) and amidst asymmetrical relations of privilege between evaluators and stakeholders and among stakeholders themselves. As Wallerstein (1999) so aptly observed, "there are many realities in the research relationship" (p. 49). Participation can thus highlight the differences in positions and status among stakeholder groups (Mercier, 1997) as well as raise other potentially unresolved power issues (House & Howe, 2000; Ryan & Johnson, 2000). Inequalities among stakeholders also can make it a challenge to ensure equitable participation (Brandon, 1998), because some stakeholders unused to having a voice may remain mute in the presence of more powerful stakeholders (Greene, 2000). Participation, the level and depth of stakeholder involvement, can thus range from low to high, depending on the diversity of the stakeholder groups involved in the evaluation process.

Whereas collaborative approaches may thus provide a more inclusive and participatory context and may in fact help mitigate some power differentials, merely inviting everyone to the table is not enough. As Schick (2002) explained:

> Power, rather than principles of logic and evidence, denies particular groups (women and members of racially "marginal" groups) legitimacy and authority to define their own experiences, needs, and

> priorities and to offer authoritative interpretations of broader social processes and structures. (p. 646)

What is thus required, as many evaluation scholars have argued, is the need to overtly and consciously address power differentials, and to understand the relationship between power and participation in the evaluative setting (Gregory, 2000). Participatory evaluation, as Rebien (1996) and Gregory (2000) have concluded, should not be naively implemented across all contexts, because it can raise a number of issues that may serve to further marginalize the very populations it was intended to benefit. As noted earlier, the evaluator's role, as trainer, facilitator, negotiator, or mediator, thus changes throughout the evaluation process to accommodate the exigencies and complexity of the evaluation and program context, and to help navigate potential power differences among participants.

CONCLUSION

In thinking about the intersection of participatory and qualitative approaches, the focus shifts to the relational and dialogic similarities and to an appreciation for contextualized meaning and understanding, as evaluators and stakeholders work together to create practical and conceptual knowledge. Thus, despite the fact that participatory evaluation embraces methodological diversity, it nonetheless embraces the fundamental principles of qualitative inquiry at a philosophical level, based on the inclusion of participants in the co-construction of knowledge and through social constructivism grounded in the program context.

What differentiates the participatory approach, however, is the nature of the relationship between evaluators and stakeholders, as they work together as partners throughout the evaluative process. The role of stakeholders thus shifts to that of co-investigator, as they become more active and engaged in decision-making as the evaluation unfolds. The role of evaluator also changes to accommodate and reflect the collaborative and more engaged interactions with stakeholders in the participatory process. Greene (2000, as cited in J. A. King & Stevahn, 2002) conceptualized the evaluator role as engaging in "moral and ethical complexities" and seeking "locations of engagement" (p. 2), thus emphasizing relationships and the contexts within which these interactions occur. Roles are thus mediated, not only by our relationships in the field, but by the nature of the relationships that we foster as we discursively co-create knowledge (Schwandt, 2002).

As a relational construct, participatory evaluation thus can be conceptualized as a dialectic process that fundamentally changes both evaluators and stakeholders, as together they become active participants in the research process. Participatory evaluation embraces fundamental principles of qualitative inquiry and explicitly moves toward a political or action-oriented focus (Burke, 1998), both relationally and in the construction (and co-construction) of knowledge.

KEY CONCEPTS

Active stakeholder involvement

Co-constructed knowledge

Collaborative partnership

Control of evaluation process

Depth of participation

Diversity among stakeholders

Emancipatory and liberatory process

Emergent data collection

Evaluation steering committee

Evaluator positionality

Holistic understanding

Local and cultural contexts

Multilateral self-awareness

Naturalistic setting

Participatory evaluation

Philosophical hermeneutics

Political perspective

Practical participatory evaluation (P-PE)

Pragmatic response

Qualitative inquiry

Relational and dialogical processes

Shared meaning and understanding

Social constructivist approach

Transformative participatory evaluation (T-PE)

Values pluralism

DISCUSSION QUESTIONS

1. Three examples of participatory evaluation are presented at the outset of the chapter. Based on these brief descriptions,

how would you characterize each example relative to the two major streams of participatory evaluation: practical participatory evaluation (P-PE) and transformative participatory evaluation (T-PE)?

2.   Identify a program with which you are familiar and that you think would be well served by a participatory approach to evaluation. Now imagine that you are asked to conduct an evaluation of the program; however, the external funder is only familiar with conventional, noncollaborative approaches to evaluation and suggests that this evaluation follow suit. In your attempt to persuade the funder to support a participatory evaluation, how might you draw on one or more of Levin's (1993) three justifications for collaborative inquiry that arise from pragmatic, political, and philosophical interests? Furthermore, how might you propose that qualitative inquiry be used to address the particular interest(s) you identify?

3.   The authors emphasize that participatory evaluation "alters the traditional roles of evaluators and stakeholders." They note the need for evaluators to "adapt their evaluative practice to local conditions and accommodate the diverse needs of the stakeholder population." As a result, the practice of participatory evaluation involves skills such as mediation, facilitation, and coaching, which may fall outside the scope of traditional research and evaluation training. Reflect on your current knowledge and skills. What aspects of participatory evaluation practice align with your existing knowledge and skills? What aspects would require further learning and development?

REFERENCES

Abma, T. A., & Widdershoven, G.A.M. (2008). Sharing stories: Narrative and dialogue in responsive nursing evaluation. *Evaluation & the Health Professions*, 28(1), 90–109.

Amo, C., & Cousins, J.B. (2007). Going through the process: An examination of the operationalization of process use in empirical research on evaluation. In J. B. Cousins (Ed.), *Process use in theory, research and practice: New directions in evaluation* (pp. 5–26). San Francisco, CA: Jossey-Bass.

Arnstein, S. R. (1969). A ladder of citizen inquiry. *Journal of the American Institute of Planners, 35*(4), 216–224.

Ayers, T. D. (1987). Stakeholders as partners in evaluation: A stakeholder-collaborative approach. *Evaluation and Program Planning, 10,* 263–271.

Bradley, J. E., Mayfield, M. V., Mehta, M. P., & Rukonge, A. (2002). Participatory evaluation of reproductive health care quality in developing countries. *Social Sciences & Medicine, 55,* 269–282.

Brandon, P. (1998). Stakeholder participation for the purpose of helping ensure evaluation validity: Bridging the gap between collaborative and non-collaborative evaluations. *American Journal of Evaluation, 19*(3), 325–337.

Brisolera, S. (1998). The history of participatory evaluation and current debates in the field. In E. Whitmore (Ed.), *Understanding and practicing participatory evaluation: New directions in evaluation* (Vol. 80, pp. 25–41). San Francisco, CA: Jossey-Bass.

Brison, D. (2007). Collaborative evaluation in a community change initiative: Dilemmas of control over technical decision making. *The Canadian Journal of Program Evaluation, 22*(2), 21–39.

Brunner, I., & Guzman, A. (1989). Participatory evaluation: A tool to assess projects and empower people. In R. F. Conner & M. Hendricks (Eds.), *International innovations in evaluation methodology: New directions for evaluation* (Vol. 42, pp. 9–18). San Francisco, CA: Jossey-Bass.

Bryk, A. S. (Ed.). (1983). Stakeholder-based evaluation. *New directions for evaluation* (Vol. 17, pp. 97–108). San Francisco, CA: Jossey-Bass.

Burke, B. (1998). Evaluating for a change: Reflections on participatory methodology. In E. Whitmore (Ed.), *Understanding and practicing participatory evaluation: New directions for evaluation* (Vol. 80, pp. 43–56). San Francisco, CA: Jossey-Bass.

Carter, S. M., & Little, M. (2007). Justifying knowledge, justifying method, taking action: Epistemologies, methodologies, and methods in qualitative research. *Qualitative Health Research, 17*(10), 1316–1328.

Chambers, R. (2003). Participation and numbers. *PLA Notes,* August, 6–12.

Chambers, R., Samaranayake, M., & Zaveri, S. (2010, October). *Participatory evaluation.* Workshop presented at the Evaluation Conclave, New Delhi, India.

Clandinin, D. J., & Connelly, F. M. (2000). *Narrative inquiry: Experience and story in qualitative research.* San Francisco, CA: John Wiley & Sons.

Cornwall, A., & Jewkes, R. (1995). What is participatory research? *Social Science & Medicine, 41*(12), 1667–1676.

Cousins, J. B., & Chouinard, J. A. (2010). *A review and integration of empirical research on participatory evaluation.* Invited keynote paper for Virtual Conference on Methodology in Programme Evaluation, University of Witswatersrand, Johannesburg, South Africa.

Cousins, J. B., & Earl, L. M. (1992). The case for participatory evaluation. *Educational Evaluation and Policy Analysis, 14*(4), 397–418.

Cousins, J. B., & Earl, L. M. (Eds.). (1995). *Participatory evaluation in education: Studies in evaluation use and organizational learning.* Washington, DC: Falmer Press.

Cousins, J. B., & Whitmore, E. (1998). Framing participatory evaluation. In E. Whitmore (Ed.), *Understanding and practicing participatory evaluation: New directions for evaluation* (Vol. 80). San Francisco, CA: Jossey-Bass.

Crishna, B. (2006). Participatory evaluation (1)—sharing lessons from fieldwork in Asia. *Child: Care, Health and Development, 33*(3), 217–223.

DeLuca, C., Poth, C., & Searle, M. (2009). Evaluation for learning: A cross-case analysis of evaluator strategies. *Studies in Educational Evaluation, 35,* 121–129.

Denzin, N. K., & Lincoln, Y. S. (1998). *Collecting and interpreting qualitative material.* Thousand Oaks, CA: Sage.

Diaz-Puente, J., Yague, J. L., & Afonso, A. (2008). Building evaluation capacity in Spain: A case study of rural development and empowerment in the European Union. *Evaluation Review, 32*(5), 478–506.

Dryden, E., Hyde, J., Livny, A., & Tula, M. (2010). Phoenix rising: Use of a participatory approach to evaluate a federally funded HIV, hepatitis and substance abuse prevention program. *Evaluation and Program Planning, 33,* 386–393.

Fetterman, D. (2001). *Foundations of empowerment evaluation.* Thousand Oaks, CA: Sage.

Fetterman, D., & Wandersman, A. (Eds.). (2005). *Empowerment evaluation principles in practice.* New York, NY: Guilford.

Feuerstein, M.-T. (1998). Finding the methods to fit the people: Training for participatory evaluation. *Community Development Journal, 23,* 16–25.

Gadamer, H.-G. (1989). *Truth and method.* New York, NY: Crossroad Publishing.

Garaway, G. B. (1995). Participatory evaluation. *Studies in Educational Evaluation, 21*(1), 85–102.

Gaventa, J., Creed, V., & Morrissey, J. (1998). Scaling up: Participatory monitoring and evaluation of a federal empowerment program. In E. Whitmore (Ed.), *Understanding and practicing participatory evaluation: New directions in evaluation* (Vol. 80, pp. 81–94). San Francisco, CA: Jossey-Bass.

Geertz, C. (1973). *The interpretations of culture: Selected essays.* New York, NY: Basic Books.

Geertz, C. (1993). *Local knowledge: Further essays in interpretive anthropology*. London, UK: Falmer.

Greene, J. C. (2000). Challenges in practicing deliberative democratic evaluation. In K. E. Ryan & L. DeStefano (Eds.), *Evaluation as a democratic process: Promoting inclusion, dialogue, and deliberation* (No. 85, pp. 27–38). San Francisco, CA: Jossey-Bass.

Greene, J. C. (2005). Context. In S. Mathison (Ed.), *Encyclopedia of evaluation* (pp. 83–85). Thousand Oaks, CA: Sage.

Greene, J. C. (2006). Toward a methodology of mixed methods social inquiry. *Research in the Schools, 13*(1), 93–98.

Greene, J. C. (2007). *Mixed methods in social inquiry*. San Francisco, CA: Jossey-Bass.

Gregory, A. (2000). Problematizing participation: A critical review of approaches to participation in evaluation theory. *Evaluation, 6*(2), 179–199.

Guba, E. G., & Lincoln, Y. S. (1989). *Fourth generation evaluation*. Thousand Oaks, CA: Sage.

Hall, B. L. (1992). From margins to centre? The development and purpose of participatory research. *The American Sociologist, 23*(4), 15–28.

Heron, J. (1996). *Co-operative inquiry: Research into the human condition*. London, UK: Sage.

Heron, J., & Reason, P. (1997). A participatory inquiry paradigm. *Qualitative Inquiry, 3*(3), 274–294.

House, E. R. (1993). *Professional evaluation: Social impact and political consequences*. Newbury Park, CA: Sage.

House, E. R., & Howe, K. R. (2000). Deliberative democratic evaluation. *New Directions for Evaluation, 85*, 3–12.

Jackson, E. T., & Kassam, Y. (1998). Introduction. In E. T. Jackson & Y. Kassam (Eds.), *Knowledge shared: Participatory evaluation in development cooperation* (pp. 1–20). West Hartford, CT: Kumarian Press.

Kelly, J. G. (2006). *Becoming ecological: An expedition into community psychology*. New York, NY: Oxford University Press.

Kimball, S., & Garrison, J. (1996). Hermeneutic listening: An approach to understanding in multicultural conversations. *Studies in Philosophy and Education, 15*, 51–59.

King, J. (1998). Making sense of participatory evaluation practice. In E. Whitmore (Ed.), *Understanding and practicing participatory evaluation: New directions in evaluation* (Vol. 80, pp. 57–68). San Francisco, CA: Jossey-Bass.

King, J. A. (2005). Participatory evaluation. In S. Matheson (Ed.), *Encyclopedia of evaluation*. Thousand Oaks, CA: Sage.

King J. A., & Stevahn, L. (2002). Three frameworks for considering evaluator role. In E. E. Ryan & T. A. Schwandt (Eds.), *Exploring evaluator role and identity* (pp. 1–16). Greenwich, CT: Information Age Publishing.

King, J. E., & Ehlert, J. C. (2008). What we learned from three evaluations that involved stakeholders. *Studies in Educational Evaluation, 34*, 194–200.

Klemm, D. E. (1986). *Hermeneutical inquiry: Volume I: The interpretation of texts.* Atlanta, GA: Scholars Press.

LaFrance, J. (2004). Culturally competent evaluation in Indian country. *New Directions for Evaluation, 102*, 39–50.

Lather, P. (1991). *Getting smart: Feminist research and pedagogy with/in the postmodern.* New York, NY: Routledge.

Lather, P. (1993). Fertile obsession: Validity after poststructuralism. *The Sociological Quarterly, 34*(4), 673–693.

Lennie, J. (2005). An evaluation capacity-building process for sustainable community IT initiatives: Empowering and disempowering impacts. *Evaluation, 11*(4), 390–414.

Levin, B. (1993). Collaborative research in and with organizations. *Qualitative Studies in Education, 6*(4), 331–340.

Lincoln, Y. S., & Guba, E. G. (1985). *Naturalistic inquiry.* Newbury Park, CA: Sage.

Lincoln, Y. S., & Guba, E. G. (2000). Paradigmatic controversies, contradictions, and emerging confluences. In N. K. Denzin & Y. S. Lincoln (Eds.), *Handbook of qualitative research* (2nd ed., pp. 163–188). Thousand Oaks, CA: Sage.

Long, N. (1992). Introduction. In N. Long & A. Long (Eds.), *Battlefields of knowledge: The interlocking of theory and practice in social research and development* (pp. 3–43). London, UK: Routledge.

MacLellan-Wright, M. F., Patten, S., de la Cruz, A. M., & Flaherty, A. (2007). A participatory approach to the development of an evaluation framework: Process, pitfalls, and payoffs. *The Canadian Journal of Evaluation, 22*(1), 99–124.

Mark, M. M., & Shotland, R. L. (1985). Stakeholder-based evaluation and value judgments. *Evaluation Review, 9*, 605–626.

McTaggart, R. (1991). When democratic evaluation doesn't seem democratic. *Evaluation Practice, 12*(1), 9–21.

Mercier, C. (1997). Participation in stakeholder-based evaluation: A case study. *Evaluation and Program Planning, 20*(4), 467–475.

Mertens, D. (2008). *Transformative research and evaluation.* New York, NY: Guilford.

Metz, M. H. (2000). Sociology and qualitative methodologies in educational research. *Harvard Educational Review, 70*(1), 60–74.

Page, R. B. (2000). The turn inward in qualitative research. *Harvard Educational Review, 70*(1), 23–38.

Patton, M. Q. (1994). Developmental evaluation. *Evaluation Practice, 15*(3), 311–320.

Patton, M. Q. (1997). *Utilization-focused evaluation* (3rd ed.). Thousand Oaks, CA: Sage.

Patton, M. Q. (2002). *Qualitative research & evaluation methods* (3rd ed.). Thousand Oaks, CA: Sage.

Patton, M. Q. (2008). *Utilization-focused evaluation* (4th ed.). Thousand Oaks, CA: Sage.

Patton, M. Q. (2011). *Developmental evaluation: Applying complexity concepts to enhance innovation and use.* New York, NY: Guilford.

Peshkin, A. (1988). In search of subjectivity—one's own. *Educational Researcher, 17*(7), 17–21.

Preissle, J. (2006). Envisioning qualitative inquiry: A view across four decades. *International Journal of Qualitative Studies in Education, 19*(6), 685–695.

Reason, P. (1999). Integrating action and reflection through co-operative inquiry. *Management Learning (Special Issue: The Action Dimension in Management: Diverse Approaches to Research, Teaching and Development), 30*(2), 207–227.

Rebien, C. C. (1996). Participatory evaluation of development assistance: Dealing with power and facilitative learning. *Evaluation, 2*(2), 151–171.

Rogers, S. J., Ahmed, M., Hamdallah, M., & Little, S. (2010). Garnering grantee buy-in on a national cross-site evaluation: The case of *Connect HIV. American Journal of Evaluation, 31*(4), 447–462.

Rossman, G. B., & Rallis, S. F. (2003). *Learning in the field: An introduction to qualitative research* (2nd ed.). Thousand Oaks, CA: Sage.

Ryan, K. E., & Johnson, T. D. (2000). Democratizing evaluation: Meanings and methods from practice. In K. E. Ryan & L. DeStephano (Eds.), *Evaluation as a democratic process: Promoting inclusion, dialogue, and deliberation; New directions in evaluation* (Vol. 85, pp. 39–50). San Francisco, CA: Jossey-Bass.

Scheurich, J. J., & Young, M. D. (2002). Coloring epistemology: Are our research epistemologies racially biased? In J. J. Scheurich (Ed.), *Anti-racist scholarship: An advocacy.* Albany, NY: State University of New York Press.

Schick, R. S. (2002). When the subject is difference: Conditions of voice in policy-oriented qualitative research. *Qualitative Inquiry, 8*(5), 632–651.

Schwandt, T. A. (2000). Three epistemological stances for qualitative enquiry: Interpretivism, hermeneutics and social constructionism. In N. K. Denzin & Y. S. Lincoln (Eds.), *Handbook of qualitative research* (2nd ed., pp. 189–213). London, UK: Sage.

Schwandt, T. A. (2002). Traversing the terrain of role, identity and self. In K. E. Ryan & T. A. Schwandt (Eds.), *Exploring evaluator role and identity* (pp. 193–207). Greenwich, CT: Information Age Publishing.

Schwandt, T. A. (2003). "Back to the rough ground!" Beyond theory to practice in evaluation. *Evaluation, 9*(3), 353–364.

Schwandt, T. A. (2007). *The Sage dictionary of qualitative inquiry* (3rd ed.). Thousand Oaks, CA: Sage.

Scriven, M. (1997). Empowerment evaluation examined. *Evaluation Practice, 18*, 165–175.

Sharkey, S., & Sharples, A. (2008). From the beginning: Negotiation in community evaluation. *Evaluation, 14*(3), 363–380.

Small, S. A., Tiwari, G., & Huser, M. (2006). The cultural education of academic evaluators: Lessons from a university-Hmong community partnership. *American Journal of Community Psychology, 37*, 357–364.

Somers, C. (2005). Evaluation of the wonders in nature: Wonders in neighbourhoods conservation education program; Stakeholders gone wild! In E. Norland & C. Somers (Eds.), *Evaluating nonformal educational programs and settings: New directions for evaluation* (Vol. 108, pp. 29–46) San Francisco, CA: Jossey-Bass.

Stake, R. E. (1975). *Evaluating the arts in education: A responsive approach.* Columbus, OH: Merrill Publishing.

Symonette, H. (2004). Walking pathways toward becoming a culturally competent evaluator: Boundaries, borderlands, and border crossings. *New Directions for Evaluation, 102*, 95–109.

Tandon, R. (1981). Participatory research in the empowerment of people. *Convergence, 14*(3), 20–29.

Taut, S. (2008). What have we learned about stakeholder involvement in program evaluation? *Studies in Educational Evaluation, 34*, 224–230.

Torres, R. T., Padilla Stone, S., Butkus, D., Hook, B., Casey, J., & Arens, S. (2000). Dialogue and reflection in a collaborative evaluation: Stakeholder and evaluation voices. In K. Ryan & L. DeStefano (Eds.), *Evaluation as a democratic process: Promoting inclusion, dialogue, and deliberation; New directions for evaluation* (Vol. 85, pp. 27–38). San Francisco, CA: Jossey-Bass.

Van Maanen, J. (1988). *Tales from the field: On writing ethnography.* Chicago, IL: University of Chicago Press.

Villarreal, M. (1992). The poverty of practice. In N. Long & A. Long (Eds.), *Battlefields of knowledge: The interlocking of theory and practice in social research and development* (pp. 247–267). London, UK: Routledge.

Wallerstein, N. (1999). Power between evaluator and community: Research relationships within New Mexico's healthier communities. *Social Science & Medicine, 49*, 39–53.

Weiss, C. H. (1998). *Evaluation* (2nd ed.). Upper Saddle River, NJ: Prentice-Hall.

2

TALES FROM THE FIELD OF QUALITATIVE EVALUATION

Successful evaluators who use qualitative inquiry in their practice begin with a solid understanding of their evaluation approach, as illustrated in Part 1, but this knowledge is coupled with an awareness that theory and practice do not always neatly align. Effective evaluators are able to read the program landscape and navigate accordingly. Part 2 of this volume addresses the place where an evaluator's theoretical and methodological training meet the real world and encounter its beautiful, complicated, complex, dynamic messiness. This nexus must be addressed because the very purpose of a qualitative evaluation is to investigate and make meaning of the normal messiness that constitutes the various perspectives, experiences, and reflections of program stakeholders.

Through in-depth case examples, new and experienced evaluators explain their thinking behind the decisions they made while working in the field. Evaluations that use qualitative inquiry purposefully portray the complexity of the experiences of many different people associated with programs and initiatives. The challenge in any evaluation, and particularly one that foregrounds qualitative inquiry, is in how to honor these various perspectives and values, while telling a story that captures how everything fits together and is more than the sum of the parts. The case studies presented in Part 2 are intentionally designed to connect evaluation theory to principles of qualitative inquiry, and to articulate how this connection relates to everyday evaluation practice.

What Does It Take to Be an Effective Qualitative Evaluator?

Essential Competencies

Laurie Stevahn and Jean A. King

Key Ideas

- Effective qualitative evaluators are essentially effective evaluators guided by and uniquely contributing to five broad areas of competence:

    Professional competence

    Technical competence

    Situational competence

    Management competence

    Interpersonal competence

- These five areas of competence are undergirded by three grounding ideas:

    A value commitment to using the qualitative paradigm

    Technical methodological expertise related to collecting, recording, and analyzing qualitative data

> The qualitative sixth sense—the ability of evaluators to interact skillfully with a wide range of others throughout an evaluation in ways that will produce trustworthy and meaningful results

■ In terms of being an effective qualitative evaluator, highly specialized sets of competencies unique to particular evaluator roles or contexts may be less important than engaging in ongoing reflection, self-assessment, and collaborative conversation about what effectiveness means given particular conditions and circumstances.

When asked about the enduring success of the weekly CBS newsmagazine *60 Minutes,* creator and executive producer Don Hewitt (2001) replied, "The formula is simple, and it's reduced to four words every kid in the world knows: Tell me a story" (p. 1), further adding, "We try always to tell it straight" (p. 11). Evaluators who use qualitative methods might well say the same: Successful practice depends on telling the story of evaluation findings and trying always to tell it straight. Broadly speaking, qualitative evaluations strive to illuminate in authentic ways the roles, relationships, responsibilities, or experiences of those who manage, lead, provide, or receive products or services in program or organizational settings, often for the purpose of determining effectiveness. What competencies do those who conduct such studies need for skillful practice?

This chapter considers what it takes to be an effective qualitative evaluator by exploring competencies for professional practice. We begin by exploring how competencies have been conceptualized in general and then provide a short history of the search for competencies in the field of program evaluation specifically. We then focus on four evaluator competency taxonomies that emerged in North America, each emerging from different orientations, but all directly focused on evaluator effectiveness. This lays the groundwork for presenting our perspective on what it takes to be an effective qualitative evaluator. The overarching point is that effective *qualitative* evaluators are essentially effective *evaluators* guided by and uniquely contributing to five broad areas of competence. Three grounding ideas undergird this point: First, qualitative evaluators make a value commitment to using the qualitative paradigm. Second, they need to have technical methodological expertise related to collecting, recording, and analyzing qualitative data. Finally, they must exhibit what we call the qualitative sixth sense—the ability of evaluators to interact skillfully with a wide range of others throughout an evaluation in ways that will produce trustworthy and meaningful results.

COMPETENCIES FOR PROFESSIONAL PRACTICE

Competencies for Professionals

Although no generally accepted definition for *competencies* (Rychen, 2001) exists, most people believe that *competence* matters in the world of work. Surely professionals should be able to demonstrate sufficient ability or expertise in any chosen field; hence the development of standards and competencies for practice across numerous disciplines. In North America, for example, educators such as teachers and administrators must meet national, state, or provincial standards for certification. In the health professions, doctors, dentists, nurses, counselors, and other specialists must demonstrate proficient knowledge and clinical skills for licensing. To practice law, attorneys must pass bar examinations mandated by governing boards. Certain business vocations such as accounting, engineering, aviation, and cosmetology, among others, also demand credentialing. Whether a teacher, surgeon, lawyer, pilot, or stylist, expecting each to acquire and demonstrate the knowledge, skills, and dispositions that support high-quality outcomes for whomever they serve—students, patients, clients, or customers—seems reasonable.

Historically, professional disciplines have identified and adopted competency taxonomies to define and guide practice in respective fields. These taxonomies attempt to articulate "complex action systems that encompass not only knowledge and skills, but also strategies and routines for appropriately applying these knowledge and skills, as well as appropriate emotions and attitudes and the effective self-regulation of these competencies" (Rychen, 2001, p. 8). Despite the potential utility of such systems—for defining a field of practice, developing effective training programs, qualifying individuals for practice, assessing performance, guiding ongoing professional development, and the like—debates continue over how best to develop and frame competencies overall. Recurring issues tend to focus on whether to (1) employ behavioral versus holistic approaches to creating competencies, (2) include desirable attitudes or dispositions along with knowledge and specialized skills, and (3) use observable/behavioral/measurable language by only including "the things you can see or hear being done" (Green, 1999, p. 7). Although reaching some degree of consensus on these issues seems unlikely in the near future, lack of agreement has not deterred the development and use of competencies across a wide array of professions, including those previously noted.

TOWARD COMPETENCIES FOR EVALUATORS

Curiously, the field of program evaluation has been slow in coming to a foundational set of competencies for evaluators—qualitative or quantitative—despite sustained interest in addressing questions of competence. Initial discussions in the late 1980s and early 1990s focused on what constitutes professionalization and whether program evaluation had matured to achieve such status. At that time Worthen and Sanders (1991) identified five distinguishing criteria for professionalism based on historical trends, comprising (1) career opportunities in the field; (2) formal preparation programs; (3) institutionalization of practice; (4) distinctiveness from other professions; and (5) methodological developments. Program evaluation seemed to qualify, given well-established evaluator training programs at various universities in the United States and Canada, robust professional organizations such as the American Evaluation Association and the Canadian Evaluation Society, professional scholarly journals such as the *American Journal of Evaluation* and the *Canadian Journal of Program Evaluation*, and adoption of *The Program Evaluation Standards* (Joint Committee on Standards for Educational Evaluation, 1994) and *Guiding Principles of the American Evaluation Association* (American Evaluation Association, 1995). Noticeably missing, however, was a widely accepted coherent set of competencies for evaluators deemed necessary to conduct evaluations effectively.

In the late 1990s, discussions relevant to competencies advanced in two ways. First, rigorous debates over whether to certify or credential evaluators, accredit training programs, or license practitioners began to appear at annual meetings of professional associations. These debates stemmed from, as well as extended, earlier discussions on professionalism, yet also more sharply focused attention on the need for evaluator competencies. Credentialing or licensing individuals as competent evaluators surely would require a common set of competencies, as would accrediting professional training programs. Although experts in the field had proposed various frameworks identifying evaluator skills and tasks (e.g., Anderson & Ball, 1978; Covert, 1992; Mertens, 1994; Sanders, 1979; Worthen, 1975) and specified content for training and professional development programs (e.g., Altschuld, 1995; Ingle & Klauss, 1980; Sanders, 1986), none were systematically derived, empirically validated, or commonly accepted as foundational.

Hence a second concern: Could evaluation professionals representing diverse evaluator backgrounds, roles, contexts, approaches, and so on across the field reach agreement on a proposed taxonomy of essential competencies for evaluators? At the turn of the century many voiced skepticism: ". . . [I]t would seem far too early to predict whether our field's conceptions will soon reach the point where there will be a cohesive core of competencies that can be widely agreed to. . . Only time will tell whether such a development is even a responsible hope" (Worthen, 1999, p. 547).

EVALUATOR COMPETENCY TAXONOMIES

In the first decade of the new millennium, evaluators began to take action toward strategically identifying, validating, and applying professional competencies. Four notable efforts emerged in North America, three aimed at program evaluators in general and one aimed at those who focus on qualitative methods specifically. Although these taxonomies have different origins, structures, and validations (summarized in Table 6.1), cross-comparisons show five broad common competency categories (summarized in Table 6.2) useful to qualitative evaluators. After briefly describing each of the four taxonomies, we will elaborate on the collective common competency domains that emerge and what they mean for competent qualitative practice. Although we recognize that taxonomies other than these four exist and incorporate into their frameworks various competencies and standards of practice pertinent to evaluators, we do not include those here because they mainly aim to accomplish other primary purposes (e.g., see *Responsibilities and Competencies*—National Commission for Health Education Credentialing, 2008; *Standard on Evaluation for the Government*

Table 6.1 Comparison of Origin/Purpose, Structure, and Validation across Evaluator Competency Taxonomies

Taxonomy	Essential Competencies for Program Evaluators (ECPE) (Stevahn, King, Ghere, & Minnema, 2005; also see King, Stevahn, Ghere, & Minnema, 2001)	Competencies for Canadian Evaluation Practice (Canadian Evaluation Society [CES], 2010)	Evaluator Competencies (International Board of Standards for Training, Performance, and Instruction [IBSTPI], 2006; Russ-Eft, Bober, de la Teja, Foxon, & Koszalka, 2008)	Professional Competencies of Qualitative Research Consultants (Qualitative Research Consultants Association [QRCA], 2003)
Origin/ Purpose	Developed for evaluators practicing at large in diverse roles and contexts across the discipline/profession; envisioned as comprehensive; may be applicable internationally	Developed for the Canadian Evaluation Society Professional Designations Program that credentials evaluators; envisioned primarily for evaluators practicing in the Canadian context; may be applicable to broader contexts	Developed for evaluators practicing in organizations, especially in human resource development envisioned for international application	Developed for qualitative evaluators practicing as external consultants; envisioned for international application
Structure	Six major competency categories classifying 61 competencies	Five major competency categories classifying 49 competencies elaborated by numerous descriptors	Four major competency categories classifying 14 competencies defined by 84 performance statements	Three major competency categories classifying 11 competencies defined by 36 descriptors
Validation	■ King et al. (2001): Multi-Attribute Consensus Reaching (MACR) process generated quantitative and qualitative input on the perceived importance of the competencies for evaluators. Purposive snowball sample (n = 31) of people involved in program evaluation in the greater Minneapolis-St. Paul region in Minnesota, USA, who represented diversity	■ Proposed competencies adapted from ECPE (Stevahn et al., 2005). ■ Crosswalk comparison of the proposed competencies with the CES Essential Skills Series (1999), CES Core Body of Knowledge (2002), Treasury Board of Canada Secretariat Competencies for Evaluators in the Government of Canada (2009), Joint Committee Program Evaluation	■ Russ-Eft et al. (2008): ■ Survey generated quantitative input (Likert-scale ratings on the perceived importance of the competencies for one's work) and qualitative input (what should be added or reworded and general comments)	■ Input from individuals within the qualitative research profession (i.e., roundtable and/or interactive presentation sessions at QRCA and joint QRCA/AQR [Association for Qualitative Research] conferences) on the relevance of proposed competencies

- across a range of demographic characteristics (i.e., evaluation experience, age, evaluation training, familiarity with evaluation standards, evaluation context/setting, professional role/job).
- Stevahn et al. (2005): Additional systematic qualitative input from evaluation professionals and graduate students (n > 100) in formal contexts (i.e., evaluation association conference sessions, university courses, professional development workshops, and consultations with the American Evaluation Association [AEA] competencies task force leader) on competency additions, revisions, deletions.
- Crosswalk comparison of the competencies with the Joint Committee Program Evaluation Standards (1994), AEA Guiding Principles (1995), and CES Essential Skills Series (1999).

- Standards (1994), AEA Guiding Principles (1995), and United Nations Evaluation Group Core Competencies for Evaluators (2008).
- CES members surveyed to obtain input on proposed competencies (2008).
- CES Chapter-based consultations to obtain further input on proposed competencies (2009).
- CES approved competencies and adopted the Professional Designations Program to credential evaluators (2009).

- Sought worldwide input from those involved in evaluation practice.
- Contacted more than 40 professional training and evaluation associations internationally, academic evaluation training programs in several countries, professional networks and listservs, worldwide contacts of IBSTPI board members, and those visiting the IBSTPI website.
- Respondents (n = 443) represented considerable diversity across a range of demographic characteristics (i.e., education, sex, age, organizational work settings/contexts, fields of expertise, evaluator role, years in evaluation, evaluation training/courses, membership in evaluation associations, geographic regions for evaluation work).

- International sample of qualitative research consultants, including QRCA members, nonaffiliated practitioners, and members of other applicable associations who represented diversity across a range of demographic characteristics (i.e., years of practice/experience; age; sex; and qualitative specialties, disciplines, and approaches).
- Input and comment from the American Evaluation Association (AEA).

Table 6.2 Cross-Comparison of Evaluator Competency Taxonomies

Common Core Competency Domains (similarities across taxonomies)	Essential Competencies for Program Evaluators (Stevahn, King, Ghere, & Minnema, 2005; also see King, Stevahn, Ghere, & Minnema, 2001)	Competencies for Canadian Evaluation Practice (Canadian Evaluation Society, 2010)	Evaluator Competencies (International Board of Standards for Training, Performance, and Instruction, 2006; Russ-Eft, Bober, de la Teja, Foxon, & Koszalka, 2008)	Professional Competencies of Qualitative Research Consultants (Qualitative Research Consultants Association, 2003)
Professional Focus Acts ethically/reflectively and enhances/advances professional practice	**1.0** Professional practice (1.1–1.6) **5.0** Reflective practice (5.1–5.5)	**1.0** Reflective practice (1.1–1.7)	Professional foundations (1–5)	8. Professional practices 10. Business practices 11. Commitment to the profession
Technical Focus Applies appropriate methodology	**2.0** Systematic inquiry (2.1–2.20)	**2.0** Technical practice (2.1–2.16)	Planning and designing the evaluation (6–9) Implementing the evaluation (10–12)	3. Conceptualization and design 4. Research 5. Interviewing 6. Analysis
Situational Focus Considers/Analyzes context successfully	**3.0** Situational analysis (3.1–3.12)	**3.0** Situational practice (3.1–3.9)	5. Demonstrate awareness of the politics of evaluation	1. Consulting 2. Content knowledge
Management Focus Conducts/manages projects skillfully	**4.0** Project management (4.1–4.12)	**4.0** Management practice (4.1–4.7)	Managing the evaluation (13–14)	9. Project management/coordination
Interpersonal Focus Interacts/communicates effectively and respectfully	**6.0** Interpersonal competence (6.1–6.6)	**5.0** Interpersonal practice (5.1–5.10)	1. Communicate effectively in written, oral, and visual form 3. Demonstrate effective interpersonal skills 14. Work effectively with personnel and stakeholders	7. Communication

of Canada—Treasury Board of Canada Secretariat, 2009; *Core Competencies for Evaluators of the UN System*—United Nations Evaluation Group, 2008).

Essential Competencies for Program Evaluators

This taxonomy emerged from a collaborative effort among four individuals at the University of Minnesota who sought to examine the extent to which evaluators—diverse across roles, work contexts, training levels, and years of experience—could reach agreement on the perceived importance of a comprehensive set of competencies necessary for program evaluation practice. Work began by exploring the possibility of creating and empirically validating evaluator knowledge, skills, and dispositions essential to effective practice (King, Minnema, Ghere, & Stevahn, 1998; King, Stevahn, Ghere, & Minnema, 1999). The effort continued by conducting a Multi-Attribute Consensus Reaching study to validate the initial set of competencies (King, Stevahn, Ghere, & Minnema, 2001), which led to revising and refining the taxonomy after systematically (1) obtaining and analyzing additional input from diverse professionals in the field and (2) conducting a cross-walk validation study that compared the taxonomy with other widely accepted standards adopted by evaluation associations in North America (Stevahn, King, Ghere, & Minnema, 2005). This taxonomy presents six major competency categories numbered 1.0 through 6.0 (see Table 6.2) that classify sixty-one specific competencies (numbered within each major category, e.g., 1.0 Professional Practice contains six specific competencies numbered 1.1 through 1.6).

Competencies for Canadian Evaluation Practice

The Canadian Evaluation Society (CES) originated and instituted the *Essential Skills Series in Evaluation* (Canadian Evaluation Society, 1999) largely for training purposes, which provided background for a series of studies subsequently undertaken to determine evaluator competencies relevant to the Canadian evaluation context. Commissioned by CES, the findings from these studies laid the groundwork for developing and adopting a set of evaluator competencies for Canadian practice (Canadian Evaluation Society, 2010). This taxonomy became foundational for designing and instituting the CES Professional Designations Program, which credentials evaluators who demonstrate evidence of accomplishing the competencies. The taxonomy presents five major competency categories numbered 1.0 through 5.0 (see Table 6.2) that classify forty-nine specific competencies (numbered within each major category, e.g., 1.0 Reflective Practice contains seven specific competencies numbered 1.1 through 1.7). Furthermore, the specific competencies are elaborated by several descriptors that depict or illustrate what each means.

Evaluator Competencies

The International Board of Standards for Training, Performance and Instruction (2006) developed and empirically validated a set of *Evaluator Competencies* for the practice of evaluation in organizations. For several decades this not-for-profit organization has systematically developed, validated, and promoted international standards to advance professional practice in areas particularly relevant to human resource development. A detailed description of the development process and validation research appears in Russ-Eft, Bober, de la Teja, Foxon, and Koszalka (2008), which sought evaluators internationally to respond to a validation survey designed to assess the importance of each competency in relation to one's work role. This taxonomy presents four major competency categories that are unnumbered (see the bulleted items in Table 6.2) that classify fourteen specific competencies (numbered 1 through 14), further defined by eighty-four performance statements.

Professional Competencies of Qualitative Research Consultants

The Qualitative Research Consultants Association (2003) developed and validated its taxonomy of evaluator competencies specifically for external evaluators hired as consultants who specialize in qualitative research, evaluation, or assessment. This not-for-profit association aims to advance the industry of qualitative research worldwide and, as such, engaged numerous rounds of international input during a 3-year development process that resulted in the final set of competencies. The taxonomy presents three major competency categories—unnumbered but presented sequentially as (1) Consulting, (2) Research, and (3) Professional and Business Practices—that classify eleven specific competencies (numbered 1 through 11 as shown in Table 6.2), each elaborated by several unnumbered descriptors that clarify meaning.

COMPETENCIES FOR QUALITATIVE EVALUATORS

Although people regularly use the term *qualitative evaluator* to describe practice, in reality an *evaluator* is neither qualitative nor quantitative; basic evaluation and methods texts emphasize the importance of choosing methods that fit a study's overarching questions and situation. In other words, the methods come second, not first. Foremost, then, a competent qualitative evaluator must be a competent evaluator, defined by the five broad competency categories that emerged from comparing and synthesizing the four competency taxonomies in the previous section. Under this overarching claim, three distinguishing features require special explication. First, a competent qualitative evaluator understands and intentionally employs a qualitative paradigm for evaluation practice. Second, a competent qualitative evaluator demonstrates technical expertise relevant to qualitative methods. Finally, a competent qualitative evaluator is attuned to social situations and skillfully interacts with people in authentic ways from start to finish. We elaborate on each of these points in the sections that follow.

CORE COMPETENCY DOMAINS

Comparing the four evaluator competency taxonomies summarized in Table 6.2 shows what is at the heart of effective qualitative evaluation practice. Clustering like items across these taxonomies illuminates five broad common core competency domains. These domains become competency categories that broadly frame what *all* evaluators need to be effective—whether qualitative, quantitative, or mixed-methods practitioners. A competent qualitative evaluator is, first and most fundamentally, a competent evaluator who expertly addresses professional, technical, situational, management, and interpersonal concerns. These core domains comprise competencies:

1. *Professional* competence—*acting ethically/reflectively and enhancing/advancing professional practice*—being honest and displaying integrity, applying professional standards,

reflecting on personal practice, continuing to develop expertise, contributing constructively to the profession at large, and so on

2. *Technical* competence—*applying appropriate methodology* —framing evaluation questions, applying appropriate designs and methods, collecting and analyzing data, attending to credibility of the data, reporting results, drawing evidence-based conclusions, and so on

3. *Situational* competence—*considering/analyzing context successfully*—attending to stakeholders and clients, respecting the uniqueness of the evaluation site, analyzing its environment and norms, addressing conflicts and political considerations, focusing on issues of organizational change, and so on

4. *Management* competence—*conducting/managing projects skillfully*—proposing and finalizing formal agreements, planning and carrying out projects in timely ways, connecting appropriately with clients, coordinating resource needs, supervising and working effectively with those involved, and so on

5. *Interpersonal* competence—*interacting/communicating effectively and respectively*—using people skills constructively (verbal and nonverbal), such as articulating clearly, listening for understanding, negotiating and resolving problems mutually, facilitating teamwork, engaging in culturally competent ways, and so on

These five domains suggest that broadly framed competency categories can provide useful guidance to qualitative evaluators as they pursue or develop training, plan and conduct evaluations, or reflect on the qualities and skills essential to their craft. In reality, trying to construct one unique set of detailed competencies exclusive to qualitative evaluation practice may be akin to searching for the holy grail: Illusive. What may matter most is recognizing one set of broad, yet essential, competency domains within which qualitative evaluators exercise unique responsibilities and make distinctive contributions. Consider the following examples:

■ The *professional* domain ethically calls those who specialize in qualitative approaches to self-disclose such expertise and inform potential clients where and when such methods would be appropriate (or not). A qualitative evaluator who acts with integrity, for example, will gracefully decline a lucrative contract offered by a government agency that quickly needs large-scale survey results to meet a legislative deadline, instead referring a well-qualified colleague who specializes in quantitative measures.

■ The *technical* domain calls qualitative practitioners to frame such questions fluently and to collect appropriate data, especially honing skills needed to conduct effective interviews, focus groups, field observations, and other methods that capture the stories, tone, nuance, depth, and texture of those providing input. A technically competent qualitative evaluator exploring evaluation possibilities with the director of a nonprofit organization, for example, may identify concerns that will require in-depth probing of service recipients, and so may suggest facilitating a series of focus groups instead of administering the quantitative questionnaire used in a previous study.

■ The *situational* domain calls on qualitative evaluators to realize the potential of qualitative analysis for better understanding the organizational and cultural context of an evaluation, identifying the interests of stakeholders, or pinpointing political considerations. A qualitative evaluator hired to assess parental trust of and satisfaction with public schools across a large urban district will realize, for example, that individual interviews with diverse stakeholders will be invaluable to understanding and navigating underlying political agendas, each of which will be in play when interpreting results, formulating recommendations, and prioritizing actions.

■ The *management* domain calls qualitative evaluators to attend to the "nuts and bolts" of organizing, storing, and accessing what easily can become a tangled mess of interview transcripts, field notes, program documents, and so forth; budgeting the evaluation appropriately for such work; justifying cost; and monitoring work to complete the job according to the timeline. A hospital's internal human resource development evaluator, for example, first prepares for the upcoming qualitative study of employee attitudes toward policies by creating guidelines for handling the interview data sheets, maintaining the confidentiality of respondents, and establishing a secure electronic database system—realizing that adjustments may be necessary as those involved reflect on what works well and what needs refinement in the evaluation process.

■ The *interpersonal* domain reminds evaluators that nearly all evaluations (especially participatory approaches) require skillful communication and constructive interaction with clients, funders, program leaders, staff, stakeholders or anyone participating in, connected to, or affected by the evaluation as it progresses. A team of qualitative evaluators hired by a local foundation to assess the effectiveness of its funded community programs, for example, will keep social skills at the forefront while working together and when interfacing with those at the various sites. Realization that clearly communicating purpose, conveying information, respectfully seeking access, deeply listening to concerns, attending to cultural norms, and constructively dealing with conflicts or tensions that may surface will be key to conducting tasks successfully in every other competency domain.

All competent evaluators share a set of general competencies, and those who call themselves qualitative evaluators must first ensure that their practice meets the standards of effective practice more generally. What, then, especially distinguishes competent *qualitative* evaluators?

COMMITMENT TO THE QUALITATIVE PARADIGM

The first distinction is a commitment to a qualitative epistemology. Labeling his or her practice *qualitative evaluation* suggests that an evaluator has accepted the qualitative paradigm to answer evaluation questions for which that paradigm is suited. The previous section detailed the ways that qualitative evaluators demonstrate general evaluator competencies with a specific qualitative orientation, for example, by collecting in-depth data when appropriate or by ensuring that qualitative data such as transcripts or field notes will be readily accessible. Although a competent qualitative evaluator must first be a competent evaluator skilled in all domains, this first distinguishing competency is a value declaration: an epistemological commitment to understanding and intentionally employing the qualitative paradigm in evaluation practice. Making a sincere commitment to the qualitative paradigm is an act of philosophical faith. Those who believe in this paradigm accept the idea of multiple realities and multiple truths, of people's uniqueness, and of the value of detailed descriptions of bounded situations that suggest overarching themes that may—or may not—be "true" or apply in other places. Not believing in one universal truth, they do not search for it, living instead in the multiple details of the specific situations in which they find themselves. As Patton (2002) wrote, ". . . the essence of qualitative inquiry is paying attention, being open to what the world has to show us, and thinking about what it means" (p. 205).

In practice a qualitative evaluator will search for situations in which qualitative methods are the appropriate way to answer the key questions of those who are commissioning the study. This means that qualitative evaluators must be able to recognize situations and contexts in which qualitative methods are appropriate; for example, where exploratory studies will help clients understand how an innovative program works, where descriptive studies will describe people's experiences in-depth, or where comparative studies can detail how programs are implemented in diverse settings. A broad base of knowledge enables qualitative evaluators to know when and where their specialized work is appropriate, including contexts with questions that demand in-depth probing or nuanced responding or where conflicts, political considerations, or hidden agendas exist. Situation analysis, then, is a critically important competency category for qualitative evaluators.

A related competency is knowing when *not* to use qualitative methods. The old saying applies: If you have a hammer, the whole world looks like a nail. Just as it is wrong to use a randomized controlled trial in settings in which a qualitative study would be more appropriate, it is wrong to use qualitative methods across the board because doing so inappropriately may result in bad or useless data. People with a deep commitment to the qualitative paradigm must not apply qualitative methods blindly in all situations, but rather choose evaluation sites and questions thoughtfully.

TECHNICAL EXPERTISE

The second distinction moves beyond a philosophical commitment to a specific set of skills. Simply stated, qualitative evaluators enact specialized skill sets within the technical competency domain grounded by an understanding of and commitment to the qualitative paradigm. These are the methodological concerns of qualitative practice that comprise (1) recognizing the value or necessity of a qualitative paradigm to adequately examine issues or address concerns; (2) focusing the study for qualitative purposes; (3) framing qualitative questions; (4) determining appropriate data sources; (5) collecting and analyzing qualitative information; and (6) interpreting and reporting results. Although detailing how qualitative experts carry out these technical tasks goes beyond the scope of this chapter (see, for example, Creswell, 2013; Miles, Huberman, & Saldaña, 2014; Patton, 2002), here we present a brief overview of key methodological components that competent qualitative practitioners will master and apply skillfully in each unique evaluation setting.

First is the ability to articulate the study's purpose and craft evaluation questions. In qualitative work perhaps the biggest challenge is to provide the type of clarity essential for guiding other technical decisions (such as design, data collection, and so on), while simultaneously allowing latitude for changes in focus or direction deemed appropriate as data are collected, analyzed, and interpreted continuously throughout the entire study—a hallmark of qualitative work. Useful and well-crafted questions will illuminate a design (evaluation plan) that can be systematically implemented, yet will signal the importance (core value) of being open and receptive to the personal perspectives and experiences of participants, attentive to voice and nuance, mindful of multiple realities, attuned to authenticity within the naturalistic setting, and driven by a desire for deeper meaning—for telling the full textured story.

Second is the ability to identify and carry out sampling, data collection, and analysis in ways that address the evaluation questions well and serve the established purposes of the study.

Noted previously, evaluators typically collect, record, and analyze data throughout a qualitative study. Findings that emerge midway should influence how evaluators proceed, mindful that evaluation budgets, timelines, resources, intended users, funder expectations, and other practical considerations also are factors in such decision making. Despite the unlimited possibilities for gathering useful information from appropriate data sources, samples, or cases—and the complexities inherent in these processes—Table 6.3 presents a brief overview of some of the most common methods that competent qualitative evaluators will apply.

Third is the ability to convey qualitative results in formats that authentically and meaningfully tell the story. Here competent qualitative evaluators will consider a range of appropriate options—some traditional, such as written reports, others nontraditional such as presentations that use images or dramatizations. The main reporting challenge lies in balancing the diverse needs or expectations of different audiences or constituencies and how best to package, deliver, and convey findings for usefulness, all the while preserving the integrity (and often multifaceted nature) of the story. Sometimes this will mean preparing different types of presentations on the same set of findings. For example, a skilled qualitative evaluator working with a native population to document growth in a community development project may present results in several formats simultaneously, knowing that culturally grounded storytelling will be the format best suited for participants and community stakeholders, an executive summary report will be most useful to the sponsoring foundation/funder, and a published journal article will best provide broad access to interested professionals and scholars working in relevant disciplines or contexts at large.

Of course, the competent qualitative evaluator always honors ethical requirements for conducting studies, attending to issues of privacy, confidentiality, consent, data ownership, participation, reporting needs, and the like when initially contracting or determining the purposes and parameters of a study. Skilled

Table 6.3 Common Methods for Qualitative Evaluators

Method (types of data)	Collecting (how to)	Recording (including useful technology)	Analyzing (options/issues across methods)
Interviews	■ Informal or formal ■ Unstructured, semi-structured, structured ■ Face-to-face or distance (Internet, telephone, other) ■ One-on-one or focus group	■ Audio or video recordings ■ Written notes (verbatim or key words/phrases) ■ Transcripts/transcriptions	■ Participant versus nonparticipant observer/analyzer (one or multiple) ■ Internal versus external analyzers (or both) ■ Use of qualitative software ■ Inductive analysis/synthesis to identify themes, patterns, recurring observances, common qualities or characteristics, unique incidents ■ Content analysis using interpretational, structural, or reflective techniques (e.g., see Gall, Gall, & Borg, 2007) ■ Triangulation for credibility, trustworthiness, authenticity ■ Emic or etic data analysis and reporting (maintain verbatim participant input versus interpret by paraphrasing/summarizing) ■ Participant or field review of analysis for accuracy, authenticity, nuance, multiple perspectives
Question-naires	■ Open-ended or categorical descriptive responses ■ Word (language) or picture (drawing) responses	■ Oral or written recordings ■ Language translations ■ Paper or electronic copies	
Docu-ments	■ Archives that contain organizational/program records ■ Mission statements, strategic plans, policies ■ Organizational charts, demographic information ■ Calendars/schedules of events/meetings ■ Meeting minutes (issues/decisions) ■ Attendance/participation records ■ Newsletters or regular announcements ■ Results of past evaluations or needs assessments	■ Coding sheets (descriptive) ■ Key messages, words, phrases ■ Time intervals	

Observations	▪ Site visits focusing on organizational/program systems or individual behaviors (personal and collective)	▪ Audio or video recordings
		▪ Script taping (ongoing written records of interactions or environmental factors/happenings)
	▪ Leadership styles, operations, communications	
	▪ Interactive networks, communication patterns, interpersonal relationships	▪ Field notes (systematic)
	▪ Performance (role, job, work)	▪ Observation sheets
	▪ Environmental factors such as social climate/morale or physical features, etc.	
Creative artifacts	▪ Photos (preexisting or newly generated by participants)	▪ Visual recordings (photos/videos) of the physical environment, tangible objects, collections, etc.
	▪ Wall posters, charts, signs	
	▪ Mottos, logos, symbols, icons, songs, mascots, cheers, or unique sayings that have meaning	
		▪ Photo or electronic copies of journals or diaries
	▪ Personal reflections, diaries, or journals	▪ Running records
	▪ Internet websites or online messages and communications	▪ Coding sheets (descriptive)
	▪ Advertising, marketing, or promotional materials	
	▪ Collections of various resources, tools, or other artifacts used in the evaluation setting	

qualitative evaluators also—like all competent evaluators—will be keenly aware of (and clearly communicate) a study's strengths and limitations. In fact, making useful inferences and drawing sound conclusions depend on this; in the end, the quality of a study, influenced by methodological choices, will determine the worthiness of results for future decisions and actions.

A related skill for the qualitative evaluator is the ability to "mix methods." In a world in which the quantitative paradigm often holds sway (e.g., in any venue where decision makers seek generalizable "truth" on which to ground their decisions), firm belief in the value of the qualitative paradigm demands that qualitative evaluators engaged in mixed-methods projects vigorously and correctly represent qualitative methods, data, analytical techniques, and reporting strategies. A brief digression is in order to clarify a long running (e.g., Greene & Caracelli, 1997b), but rarely emphasized misunderstanding. Novices to the field sometimes discuss "mixed methods," referring to the use of both qualitative and quantitative data collection techniques, but then mistakenly assume, for example, that surveys represent the quantitative and interviews the qualitative. But a paradigm and a method are not the same thing. A survey can have both quantitative (e.g., forced-choice response) and qualitative (e.g., open-ended or fill-in-the-blank) items. In some settings, an interview may consist entirely of an interviewer reading a quantitative survey aloud to a respondent and writing in individuals' answers for them, which is hardly qualitative in nature. What are often called mixed methods, then, are in reality "mixed paradigms," and there are several different ways to mix them (Greene, 2007; Greene & Caracelli, 1997a; Tashakkori & Teddlie, 2010; Teddlie & Tashakkori, 2009). Knowing this, a qualitative evaluator must be skilled in the use of mixed-methods designs, ensuring that the qualitative component—the use of qualitative methods and their results—builds appropriately on the philosophical assumptions of the paradigm in meaningful ways and that their special characteristics are not lost in the process of mixing paradigms.

THE QUALITATIVE SIXTH SENSE

The third distinction for qualitative evaluators is neither philosophical nor technical; to our knowledge it is not even documented in the literature. It relates to the fact that these evaluators become key actors in an evaluation setting, responsible for data collection and analysis that is highly person- and context-dependent. (There are, of course, challenges in collecting quantitative data as well, but they are of a different type.) What distinguishes highly competent qualitative evaluators, finally, is what we would call an overall sixth sense. This could go by many names—"interpersonal skills," "antennae," "extrasensory perception (ESP)," or, to quote two classic teacher education sources, "withitness" (Kounin, 1970) or even "crap detector" (Postman & Weingartner, 1969). It involves an evaluator's ability to connect with people in an authentic way and to truly perceive the realities of a situation. The idea of an avatar, a movable three-dimensional image brought to life in the movie of the same name, provides an apt image for the qualitative evaluator. Like an avatar, the qualitative evaluator becomes part of the program experience, speaking with staff and participants and potentially engaging in program activities, but often as someone distinctly separate from the program who eventually will leave the scene (certainly true for external evaluators, and somewhat also for internal evaluators who do not regularly work in the programs they evaluate). The ability to blend in and become accepted—to pass—is critical to the quality of the eventual process and outcomes of the evaluation.

Regardless of the approach or the issues faced, competent qualitative evaluators must, therefore, understand and be able to skillfully demonstrate high-quality interpersonal skills and to know that they are gathering data worth analyzing. At the beginning of a study and throughout, this requires facilitating interaction around thoughts for the study, being culturally appropriate, negotiating with clients, and documenting the process. As the study progresses, the evaluator may need to collaborate with various groups to gain access for data collection, to listen carefully and ask probing questions, and perhaps to resolve conflicts that arise as a result of the evaluation. At the end of a study, regardless of report format, written and oral communication skills become important to accurately convey results—to "tell the story"—in a meaningful and effective manner.

How can evaluators be sure that their sixth sense is operating? Consider one evaluator's nightmare when he learned at the conclusion of a study, only after submitting the final report, that to ensure a program's continued funding, the interpreter for multiple focus groups had warned respondents not to say anything bad about their program! Various procedures—member checks, analytical debriefing conversations, audits, processing social interactions, and ongoing self-reflection—can provide supportive sixth-sense evidence. Continuing caution and sensitivity are always appropriate, however, as interpersonal competencies interact with and affect all others, especially situational analysis, project management, and even the technical competencies involved in framing studies and collecting qualitative data.

CONCLUSION

Based on four sets of competencies for professional evaluation practice, this chapter has argued that to be an effective qualitative evaluator is to first be a competent evaluator. Beyond this, competent qualitative evaluators have three distinctive features: (1) an enduring commitment to the qualitative paradigm; (2) the technical expertise required by the skilled use of qualitative methods; and (3) a special "sixth sense" that ensures both a high-quality process and outcomes for qualitative evaluation studies. The importance of qualitative evaluators knowing themselves and being able to convey their approach and unique skills to their clients cannot be overstated. In the end, highly specialized sets of competencies unique to particular evaluator roles or contexts may be less important than engaging in ongoing reflection, self-assessment, and collaborative conversation about what effectiveness means given particular conditions and circumstances.

KEY CONCEPTS

American Evaluation Association

Canadian Evaluation Society

Competencies

Criteria for professionalism

Epistemological commitment

Guiding Principles for Evaluators

Interpersonal domain

Management domain

Professional domain

Program Evaluation Standards

Qualitative data

Qualitative evaluator

Qualitative methods

Qualitative paradigm

Qualitative Research
Consultants Association

Qualitative results

Situational domain

Sixth sense

Taxonomies

Technical domain

DISCUSSION QUESTIONS

1. Part 2 of this volume is devoted to practicing evaluators describing how they actually conduct evaluations. After reading each chapter, describe how the author displayed—or did not display—the five core competency domains: professional competence, technical competence, situational competence, management competence, and interpersonal competence.

2. The concept of a "sixth sense" is familiar to evaluators who embrace qualitative inquiry in their practice, but is not addressed in the literature. As you read the cases presented in Part 2 of this volume, identify how the evaluators effectively used their sixth sense to carry out their evaluations. Think about a time when you relied on your sixth sense; describe the circumstances and how you used your sixth sense to make decisions and navigate the situation.

3. The authors state that a competent qualitative evaluator will consider a range of options for reporting findings. Discuss situations that would lend themselves to a nontraditional method of reporting (i.e., not a typical written report). How would you negotiate a nontraditional approach with the sponsor of the evaluation?

REFERENCES

Altschuld, J. W. (1995). Developing an evaluation program: Challenges to the teaching of evaluation. *Evaluation and Program Planning*, *18*, 259–265.

American Evaluation Association, Task Force on Guiding Principles for Evaluators. (1995). Guiding principles for evaluators. In W. R. Shadish, D. L. Newman, M. A. Scheirer, & C. Wye (Eds.), *Guiding principles for evaluators: New directions for program evaluation* (Vol. 66, pp. 19–26). San Francisco, CA: Jossey-Bass.

Anderson, S. B., & Ball, S. (1978). *The profession and practice of program evaluators*. San Francisco, CA: Jossey-Bass.

Buchanan, H., Kuji-Shikatani, K. & Maicher, B. (2009). *CES professional designations project chronology*. Retrieved from http://evaluationcanada.ca/txt/20090531_chrono_designations.pdf

Canadian Evaluation Society. (1999). *Essential skills series*. Available at http://www.evaluationcanada.ca

Canadian Evaluation Society. (2010). *Competencies for Canadian evaluation practice*. Available at http://www.evaluationcanada.ca/txt/2_competencies_cdn_evaluation_practice.pdf

Covert, R. W. (1992, November). *Successful competencies in preparing professional evaluators*. Presented at the annual meeting of the American Evaluation Association, Seattle, WA.

Creswell, J. W. (2013). *Qualitative inquiry and research design: Choosing among five approaches* (3rd ed.). Thousand Oaks, CA: Sage.

Gall, M. D., Gall, J. P., & Borg, W. R. (2007). *Educational research: An introduction* (8th ed.). Boston, MA: Pearson Education Allyn and Bacon.

Green, P. C. (1999). *Building robust competencies: Linking human resource systems to organizational strategies*. San Francisco, CA: Jossey-Bass.

Greene, J. C. (2007). *Mixed methods in social inquiry*. San Francisco, CA: Jossey-Bass.

Greene, J. C., & Caracelli, V. J. (Eds.). (1997a). *Advances in mixed-method evaluation: The challenges and benefits of integrating diverse paradigms; New directions for program evaluation* (Vol. 74). San Francisco, CA: Jossey-Bass.

Greene, J. C., & Caracelli, V. J. (1997b). Defining and describing the paradigm issue in mixed-method evaluation. In J. C. Greene & V. J. Caracelli (Eds.), *Advances in mixed-method evaluation: The challenges and benefits of integrating diverse paradigms; New directions for program evaluation* (Vol. 74, pp. 5–17). San Francisco, CA: Jossey-Bass.

Hewitt, D. (2001). *Tell me a story: Fifty years and 60 Minutes in television*. New York, NY: PublicAffairs.

Ingle, M. D., & Klauss, R. (1980). Competency-based program evaluation: A contingency approach. *Evaluation and Program Planning, 3,* 277–287.

International Board of Standards for Training, Performance, and Instruction. (2006). *Evaluator competencies.* Available at http://www.ibstpi.org

Joint Committee on Standards for Educational Evaluation. (1994). *The program evaluation standards* (2nd ed.). Thousand Oaks, CA: Sage.

King, J. A., Minnema, J., Ghere, G., & Stevahn, L. (1998, November). *Evaluator competencies.* Presented at the annual meeting of the American Evaluation Association, Chicago, IL.

King, J. A., Stevahn, L., Ghere, G., & Minnema, J. (1999, November). *"And the verdict is . . ." An exploratory study of perceived evaluator competencies.* Presented at the annual meeting of the American Evaluation Association, Orlando, FL.

King, J. A., Stevahn, L., Ghere, G., & Minnema, J. (2001). Toward a taxonomy of essential evaluator competencies. *American Journal of Evaluation, 22*(2), 229–247.

Kounin, J. S. (1970). *Discipline and group management in classrooms.* Oxford, UK: Holt, Rinehart & Winston.

Mertens, D. M. (1994). Training evaluators: Unique skills and knowledge. In J. W. Altschuld & M. Engle (Eds.), *The preparation of professional evaluators: Issues, perspectives, and programs; New directions for program evaluation* (Vol. 62, pp. 17–27). San Francisco, CA: Jossey-Bass.

Miles, M. B., Huberman, A. M., & Saldaña, J. (2014). *Qualitative data analysis: A methods sourcebook.* Thousand Oaks, CA: Sage.

National Commission for Health Education Credentialing. (2008). *Responsibilities and competencies.* Available at http://www.nchec.org

Patton, M. Q. (2002). *Qualitative research and evaluation methods* (3rd ed.). Thousand Oaks, CA: Sage.

Postman, N., & Weingartner, C. (1969). *Teaching as a subversive activity.* New York, NY: Delta.

Qualitative Research Consultants Association. (2003). *Professional competencies of qualitative research consultants.* Available at http://www.qrca.org

Russ-Eft, D., Bober, M. J., de la Teja, I., Foxon, M. J., & Koszalka, T. A. (2008). *Evaluator competencies: Standards for the practice of evaluation in organizations.* San Francisco, CA: Jossey-Bass.

Rychen, D. S. (2001). Introduction. In D. S. Rychen & L. H. Salganik (Eds.), *Defining and selecting key competencies* (pp. 1–15). Seattle, WA: Hogrefe and Huber.

Sanders, J. R. (1979). The technology and art of evaluation: A review of seven evaluation primers. *Evaluation News, 12,* 2–7.

Sanders, J. R. (1986). The teaching of evaluation in education. In B. G. Davis (Ed.), *Teaching evaluation across the disciplines: New directions for program evaluation* (Vol. 29, pp. 15–27). San Francisco, CA: Jossey-Bass.

Stevahn, L., King, J. A., Ghere, G., & Minnema, J. (2005). Establishing essential competencies for program evaluators. *American Journal of Evaluation, 26*(1), 43–59.

Tashakkori, A., & Teddlie, C. B. (Eds.). (2010). *Sage handbook of mixed methods in behavioral research* (2nd ed.). Thousand Oaks, CA: Sage.

Teddlie, C. B., & Tashakkori, A. (2009). *Foundations of mixed methods research: Integrating quantitative and qualitative approaches in the social and behavioral sciences.* Thousand Oaks, CA: Sage.

Treasury Board of Canada Secretariat. (2009). *Standard on evaluation for the government of Canada.* Available at http://www.tbs-sct.gc.ca

United Nations Evaluation Group. (2008). *Core competencies for evaluators of the UN system.* Available at http://www.unevaluation.org /evaluatorcorecompetencies

Worthen, B. R. (1975). Some observations about the institutionalization of evaluation. *Evaluation Practice, 16*, 29–36.

Worthen, B. R. (1999). Critical challenges confronting certification of evaluators. *American Journal of Evaluation, 20*, 533–555.

Worthen, B. R., & Sanders, J.R. (1991). The changing face of educational evaluation. *Theory Into Practice, 30*, 3–12.

Zorzi, R., McGuire, M., & Perrin, B. (2002). *Canadian Evaluation Society project in support of advocacy and professional development: Evaluation benefits, outputs, and knowledge elements.* Toronto, ON: Zorzi & Associates.

Dealing with Asymmetric Relations between Stakeholders

Facilitating Dialogue and Mutual Learning through Qualitative Inquiry

Vivianne E. Baur and Tineke A. Abma

Key Ideas

■ Evaluators need to be self-reflexive and aware of their backgrounds, experiences, skills, roles, perspectives, and values; these inherently become part of the evaluation context.

■ The process of facilitating dialogue between stakeholder groups can lead to mutual learning when the evaluator creates a safe environment that allows for the building of trust and tailors the dialogic process to particular stakeholder communication styles.

■ Qualitative inquiry, particularly using a design that is emergent and responsive to stakeholder needs, can be used to address power imbalances between stakeholder groups by uncovering tensions, giving voice to marginalized groups, and fostering mutual learning.

■ The evaluator's interpersonal and communication skills play an important role in the way stakeholders see and relate to the evaluator and the evaluation process.

As an evaluator, what do you do when you enter into a situation in which prevailing power imbalances run counter to a legislative mandate for a greater client voice in service delivery? In this chapter, we present the approach we took in an evaluation of the interactions between resident councils and managers in care homes for older people. We will share the challenges we encountered and the lessons we learned about the use of qualitative inquiry in facilitating dialogue and mutual learning between stakeholders. We address questions such as: How do evaluators navigate design decisions? How do evaluators uncover tacit tensions between stakeholders in a way that brings them closer together instead of driving them apart? How can evaluators ensure that all voices are heard and genuine dialogue takes place in a context in which some voices tend to be dominant and others tend to be marginalized?

But first, let us tell you a bit about ourselves as evaluators, including the insights and approaches that inspire us and inform our thinking and practice. We believe that this is the basis of understanding qualitative evaluation: Knowing who you are as an evaluator, what value-committed stance you hold, and what your outlook is on the overall aim and practice of conducting evaluation.

EVALUATORS' OUTLOOK AND IDENTITY

Transformative Paradigm in Qualitative Inquiry

Our work is strongly inspired by what is called a transformative paradigm in research and evaluation (Mertens, 2009). This paradigm reflects a value-committed stance on the part of evaluators working for social justice, equality, empowerment, and emancipation (Greene, 2006). The methodology we used in this project was a responsive, democratic, and participatory approach to evaluation that can be interpreted as a transformative participatory evaluation (Cousins & Whitmore, 1998; see also Chouinard and Cousins, Chapter 5, this volume). Our approach was responsive, because it originated from the issues and concerns of the various stakeholders and aimed to enhance the mutual understanding between stakeholders through dialogue (Guba & Lincoln, 1989). Our approach was democratic, because we engaged stakeholders as partners in the evaluation process. It was transformative, because we endeavored for social change and "to empower people through participation in the process of constructing and respecting their own knowledge" (Cousins & Whitmore, 1998, cited in King, 2007). As evaluators, we are committed to affecting democratic social change, because we believe that human life can flourish when diversity and differences between people are given equal "space" in organizations and in society. In this project, we strove for social change (improvements in the interactions between and practices of resident councils and managers) based on experiential knowledge shared by multiple stakeholders. Against this background, we distinguished the need for relational empowerment of resident councils and approached this as another goal of our evaluation project. The idea of relational empowerment (VanderPlaat, 1999) seemed appropriate here, because it is based on the acknowledgment that people exist in relation to each other. In this concept, power is not given to one party by the other, or taken by one party from the other, because this would only confirm the existence of power imbalances. Therefore, empowerment is relational in that the interactions between people become more equal as they learn from each other and start to work together and divide power, based on a mutual understanding of each other's backgrounds, values, and perspectives.

Responsive Evaluation and Hermeneutic Dialogue

The roots of responsive evaluation lie in the 1970s. Calling for a wider scope for evaluation than mere goal-oriented evaluation, Stake (1975) introduced a responsive approach as part of his vision for educational research and evaluation (see also Schwandt and Cash, Chapter 1 of this volume). Central to this vision is the broadening of evaluation criteria to include as many stakeholder issues as possible, unlike evaluation models that merely include the goals and intentions of policy makers. In responsive evaluation, processes, backgrounds, and judgments are included as well, rather than a focus on simply measuring outcomes (Abma & Stake, 2001; Stake, 2004). These ideas have been further developed by others: Guba and Lincoln (1989), for example, built on Stake's work, proposing an interactive approach in which stakeholder issues are a departure point for negotiation to enhance mutual understanding and consensus. In our project, we used a particular version of responsive evaluation, linking the responsive evaluation paradigm (Guba & Lincoln, 1989; Stake, 1975) to insights about narratives, storytelling, and ongoing dialogues in evaluation (Abma, 2003, 2007; Abma & Widdershoven, 2005, 2006; Widdershoven, 2001).

In particular, we used insights about hermeneutic dialogue to engage stakeholders in a learning process to help them better understand themselves and each other, and hence empower them to place their own viewpoints in perspective. A hermeneutic perspective on human life inspires us to listen to people's narratives about their experiences as a process for understanding. Through stories, people make sense of their world and are interconnected with each other (Josselson & Lieblich, 1999). Hermeneutic dialogue takes the complexity of human life (embedded in their stories and experiences) as a starting point for mutual learning processes in which all stakeholders change by way of interaction with one another (Widdershoven, 2001). Learning and change occur when people extend their horizons by appropriating new perspectives. We understand dialogue in this hermeneutic sense as an ongoing and cyclical process among stakeholders, aiming at reciprocal understanding and acceptance. For instance, stakeholders may gain a better understanding of a given programmatic activity or practice through the combination of various perspectives.

Responsive evaluation in this dialogical interpretation, aiming for mutual understanding, consists of four methodological steps (Abma & Widdershoven, 2006). These steps are (1) creating social conditions, (2) generating stakeholder issues, (3) facilitating dialogue among homogeneous groups of stakeholders, and (4) facilitating dialogue among heterogeneous groups of stakeholders. Homogeneous in this sense does not mean that these stakeholders are all the same. However, the accent is on the shared perspectives and positions that they have in common. This way, the exchange of experiences and a deepening of mutual understanding can be enhanced. The experiences that are shared by the stakeholders in homogeneous dialogue groups become input for the subsequent heterogeneous dialogue. The distinction between homogeneous and heterogeneous dialogue is particularly useful for situations in which power imbalances exist between stakeholders (Baur et al., 2010b; Nierse & Abma, 2011).

Personal Identity

Of course, evaluators are human beings in the first place, with their own personal identity, character, and educational and social background. With the narrative turn in social sciences, ideas about researchers' neutrality and objectivity have been challenged (Denzin, 1997; Ellingson, 2006). We are never distant, impersonal observers of practice; our character, our emotions, and personal convictions all interact with the realities we research. Moreover, we are part of these realities. Our interpersonal and communication skills play an important role in the way others (including the stakeholders in an evaluation project) see us and relate to us. Therefore, we think evaluators should be self-reflexive and aware of their own "backpack" of opinions, backgrounds, experiences, vulnerabilities, skills, and perspectives that they bring with them to the evaluation context. So, let us introduce ourselves before we continue with this chapter.

We are: Vivianne Baur, a junior researcher who works on various evaluation projects concerning the deliberative democratic participation of older people in residential care homes, which bring people with diverse perspectives and experiences together in a way that fosters their mutual understanding and collaboration; and Tineke Abma, a senior researcher who has spent more than twenty years in the academy focusing on developing a theory and methodology for evaluation suited to our contemporary society, where expert knowledge no longer automatically has an authoritative status.

THE PROJECT

Setting

We were asked by a residential care and nursing home organization in the Southern Netherlands, called Horizon (pseudonym), to evaluate the participation of client councils in strategic policy processes. At the time of the evaluation, Horizon managed facilities in eight separate locations. In total, the organization housed 3,316 residents and employed a total of 1,085 full-time equivalent employees. Two locations were nursing homes for older people with physical or mental health problems. The other six locations consisted of residential care, sometimes combined with sheltered home facilities. Throughout the whole organization, the average age of residents was high (80+). Every location had its own local client council. These resident councils consisted of residents and relatives. Two resident councils in the nursing homes formed an exception: These consisted solely of relatives (spouses and partners) and volunteers, because of the high degree of physical and mental impairments of the residents. In addition to these eight local resident councils, the organization instituted a central resident council to cover more complex and overarching policy issues. The central council consisted of two representatives from each local resident council. Only relatives and volunteers were allowed to serve on the central council, because it was considered too much of a burden (in terms of energy, time, and content) for residents to participate.

Occasion for Evaluation

We conducted the evaluation over a period of six months in 2006. We held the first inventory conversations with key figures in the organization to get to know the setting and to determine the main issues that would define the evaluation goals and initial design. These inventory conversations are important, because they form the very basis of the evaluation: Why do stakeholders want this evaluation, what exactly do they want to have evaluated, what issues (from diverse perspectives) caused the request for evaluation?

The needs of this project aligned with our evaluation interests, experience, and values. After the inventory conversations with key stakeholders, the decision was made to conduct a responsive evaluation. This choice was based on the situation that gave cause for the evaluation: A member of the central resident council had written a letter to the board of directors, ringing the alarm about the central resident council's lack of actual influence on policy issues. According to this letter, the central resident council was overwhelmed with information about complex issues and being asked to respond to important policy matters in very short periods of time. Moreover, the author of the letter felt that decisions had already been made by the board of directors in advance of the central resident council's deliberations. The letter ended with the statement that the author did not know how this could be changed. In reaction, the board of directors discussed this letter with the central resident council, and they concluded that something had to be done.

In our inventory conversations, other key stakeholders mentioned issues similar to those raised by the central resident council. Resident councils were mandated by law in the 1990s (*Wet Medezeggenschap Clienten Zorgsector*), to provide clients in the social and care sector with legal and democratic rights to participate in policy and practice through advice and assent. However, stakeholders with whom we spoke felt that the resident councils lacked influence, and they pointed to the need to rebalance power relations among the stakeholders in this project (resident councils and managers). Therefore, we proposed a responsive evaluation that would address the interactions between Horizon's resident councils and managers and would also facilitate relational empowerment of these two stakeholder groups. In the sections that follow, we describe how we negotiated the evaluation approach with the board of directors. Later in this chapter, we discuss how we managed stakeholders' expectations.

Issues to Be Addressed

Managers, as well as resident council members, expressed the feeling that resident councils lacked influence. Managers ascribed this lack of influence mainly to resident council members' limitations in thinking and speaking about complicated policy issues. Resident councils attributed their lack of influence to the fact that they were given information too late, after policy decisions had already been made. Furthermore, resident councils felt overwhelmed by reports that contained policy makers' difficult jargon. These aspects were also illustrative of the communication problems between resident councils and managers. Resident councils wanted to speak about the "small" issues that affected the quality of life of clients (such as the temperature of the potatoes served at meals), whereas managers found themselves in a difficult position where they were obliged (by law) to speak with resident councils about amalgamations, budgets, and annual accounts. The co-mingling of these shortcomings and legal expectations of the collaboration were never expressed in public but were evident behind the scenes through numerous complaints and reproaches. As evaluators, we had to bring these issues out in the open in a way that would bring resident councils and managers closer together instead of driving them further apart. Therefore, the project design we chose was based on enhancing mutual understanding and relational empowerment.

Project Design

The project design was emergent, as is common for qualitative inquiry. An emergent design is important because it allows evaluators to tune in to the specific dynamics of the evaluation context (i.e., interactions with and among stakeholders, issues at hand, and value systems involved). Evaluators cannot know beforehand what multiple realities exist in the evaluation setting and how these realities and patterns will shape the process and outcomes of the inquiry (Lincoln & Guba, 1985). We used the methodological steps of responsive evaluation to guide the project design process (Abma & Widdershoven, 2006). The exact moment and content of the steps that are to be taken according to a responsive evaluation framework are not fixed beforehand. These emerge from the conversations of the evaluator with the stakeholders, and thus the design is emergent (Abma, 2005).

The project consisted of two main stages: homogeneous consultation and heterogeneous dialogue. These stages of the development of relational empowerment are important to distinguish. During a homogeneous consultation, stakeholders develop "their voice" and gain a sense of empowerment in the safe and comparatively intimate environment of peers (Baur et al., 2010a; Nierse et al., 2011). In this project, for example, we organized homogeneous consultations in the form of a focus group with four managers and a storytelling workshop with fourteen members of resident councils to enable stakeholders to articulate their perspectives in "safer" peer-based settings. Thereafter, resident council members and managers were brought together in a heterogeneous dialogue, which was a storytelling workshop as well, to create mutual understanding and a joint agenda for practice improvements. (The storytelling workshops are discussed in greater depth toward the end of the chapter, specifically in terms of how they were used to address asymmetric relations between stakeholders. For a detailed account of the activities and processes used to conduct storytelling workshops, please see Abma and Widdershoven, 2005).

How these methodological choices emerged is described in the following section. We discuss what challenges we encountered in this project, how we dealt with them, and what we learned about qualitative evaluation in the process. Even though these lessons are based on this specific project, we believe that the challenges we encountered are recognizable for other qualitative researchers and evaluators as well. We do not aim to give *the* answer to these challenges. Rather we would like to share the lessons learned with you, the reader, so you may experience them vicariously and gain knowledge as a result.

EVALUATORS' METHODOLOGICAL CHOICES AND ACTIONS

Negotiating with Commissioners, Managing Expectations, and Exploring Underlying Values

In the contract phase, no defined evaluation plan existed. Indeed, at every stage of the project, we negotiated with the stakeholders about what steps had to be taken next. At the very start of the project, we spoke with the board of directors. In this contract phase of the project, we also conducted inventory conversations with the chair and secretary of the central client council and a member of the management team. In these conversations, we asked these key figures about their experiences and perspectives on the participation of resident councils. The conversations were open-ended and left plenty of room for the persons consulted to express their opinions. Striking just the right tone in conversations like this can be tricky. An important element of the success of these conversations was that we not only listened very carefully to what these key figures had to say, but also shared with them some information about ourselves, our work, and ideas about how people with diverse perspectives in organizations can learn from each other. It helped to share some examples of successful evaluation projects in which the starting situation (a specific stakeholder group lacking influence) was similar to what we encountered in this organization. This enabled the inventory conversations to serve not just as a way for us to get to know the organization, its people, and their issues; they also became a way for the stakeholders to get to know the person behind the evaluator and to learn that possibilities exist for overcoming the challenges they experienced.

Based on these inventory conversations with some of the stakeholders, a responsive evaluation project design was developed. The inventory conversations had made clear what issues resident councils and managers experienced (lack of influence and communication problems) and that there seemed to be a tension between the legislative mandate for a greater say of residents and the realities that confronted resident councils and managers. To surface unspoken tensions, the overarching evaluation question was open-ended so that the stakeholders would feel they were given room to express their own experiences and perspectives. The question was: *"How do the stakeholders experience the client councils and their collaboration with the management of Horizon?"* Our proposal was to systematically map the experiences of resident councils and managers through interviews, homogeneous consultation, and heterogeneous dialogue, to enhance mutual understanding and relational empowerment.

This proposal was shared with the board of directors and central resident council. They, as commissioners of the evaluation, wanted to find practical solutions to the frustrations of the stakeholders and identify ways to improve their joint practice. As such, enhancing mutual understanding and empowerment was not the first aim for the board of directors, nor for the central resident council. However, we were convinced that this study would be especially valuable if it focused on the interactions of the stakeholders and their relational empowerment because we heard from the board and council members, as well as from other key stakeholders (a member of the management team, the secretary, and the chair of the central resident council) what the main problems were in practice. This proposal was discussed with the board of directors and the central resident council. They were open to our approach, and after we explained why we thought it would be important to focus on mutual understanding and empowerment, they agreed with us. However, they also emphasized the need for practical and concrete solutions to the frustrations of stakeholders, such as recommendations for a communication structure (between local client councils and managers, and between the central client council and board of directors) that would lead to more effective communication.

We discussed with them the possibility of combining the aim of formulating concrete recommendations concerning the practice of resident councils and managers with the aim of enhancing mutual understanding and relational empowerment. This was not a real distinction for us as evaluators, because the methodological steps of responsive evaluation (grounded in a transformative paradigm) led to the formulation of a joint action agenda by stakeholders. This joint action agenda was exactly what the commissioners were looking for: concrete recommendations to improve practice, firmly rooted in the perspectives and experiences of stakeholders and co-produced (and thus carried) by the stakeholders themselves. However, from our perspective, a joint action agenda can only come into existence when the foregoing steps (homogeneous consultation and the development of an intimate and a political voice) have been taken, because power imbalances have to be addressed first. The commissioners were open to our argument, and they agreed that the combination of these two (not so distinct) purposes would give the evaluation depth and strength. We thus came to an agreement that the study would have a twofold aim: (1) to improve the co-production of the policy-making process by managers and resident council members and (2) to enhance the mutual understanding and relational empowerment of managers and client council members.

Evaluator–Stakeholder Relationships

We wanted to create a commitment to the project by all of the relevant and affected groups, and thus we held interviews with all resident councils (collectively with the councils, as well as with some individual members), managers, and some other staff. This approach helped us learn about the stakeholders' perspectives on how the practice of resident councils was experienced by several groups in Horizon. This also prevented the perception of the evaluation as having one-sided loyalty or partiality to any of the stakeholder groups.

As we conducted interviews, we recognized and documented tensions and asymmetric relations between resident councils and managers. These interviews corresponded to the previous inventory conversations with key stakeholders that made us realize that power imbalances were at the root of the problem. The interviews shed light on frustrations and distrust among resident councils and managers, which impeded interactive policy planning. These interviews started with the question of how the respondents themselves experience the interactive policy processes of resident councils in Horizon. The interviews were conducted in a conversational style to allow room for expression of all aspects of the lived experiences of the stakeholders. We also held group interviews with resident councils. We tape-recorded the interviews and analyzed them thematically. We summarized the citations and sent them back to the stakeholders as a member check (Guba & Lincoln, 1989).

We learned that these in-depth interviews helped us build trust with stakeholders, because we demonstrated that we took their stories and experiences seriously. Accordingly, the interviews provided a way to build rapport with the resident council members and managers we interviewed. Qualitative interviews are much more than simply a way of gathering data. Especially in the context of asymmetric relations, interviews can be used to give voice to marginalized groups (Abma, 2006a). As a result, interviews can become a vehicle to recognize individuals as autonomous persons worthy of respect (Koch, 1996, 2000). The interviewer can approach interviews as a form of "reciprocal dialogue," a way of building equal communication between researcher and participant or evaluator and stakeholder (Yassour-Borochowitz, 2004). By sharing interpretative insights with interviewees, the evaluator creates room for communicative action and solidarity. This approach allows for the authentic voices of people involved to be heard and more deeply understood. In the process, interviewees may arrive at an understanding of their identities set within a broader perspective (Yassour-Borochowitz, 2004).

During this project, we had to take up various roles as evaluators. The role that the evaluator plays at different points in the process has to be flexible and follow the dynamics of the evaluation context. Roles include being an interpreter, educator, facilitator, and Socratic guide (Abma, 2006a). In the role of interpreter, the evaluator endows issues with meaning. This was what we did especially in the first stage of the evaluation, when we negotiated with the commissioners about the aims of the project. We interpreted what the issues stakeholders shared with us meant for the interaction between resident councils and managers. Furthermore, as an educator, the evaluator supports the development of mutual understanding between stakeholders by explicating the various experiences to the groups that are involved. We played this role in the homogeneous consultation meeting with managers, when statements that were based on the experiences of resident council members were used for discussion. When the evaluator organizes dialogue, he or she takes up the role of facilitator. During the heterogeneous storytelling workshop, we had to facilitate the interactions between the participants so that room for dialogue was enhanced.

Finally, the evaluator can act as a Socratic guide, probing taken-for-granted ideas, final truths, and certainties, thus bringing new perspectives to the situation (Schwandt, 2001). For example, we saw that resident councils and managers held some negative presumptions about each other, such as resident council members thinking that managers did not want to give them a real influential position in interactive policy making, or managers rejecting the resident council because of a supposed lack of members' competency in policy making. In our role as Socratic guides, we probed these ideas, asking the stakeholders to think of examples on which these ideas were based and also asking for examples that would show the opposite. Through this evaluation, the stakeholders discovered that managers sincerely and eagerly awaited a critical, influential, and autonomous resident council and that resident council members had more capacity to put real issues on the policy agenda than the managers expected. Both stakeholder groups learned that they had to change their ways of thinking about the other, which would enable the other to be a better resident council member or a better manager.

Balancing Power Dynamics
The context of this evaluation featured asymmetric relations between resident councils and managers. After the board of directors and the central resident council agreed that this project would also aim to enhance mutual understanding and relational

empowerment, we had to find a way to accomplish this. Based on prior experience with responsive methodology, we decided to organize homogeneous meetings with resident council members and managers first, before bringing them together in a heterogeneous meeting (Abma, 2006a, 2006b; Abma & Widdershoven, 2006). Several qualitative methods can be used for facilitating homogeneous groups, such as storytelling workshops, focus groups, or creative workshops (Abma & Broerse, 2007). What technique evaluators choose depends on the goals that are to be reached and the communication style of the stakeholders.

Because we wanted to create a basis for mutual understanding and relational empowerment through hermeneutic dialogue, storytelling seemed to be a valuable approach for the homogeneous meeting with resident council members, and for the heterogeneous meeting with resident council members and managers together. As evaluators, our belief is that emotions play a role in human life and should be given space, since they reveal stakeholder values, what people find important, and what they do not find important. Emotions complement cognitions and opinions. For example, people may say that they find participation important (cognitive opinion), but they do not act as if they do (meaningful action). Cognitive questions and answers are thus not very helpful for developing an understanding of the emotions associated with participating in client councils. Barnes (2008) argued that emotions form the basis for social movement and motivations for participation as they point at structural relationships of power and status. In this respect, sharing personal experiences and allowing emotional expressions are important in developing social action (Barnes, 2008). Emotions and experiences can come to the fore through stories, because people can be considered "embodiments of lived stories" (Clandinin & Connelly, 2000); stories reveal a personal standpoint and morality (Abma, 1999; Widdershoven, 2001). Storytelling is considered to be an ontological condition of human life; we use stories to impose order on our experiences and emotions and make sense of actions in our lives (Phoenix & Sparkes, 2009). Narratives and stories create meaning, emotion, memory, and identity (Rappaport, 1995). Therefore, in the homogeneous group with resident councils, we used storytelling and narratives to illuminate their issues and underlying value commitments (Abma, 2003).

The separate homogeneous meetings of resident councils and managers were a significant step toward balancing the asymmetric relations between these two groups. We argue that marginalized groups first need to develop their own voice before they enter into dialogue with other stakeholders (Baur et al., 2010b; Nierse & Abma, 2011). This is a means of creating a safe and open climate for stakeholders and it gives room for the development of an understanding of collective experiences within their "own" group of stakeholders. Homogeneous meetings thus contribute to the development of empowerment within this group (Baur & Abma, 2011; Nierse & Abma, 2011).

The heterogeneous group meeting in which the diverse stakeholder groups come together and dialogue between them is facilitated was the next step in our attempt to bring the differing perspectives of resident councils and managers closer together. Genuine dialogue requires openness, respect, trust, and the engagement of all stakeholders (Abma et al., 2009). In a heterogeneous dialogue, the qualitative evaluator should be sensitive to power imbalances and subtle processes of exclusion (Abma et al., 2009; Mertens, 2002). Therefore, in the heterogeneous meeting, we started with the perspective of the stakeholder group with the least influence, the resident councils.

For the heterogeneous storytelling workshop, evaluators necessarily (because of limitations of space and dialogical power) have to make a selection of participants. We specifically selected individual stakeholders for the heterogeneous dialogue who had shown in the interviews and during the homogeneous phase to be articulate, constructively critical, assertive, and open to the opinions and experiences of others. This does not mean that other perspectives, such as being less positively formulated or less open to other views, were ignored. These also had a place in the dialogue. We inserted these voices in the stories that were used for dialogue. This helped to speak about frustrations and tensions in an open, safe, and friendly atmosphere. Consequently, our evaluation went beyond the problematic issues of stakeholders and explored solutions, practice improvements, and new possibilities. Using the format of a storytelling workshop thus is a means to give voice to all stakeholders even with resource constraints.

Dialogue and Communication Styles

The choice of a certain technique for dialogue with and between stakeholders is also informed by the communication style and dynamics of the stakeholders. Thus, qualitative evaluators can engage stakeholders in homogeneous dialogues by tuning in to their specific style of communication (Baur et al., 2010a). In our evaluation, in the dialogue group with the members of resident councils, we chose to focus on their stories. This was because storytelling sheds light on underlying emotions and values, which need to be understood to enhance relational empowerment. Another reason for choosing the format of a storytelling workshop was that we noticed during the first phase of the evaluation that the members of resident councils were mostly older persons (age sixty-five plus). In their communication (informally as well as during interviews), these persons shared their personal stories (who they are, their motivations for being members of a resident council, their positive and negative experiences) in a lively manner and with ease. They liked to talk with the evaluator and took time to do so elaborately. Storytelling seemed to be their natural way of communicating. Therefore, we chose this as a guiding principle for the homogeneous meeting with resident council members.

Managers communicated differently than resident council members. They tended to be more focused and clear in the expression of their issues. Therefore, we chose the format of a focus group for the homogeneous gathering with the managers. This focus group featured statements based on the experiences of both managers and resident councils that had arisen in the first and second stage of the project. Focus group participants then had the opportunity to react to these statements. By defending or opposing specific statements regarding the resident councils, managers found themselves trying to convince each other of the councils' value. Thus, the managers deepened their own perspectives but also were introduced to the perspectives of the resident councils.

In the heterogeneous meeting, we facilitated the dialogue between resident council members and managers. We did this by choosing the format of a storytelling workshop again, because this was also a good way of expressing differences between stakeholders in a non-offensive way. At the same time, listening to a story evokes the sharing of one's own experiences that relate to the content of the story (by either existing similarities or differences). In the heterogeneous storytelling workshop, the diverse perspectives (resident councils, managers, and board of directors) were shared through stories that reflected each perspective. The stories reflected the ambiguous nature of practice, illuminating both the tensions and strengths of the resident councils' and managers' joint practice. The stories were created by us and written down in first person, based on aspects that came to the fore during the interviews and the homogeneous meetings. By starting off with the stories of resident councils, their perspectives were given a central place in the heterogeneous storytelling workshop. This way, the less powerful stakeholders' feelings of security, acknowledgment, and being heard were supported, so that the conditions for genuine dialogue (openness, respect, inclusion, and engagement) could be created (Abma, 2006a; Abma et al., 2001; Greene, 2001).

During the heterogeneous dialogue, resident councils and managers learned from each other that they shared an important interest, namely, the well-being of the residents. Because they had mostly focused on their differences before, hearing the perspectives and experiences from the other stakeholder group created a new understanding and possibilities for the future. This discovery motivated the participants to jointly sketch some prerequisites for a good and constructive participation process in the form of a joint action agenda. Thus, dialogue served as a vehicle for finding common ground in the context of asymmetrical relations. This joint agenda could only be formulated on the basis of mutual understanding and on the new insights of the resident council members and managers related to the acknowledgment that they needed each other to further develop their collaboration. This was not seen as an instrumental need (in terms of dependency), but as an intrinsic value of interdependence and the mingling of diverse forms of knowledge and experiences.

CONCLUSION

In this chapter we have described an evaluation project in which we confronted the challenging existence of asymmetric relations between stakeholders. Instead of considering this as a barrier for our evaluation, we embraced balancing these power relations as one of the aims of our evaluation. We did this because we strive for socially just practices in care organizations and because we believed that the existence of asymmetric relations was so omnipresent in this context that we would not reach any significant results with our evaluation if we did not address this reality. We argue that the methodological choices we made as qualitative evaluators all contributed to the balancing of power dynamics in this evaluation context. Thus, our answer to the question "What do you do when you enter into a situation in which prevailing power imbalances run counter to a legislative mandate for a greater say of clients in service delivery?" is that you, as an evaluator, first reflect on your own outlook and identity. What is it you want to accomplish with this evaluation, and why? Second, negotiation with commissioners and key stakeholders is needed to agree on the aims of the evaluation. As an evaluator you can have an explicit value-committed stance toward the evaluation; however, you must share this stance with the commissioners and other stakeholders and at the same time listen to their wishes and expectations. Furthermore, by first organizing homogeneous meetings with stakeholders, marginalized groups are given space to develop voice and empowerment. Another lesson learned from this evaluation is that, as a qualitative evaluator, you have to consider the communication styles of the stakeholders to extract the most accurate data and to support the sharing of diverse perspectives and voices. For some stakeholders, storytelling can be a vehicle for dialogue and mutual understanding. Finally, as an evaluator, you have to be sensitive to the dynamics of the project and the stakeholders and shift roles when needed. By bringing these principles into practice, qualitative evaluators can make a valuable contribution to enhancing mutual understanding and relational empowerment between stakeholders.

KEY CONCEPTS

Asymmetric relations	Emergent design
Authentic voices	Evaluator roles
Communication styles	Hermeneutic dialogue

Heterogeneous groups

Homogeneous groups

Joint action agenda

Mutual understanding

Reciprocal dialogue

Relational empowerment

Responsive evaluation

Storytelling

Transformative paradigm

Transformative participatory evaluation

DISCUSSION QUESTIONS

1. This chapter serves as a good example of the concept that evaluators are stakeholders, too, as the authors clearly state their interests, positions, and value stance when describing their approach to the evaluation. How, if at all, do you think these affected the outcome of the evaluation? What other approaches might have worked in this situation?

2. The authors found a "receptive ear" for addressing power issues when they negotiated with the board of directors and the central resident council. If you, as an evaluator, encountered a similar situation but the people commissioning the evaluation were not receptive, how might you proceed? Discuss how an evaluator can account for the group with less positional power while assisting stakeholders to arrive at a solution acceptable to all.

3. How is evaluation use promoted in this chapter? In what ways do the authors promote learning, and is this a form of evaluation use? Can you think of other ways the authors might have promoted evaluation use with the Horizon stakeholders?

REFERENCES

Abma, T. A. (1999). Introduction. In T. A. Abma (Ed.), *Telling tales: On narrative and evaluation (advances in program evaluation)* (Vol. 6, pp. 1–27). Greenwich, CT: JAI.

Abma, T. A. (2003). Learning by telling: Storytelling workshops as an organizational learning intervention. *Management Learning, 34*(2), 221–240.

Abma, T. A. (2005). Responsive evaluation: Its meaning and special contribution to health promotion. *Evaluation and Program Planning*, *28*, 279–289.

Abma, T. A. (2006a). The practice and politics of responsive evaluation. *American Journal of Evaluation*, *27*(1), 31–43.

Abma, T. A. (2006b). Social relations of evaluation. In I. F. Shaw, J. C. Greene, & M. M. Mark (Eds.), *Handbook of evaluation: Programme, policy and practice* (pp. 184–199). London, UK: Sage.

Abma, T. A. (2007). Situated learning in communities of practice: Evaluation of coercion in psychiatry as a case. *Evaluation*, *13*(1), 32–47.

Abma, T. A., & Broerse, J. (2007). *Zeggenschap in wetenschap: Patiëntenparticipatie in theorie en praktijk. [Having a say in science. Patient participation in theory and practice]*. Den Haag: Uitgeverij LEMMA.

Abma, T. A., Greene, J. C., Karlsson, O., Ryan, K., Schwandt, T. A., & Widdershoven, G.A.M. (2001). Dialogue on dialogue. *Evaluation*, *7*(2), 164–180.

Abma, T. A., Nierse, C. J., & Widdershoven, G.A.M. (2009). Patients as partners in responsive research: Methodological notions for collaborations in mixed research teams. *Qualitative Health Research*, *19*(3), 401–415.

Abma, T. A., & Stake, R. E. (2001). Responsive evaluation: Roots and evolution. In J. C. Greene & T. A. Abma (Eds.), *Responsive evaluation: New directions for evaluation* (Vol. 92, pp. 7–22). San Francisco, CA: Jossey-Bass.

Abma, T. A., & Widdershoven, G.A.M. (2005). Sharing stories: Narrative and dialogue in responsive nursing evaluation. *Evaluation and the Health Professions*, *28*(1), 90–109.

Abma, T. A., & Widdershoven, G.A.M. (2006). *Responsieve methodologie: Interactief onderzoek in de praktijk [Responsive methodology: Interactive research in practice]*. Den Haag: Uitgeverij LEMMA.

Barnes, M. (2008). Passionate participation: Emotional experience and expressions in deliberative forums. *Critical Social Policy*, *28*(4), 461–481.

Baur, V. E., & Abma, T. A. (2011). "The taste buddies": Participation and empowerment in a residential home for older people. *Ageing and Society*, *32*, 1055–1078.

Baur, V. E., Abma, T. A., & Widdershoven, G.A.M. (2010a). Participation of marginalized groups in evaluation: Mission impossible? *Evaluation & Program Planning*, *33*(3), 238–245.

Baur, V. E., van Elteren, A.H.J., Nierse, C. J., & Abma, T. A. (2010b). Dealing with distrust and power dynamics: Asymmetric relations between stakeholders in evaluation. *Evaluation*, *16*(3), 233–248.

Clandinin, D. J., & Connelly, M. (2000). *Narrative inquiry: Experience and story in qualitative research*. San Francisco, CA: Jossey-Bass.

Cousins, J.B., & Whitmore, E., (1998). Framing participatory evaluation. In E. Whitmore (Ed.), *Understanding and practicing participatory evaluation: New directions for evaluation* (Vol. 80). San Francisco, CA: Jossey-Bass.

Denzin, N. (1997). *Interpretive ethnography.* Thousand Oaks, CA: Sage.

Ellingson, L. L. (2006). Embodied knowledge: Writing researcher's bodies into qualitative health research. *Qualitative Health Research, 16*(2), 298–310.

Greene, J. C. (2001). Dialogue in evaluation: A relational perspective. *Evaluation, 7*(2), 181–187.

Greene, J. C. (2006). Evaluation, democracy, and social change (pp. 118–140). In I. Shaw, J. Greene, & M. Mark (Eds.), *The Sage handbook of evaluation.* Thousand Oaks, CA: Sage.

Guba, E. G., & Lincoln, Y. S. (1989). *Fourth generation evaluation.* Newbury Park, CA: Sage.

Josselson, R., & Lieblich, A. (1999). *Making meaning of narratives: The narrative study of lives* (Vol. 6.) Thousand Oaks, CA: Sage.

King, J. (2007). Making sense of participatory evaluation. *New Directions for Evaluation, 114*, 83–86

Koch, T. (1996). Implementation of a hermeneutic inquiry in nursing: Philosophy, rigor and representation. *Journal of Advanced Nursing, 244*, 174–184.

Kocht, T. (2000). "Having a say": Negotiation in fourth generation evaluation. *Journal of Advanced Nursing, 31*(1), 117–125.

Lincoln, Y. S., & Guba, E. G. (1985). *Naturalistic inquiry.* New York, NY: Sage.

Mertens, D. M. (2002). The evaluator's role in the transformative context. In K. E. Ryan & T. S. Schwandt (Eds.), *Exploring evaluator role and identity* (pp. 103–119). Greenwich, CT: IAP.

Mertens, D. M. (2009). *Transformative research and evaluation.* New York, NY: Guilford.

Nierse, C. J., & Abma, T. A. (2011). Developing voice and empowerment: The first step towards a broad consultation in research agenda setting. *Journal of Intellectual Disability Research, 55*(4), 411–421.

Nierse, C. J., Schipper, K., Van Zadelhoff, E., Van de Griendt, J., & Abma, T.A. (2011). Collaboration and co-ownership in research: Dynamics and dialogues between patient research partners and professional researchers in a research team. *Health Expectations.* doi: 10.1111/j.1369–7625.2011.00661.x

Phoenix, C., & Sparkes, A. C. (2009). Being Fred: Big stories, small stories and the accomplishment of a positive ageing identity. *Qualitative Research, 9*(2), 83–99

Rappaport, J. (1995). Empowerment meets narrative: Listening to stories and creating settings. *American Journal of Community Psychology*, *23*(5), 795–807.

Schwandt, T. A. (2001). A postscript on thinking about dialogue. *Evaluation*, *7*(2), 264–276.

Stake, R. E. (1975). To evaluate an arts program. In R. E. Stake (Ed.), *Evaluating the arts in education: A responsive approach* (pp. 13–31). Columbus, OH: Merrill.

Stake, R. E. (2004). *Standards-based and responsive evaluation*. Thousand Oaks, CA: Sage.

VanderPlaat, M. (1999). Locating the feminist scholar: Relational empowerment and social activism. *Qualitative Health Research*, *9*(6), 773–785.

Widdershoven, G.A.M. (2001). Dialogue in evaluation: A hermeneutic perspective. *Evaluation*, *7*(2), 253–263.

Yassour-Borochowitz, D. (2004). Reflections on the researcher-participant relationship and the ethics of dialogue. *Ethics & Behavior*, *14*(2), 175–186.

Balancing Insider-Outsider Roles as a New External Evaluator

Norma Martínez-Rubin and Stuart Hanson

Key Ideas

- It is important for evaluators to balance their understanding of the issues facing a community with how the community itself makes sense of the issues before it.

- Leveraging intimate knowledge of a community is important if an evaluator wants to build a collective commitment to cultural sensitivity among stakeholders, to foster trust, and to give voice to program participants.

- An evaluation is a quest in which a study design and protocols are set to guide the roads to be taken. However, it is important for evaluators to remain open to what might occur within the context of following those protocols.

In 2005, the Department of Administration of Sunrise Health Systems (pseudonym), a large, integrated health care system, contracted with the Center for Applied Local Research and Evaluation Focused Consulting to conduct a community assessment on childhood obesity among Latino families in four

Southern California counties. As may often be the case for evaluations conducted by those who lean toward qualitative inquiry, this project became a personal journey for me, Norma Martínez-Rubin. I am a Latina health educator who has taken on the role of an evaluator/researcher. As such, I thought I was perfectly suited to be part of this community assessment. Little did I know the personal discoveries I would encounter as a result of the relationships I built with my colleague, Stu Hanson; the various staff of Sunrise Health Systems with whom we worked; and the participants of our community assessment: Latino families and health care professionals. But first, some background.

Since 1994, many private, not-for-profit hospitals in California have been obligated to provide "community benefits in the public interest" in exchange for their tax-exempt status. (See SB 697 for further information regarding the types of institutions subject to this requirement.) Each hospital is required to (1) conduct a community needs assessment every three years; (2) develop a community benefit plan in consultation with the community; and (3) submit a copy of the plan to the Office of Statewide Health Planning and Development (SB 697). To fulfill this obligation, the Department of Administration of Sunrise Health Systems contracted with the Center for Applied Local Research (C.A.L. Research) to conduct a community needs assessment related to childhood obesity among Latino families in four Southern California counties: Los Angeles, Orange, San Bernardino, and San Diego. Beyond a community needs assessment, the project was also designed to inform the community benefit plan to reduce and prevent childhood obesity. This community benefit plan would ultimately be carried out by the staff of Sunrise's Regional Community Outreach Department. Stu Hanson of C.A.L. Research was the key contact for the project; I was an external consultant brought in to co-develop and implement the assessment. Stu and I worked closely as a team.

Ordinarily, a health educator conducts a community needs assessment (Altschuld & Kumar, 2005) to identify what the particular community knows (and does not know) about a given health situation. The community assessment we conducted would serve as the basis of Sunrise's outreach to the community. We started with the assumption that the professional community has determined that a problem merits the allocation of resources and that an effective intervention is possible. There is a tacit expectation that community members will voluntarily participate and act to decrease the prevalence of the problem at hand. In other words, we started with the assumption that, based on health statistics, pediatric obesity was a problem in the Latino community; our responsibility was to discover how Latinos understood the issue and gather their ideas about how to best address the concern.

RESPONDING TO THE SPONSORING ORGANIZATION'S REQUEST FOR PROPOSALS

As a nonprofit integrated health care system that provides services and public health promotion, Sunrise Health Systems is an integral part of many of the California communities covered in this assessment. As such, although community assessments are statutorily required, the practice is actually part of their business plan. Five distinct groups, including three Sunrise departments, were stakeholders in the community needs assessment we conducted. The Community Public Relations Department had a stake in ensuring that the study was sensitive to their concerns in working with various community groups. The Department of Administration, which coordinates grant funding with local and regional organizations, issued the contract to C.A.L. Research.

The third stakeholder, the Community Outreach Department (COD), had a major interest in the project for two reasons: First, the outreach staff, including a senior educator designated to work with the evaluation team, had strong ties with health educators in Southern California's public health sector, as well as with coalitions of community organizations and charitable foundations. Second, COD health educators would use the results of the community needs assessment to subsequently develop a health education plan for the targeted community.

Participating in this study as a member of the professional community of evaluators presented an opportunity for me to bridge the professional expertise I possess as a health education practitioner with my recently adopted role of researcher/evaluator. I was eager to involve community members in the design of programs to be developed according to the messages they identified as necessary, with the wording they wanted to hear, through the channels they found accessible, and to which they would pay attention. It was rewarding to think that the educational programming that would be designed would be informed by the responses derived from our work.

In developing our proposal, we began by thinking about and identifying the community of interest. Should we study a community living or working in a certain geographic area? Should we study a group of people brought together by common demographic characteristics? Do we study the people who have come together and share a common ancestral origin or culture and happen to occupy a certain geographic area? For this project, the "community" was overtly defined by ethnic similarities and geographic area of residence. The ethnic categorization for the study group was Latinos, and the defining boundaries were the political and civic boundaries of four counties (Los Angeles, Orange, San Bernardino, and San Diego) in Southern California. By *Latino*, we mean people who self-identify as having a family of origin from one or more countries in Latin American. No distinction was made in this study about country of birth. The Latino participants in the community needs assessment became our fourth stakeholder group.

Our fifth stakeholder group included the local public health experts and officials from whom we needed information. This group contributed an essential understanding of childhood obesity from a professional public health perspective. This group could also provide insight about the health promotion and education that had been or was being implemented in the four counties.

The proposal we submitted was designed to explore familial and environmental factors in Latino communities that supported healthy dietary habits and physical activity that reduced and prevented childhood obesity. Five key evaluation topics were explored, using three distinct strategies. First, the extent and distribution of childhood obesity among Latinos in the region was explored through an environmental scan of pediatric overweight in the target communities. Focus groups with adult Latino family members and semi-structured key informant interviews with local public health experts and officials were designed to obtain the perspectives of both program providers and program participants for the remaining four topics. Specifically, we wanted to explore (1) how beliefs and attitudes about diet and health varied within and among Latino communities; (2) what health education messages and other interventions have been tried and how they were perceived to work; (3) what barriers may have impeded successful implementation of these efforts; and (4) new solutions that might have promise.

Stu and I had several important considerations in writing the proposal. The protocols were refined to accommodate the length of time Stu and I agreed would be reasonable and feasible for semi-structured key informant interviews and focus groups. Being reasonable meant keeping in mind the potentially intrusive nature of semi-structured interviews that we wanted to conduct with key staff, who had busy work schedules. Considerations for the focus groups meant including sufficient time for the following: (1) to explain the paperwork required to demonstrate that informed consent was undertaken; (2) to inform our study participants that their involvement was voluntary, and they had the option of not participating in the study without jeopardizing the benefits and services they were receiving from Sunrise Health Systems; and (3) to allow time to respond to participants' questions when my explanations as focus group facilitator required further clarification. When we used the term feasible, we meant that the time available for both modes of inquiry—the semi-structured phone interviews and the in-person focus groups—would yield data from a cross-section of four counties and a representative sample of the Latino community. As it turned out, the COD outreach staff provided Stu and me with a roster of key contacts from school districts, community-based organizations, and health clinics. Stu and I interviewed them by phone. Ultimately, the sample of focus group participants was a convenience sample drawn from community members invited to attend the focus groups by members of community-based organizations that had working relationships with COD staff members.

In addition, the instructions provided by Sunrise administrators included some specific requirements. For the environmental scan, they wanted the portrayal of risk of childhood obesity to be broken down by racial/ethnic group (Latino versus all other groups) and age (children aged under five and children aged five to twenty) for the entire six-county Southern California region

(Los Angeles, Kern, Orange, Riverside, San Bernardino, and San Diego) and to break out the densely populated Los Angeles area into five planning areas. The focus group and key informant samples, however, were limited to Latino parents and health planners and experts in just four counties (Los Angeles, Orange, San Bernardino, and San Diego). This smaller target area was identified because of three factors: (1) budgetary constraints, (2) Sunrise's relatively small presence in Riverside and Kern Counties, and (3) the scarcity of community health educators and planners known to COD outreach staff in these same counties. In effect, the environmental scan statistically addressed the entire region (i.e., the six counties), but the project's limited resources were concentrated on the areas in which Sunrise Health Systems had a significant presence and their outreach staff had formed strong working relationships with partners and stakeholders.

Several more subtle considerations drove the process. The COD outreach staff wanted to reach out to key community leaders and health professionals with whom staff either wished to initiate or had established relationships. Of particular interest was the inclusion of community outreach workers (*promotoras*) who had a history of working with the target population of Latino families. The outreach staff also found it opportune to involve agencies with whom they had previous relationships so as to advance, on a broad level, collaboration required to systematically address pediatric obesity. They further recognized the strength of the hospital's clinical expertise and their ability to contribute to community-based outreach and education. The new consideration they wanted to explore in this community assessment was what new educational experiences and messages the Latino community would find acceptable and how other organizations could contribute to future educational initiatives.

For Stu and me, both very aware of the budget, having COD staff identify organizations that could recruit the participants for the focus groups and the key informant interviews was a boon because this process is frequently labor-intensive. Conversely, as evaluators we had an ethical stake in ensuring the representativeness of the focus group and key informant samples, as well as a financial and logistical stake in ensuring that focus groups sites were grouped by location and date. We addressed this problem by giving the COD staff a fixed choice of available dates for travel to the target communities. We also made sure that the organizations that recruited focus group participants represented the array of community services that parents would possibly access: elementary schools, community centers, and health clinics. Faith-based organizations were purposefully excluded, because Sunrise outreach staff had not established formal relationships with any of them for nutrition programs or health education.

We needed to establish and maintain a collegial working relationship with our client. We were well aware of the critical role Sunrise Health Systems has played in health promotion in Southern California. We began our consulting engagement by explicitly recognizing the long-term experience that Sunrise staff had in the public health field. The work we embarked on was part of a continuum of services to be further developed by the COD department. The results from our work were expected to inform future community education approaches and prospective collaborative efforts with existing and new partner organizations. Though we might not necessarily be involved in that future work, our contribution as evaluators was influenced by the professional beliefs that what we do not only matters for the duration of a project, but has implications in our respective professional disciplines and alliances. Also, as external consultants, our professional reputations depend on quality work.

Because we were cognizant of the role that our work would play in ongoing health promotion efforts in Southern California, we approached the contract with an attitude of flexibility. This was helpful, because we discovered three months after the award of the contract that we were to revise the work plan. The revisions were resolved after a few phone conversations with the administrative staff (the study sponsor) and an onsite, in-person meeting that involved three levels of staff (program, administrative, and contractual), Stu, and me.

During this revision meeting we were able to establish our collective commitment to cultural sensitivity relative to the study population: Latino families. As it turned out, I had met, though never had a working relationship, with one of the administrative staff members more than a decade earlier, when we were both employed by another organization in the area. Having that shared experience provided an additional sense of collegiality, which was particularly important to me as a Latina professional and relative newcomer to the field of evaluation. Our shared ethnic and professional backgrounds assisted in the development of the final, more refined evaluation protocols, and the group's collective commitment to cultural sensitivity was maintained through to the completion of the study report.

Now that I had a bit more of a professional connection, I thought it important to build and maintain a trusting work relationship with the people who would use the results of our community needs assessment. The COD outreach staff, Stu, and I were all interested in delving into more than a superficial inquiry of childhood obesity in the Latino community. We all wanted to pay attention to the cultural nuances that intersperse the evaluation context. These included inquiry about disease conditions, cultural beliefs related to health, and socioeconomic factors that contribute to health status and social integration. Integral to this collective value was the careful selection of Spanish language terminology in our focus group protocol that would have broad meaning across Latin American nationalities, something I expected to find among study participants, whether they were the parents or community outreach workers (*promotoras*) who participated in one of the fifteen focus groups we scheduled to occur in a wide variety of locations, including schools, community centers, and participants' homes.

The focus group and key informant data collection instruments and protocols were carefully designed and reviewed to address both the intent of the study and respect for the participants. Invitations to participate, informed consent procedures, incentives, foods for the focus groups, and every other aspect of participant involvement were designed to maximize the amount and quality of information obtained, while reducing costs and the burdens associated with participation in our study (Krueger & Casey, 2000). Above all, focus group recruitment materials were meant to develop trust between Sunrise Health System and Latino families, health professionals, local government, and community organizations in the region. This was considered important because our findings would inform future educational activities to be conducted in the very communities from which we were soliciting information; we all thought that building community relationships was of equal importance to the educational content of future efforts.

Focus groups protocols were written in both Spanish and English so as to be sensitive to the language preferences of our participants. The questions covered a range of content areas. Specifically, we explored the perceived causes of childhood obesity in the Latino community. We then solicited possible solutions from the focus group participants, and existing health education messages were also presented and examined.

The COD and administrative staffs carefully reviewed all phases of the evaluation project, including the scope of the environmental scan, the focus group and key informant samples, data collection protocols, and the analysis and reporting of our findings. Clearly, although the study was designed to find answers to key questions about childhood obesity, the way in which the project was conducted was engineered to develop and maintain linkages with Sunrise's partners and stakeholders.

THE USE OF QUALITATIVE INQUIRY

What the study sponsors were interested in obtaining from the Latino community, and what I was eager to assist in obtaining, was parental and community input toward the sponsor's future educational programming on prevention and reduction of childhood obesity. We were interested in knowing how parents provided food and encouraged physical activity of their children, given their family resources and familiarity with community-based and institutional resources, for example, schools, parks, civic organizations. We were also interested in their identification of gaps in services and what they believed would be the best approaches for the Sunrise Health Systems COD to use in the future to inform them about preventing and reducing childhood obesity. Because of this, we knew from the beginning that our primary approach to meet these expectations would involve qualitative inquiry.

Qualitative inquiry provided us the opportunity to explore immediate responses to the evaluation questions and to delve further through moderated probes guided by group dynamics. Interviews and focus groups allowed for open-ended questions, response variations, spontaneous reactions, and verbal and nonverbal indications of the relevance and significance of the topic at hand. We were interested in soliciting participants' comments, opinions, and suggestions on an issue for which scant data were available. We anticipated low literacy levels and language differences between the study sponsor and the community members. This awareness was particularly important because when there are presuppositions about the community of study that might interfere with participation, the evaluators need to seek a data collection approach that best respects the relationship between program staff and the participants.

As a Latina myself, I was particularly aware of the heterogeneity among Latinos with regard to national origin and length of stay in the United States. As such, there exist various levels and nuances associated with acculturation. Likewise, family characteristics—including, but not limited to number of children, income levels, and preferred language spoken at home and outside—result in differences within the Latino population (Lara, Gamboa, Kahramanian, Morales, & Hayes Bautista, 2005). I recognized that while we were on a quest for findings about a community often characterized simply by national origin (i.e., with ancestral roots in Latin America), we were presented with an opportunity to obtain participants' varied responses to the study questions. Given this purpose, we knew how important it would be to solicit information in an open-ended manner. I also knew how important it would be to create a comfortable and respectful atmosphere for the focus groups so that we could simulate informal discussions commonly held among friends and neighbors. What an opportunity!

PERSONAL INFLUENCES ON EVALUATION DESIGN

My personal history makes me aware of the appreciation for food in family life. Food is important not only for basic sustenance, as preached in religious affairs, but for its role in the celebrations marking birthdays and other milestones that involve family members, extended family, friends, and neighbors. Moreover, food availability can represent an abundance of health and wealth. The value of food as a social connector and symbol of an enriched life is evidenced by the large quantities of food found in social events (e.g., banquets, potlucks, and food bars for weddings and *quinceañeras,* the traditional celebrations for a Latina fifteen-year-old girl, which are much grander than birthday celebrations held in earlier years and represent a rite of passage from childhood to a more mature life phase). The enjoyment of a variety of food can represent a sense of being cosmopolitan. Its contribution to physical growth yields further social value to those who can show they are able to afford such lavish displays.

Conversely, my formal training as a health educator has exposed me to the value of examining the nutritional value of food and the physiology of food intake—the physics of energy gained and expended and the balance necessary to maximize biological efficiency. In contrast to the social values placed on food, the study of nutrients, vitamins, proteins, and minerals can mitigate one's interest in experimenting with one more helping of food or drink that possibly (and literally) tips the scale of a nutritionally balanced meal.

My questions at the outset of the project included: Might that same balancing act be a consideration for the parents we were to recruit for the study focus groups? What key educational messages would be most relevant to them so as to influence their decisions about food, food purchases, and nutrition education? What were the communication channels to which they would be most receptive? Who were the individuals they trusted and regarded as credible sources of information about obesity and its prevalence among children? What did they know about childhood obesity and how did they already use that information on a daily basis? These questions formed the foundation for the questions posed in the focus groups.

TRENDS IN HEALTH EDUCATION

At the time when Sunrise Health Systems issued a call for proposals for the community assessment, the public health and medical literature already had identified childhood obesity as an epidemic. Coalitions of public and private organizations had formed to address what was once recognized primarily as a problem of adulthood. There was also interest in addressing the problem systematically and with an environmental perspective, involving many entities that might play a role in reducing an increasingly prevalent, but preventable, condition.

The social and political context was also shifting to bring increased attention to childhood obesity. California became the first state to ban the sale of soft drinks in middle and elementary schools, over the objections of the beverage industry. In 2005, a legislative proposal was made to update and expand nutritional standards for food sold in school vending machines and snack bars.

For a health care organization focused on maintaining low health service costs by preventing the need for their use, it made economic sense for Sunrise Health Systems to invest in an evaluation that would inform the direction of their health education and clinical programs aimed at preventing and reducing childhood obesity. What was less clear, and of great interest to the study sponsors, was the general perception of childhood obesity as a problem among Latino parents. If childhood obesity was perceived as a problem, how would the Latino community in Southern California understand it and prefer it be addressed?

DELVING INTO THE FORMALITY OF EVALUATION DESIGN

With this backdrop, I became the project director of the community assessment for Latino-focused pediatric overweight prevention education programs. I learned in the course of the fourteen-month study that as much as one desires to place collegiality above personal motivations, how decisions are made reflects many things, including conviction, organizational hierarchies, and unknowns that remain mysteries. Still, one proceeds in the interest of discovery, exploration, and a focus on obtaining useable information that stems from the questions driving the evaluation. Identifying appropriate ways to tactfully communicate disagreements, politely remind sponsors of study limitations, or let go of matters that are not within the scope of the work are at times fascinating (albeit unnerving) parts of the learning process. Needless to say, these issues can, if not addressed, become hindrances to progressing with the study.

A community needs assessment is about going from a beginning—during which there is a discovery about study sponsors' interests relative to what is presented in the call for proposals—to obtaining information that will respond to evaluation questions. After all, it is an evaluation. It is a quest in which one sets a study design along with protocols to guide the roads to be taken, but nonetheless remains open to what might occur within the context of following those protocols.

Stu and I were always together on phone communications with the COD and administrative staff, which allowed for immediate, joint responses to evaluation-related matters (e.g., logistics, approval status on protocols, scheduling of interviews or focus groups, explanations of the rationale for our line of inquiry). Because the content of these calls was subject to being forgotten, particularly when the various parties had multiple responsibilities on a number of concurrent projects, I carefully documented these ongoing communications.

DATA COLLECTION, ANALYSIS, AND REPORTING

As we entered into the data collection portion of the study, we were not particularly concerned about sensitive information being revealed by our study participants. We had excluded certain components that would have required us to broach topics possibly deemed controversial or challenging to discuss among strangers: adolescence, puberty, sexual and emotional developmental phases, drugs, child abuse. Discussing parental rearing practices related to pediatric obesity might have felt uncomfortable to the focus group participants, but no one opted out after beginning the group discussions, nor did anyone make an overt statement leading me to believe that either the questions posed or the ensuing discussions were insensitive, uncomfortable, or offensive.

The key informant interviews were another matter. Stu and I gave thought to the possibility that key informants might say something unfavorable about their prior working relationships with Sunrise Health Systems. If they did have unfavorable experiences in working with Sunrise, it was important to surface those during the study process. That said, we subsequently realized that since the COD outreach staff had indirectly identified the individuals to be included in the focus groups and directly identified those for the telephone interviews, we might be less likely to encounter unfavorable experiences. We introduced ourselves as external evaluators and reiterated the confidential nature of the interview in an effort to create the best possible conditions for candor. We presented in our interview guide, as is standard practice in phone interviews, the option for the interviewee to end the interview when they felt it necessary. In addition, to maximize the efficient use of phone time and offer participants time to consider the questions ahead of time, we sent the interview guide to participants in advance of a scheduled interview, expecting that they would review it and prepare their responses.

Although we thought we had attended to every detail before data collection, we quickly discovered a difference in understanding between the "professionals" and study participants. On several occasions, participants made statements referring to the focus group as "classes." The first time it happened, I quickly realized that this misunderstanding should not have been a surprise. The community residents had prior experience attending health education classes or workshops presented or organized by Sunrise Health Systems; our purpose was quite different. To avoid possible confusion, my introduction during the focus groups that I facilitated was adjusted to include a statement or two about the purpose of the study. I explained that we wanted to hear from them about their ideas related to childhood obesity. I also stressed the voluntary nature of participation when distributing and explaining the paperwork involved before any further discussion about the crux of the group gatherings.

As a follow-up, Stu and I further reflected on the misunderstanding about the nature of the focus groups. We maintained that the focus groups were largely made up of people whose life experiences had not provided them with ample opportunities in which their opinions were solicited for program design. Approximately 44 percent reported having less than a high school education, and 33 percent reported less than $10,000 as annual household income. Furthermore, their experiences with Sunrise Health Systems had likely been receiving hospital services or attending health education classes, not as consultants to services that are designed for them by professionals. The dynamic verbal interaction and exchange involved in making focus groups effective as a data collection method can be foreign to people unaccustomed to contributing their thoughts, comments, or opinions in public. Yet for our purposes, the dynamic exchange was absolutely essential.

We relied on the availability of healthy snacks and beverages that were culturally familiar brand name products to initiate conversations about food. These items were displayed for group participants when they entered the community rooms, school resource areas, or other gathering places where we met. Further attempts at inciting participants to share their experiences included explaining that the focus group would function as a group discussion or *platica* among parents. I used the formal term *Usted* to address participants rather than the familiar *tu* as a respectful way (in Spanish) of addressing people recently met from whom information would be solicited. The formal way of addressing members of the group did not prevent me from also occasionally using colloquial expressions to draw out perceptions of obesity. For example, talking about being *gordito y lleno de vida* or chubby and full of life tested people's acceptance of the connection between fullness and girth as an indicator of overweight or recognition that *estar lleno de vida* ("being full of life") is not necessarily linked to the health burdens associated with extra weight.

We also provided monetary incentives that were a token means of compensating participation. Gift cards to local retail and food outlets were provided to focus group participants as a symbolic exchange for time spent in a setting organized by community agency representatives and the Sunrise outreach staff. In essence, we attempted through several means to make participants feel that we valued their time, experiences, and presence at the focus groups.

The demographic questions we asked were minimal. We tried to ask the questions in order of sensitivity. The seven questions we needed answered to provide an overall profile of the groups were zip code, age, gender, number of children, highest level of education attained, employment description, and income. These were collected on individual sheets of paper, without name identification and apart from the signed consent forms we required of each participant. When participants were unable to read or write, we accepted noncompletion of the forms, and they acknowledged their consent by remaining in the group.

The focus groups were not the only source of misunderstanding about the evaluation's purpose. Despite the efforts to obtain balanced and thoughtful responses to all of our questions, some unanticipated events occurred in the key informant interviews as well. In some instances, the key informants interviewed by phone used the opportunity to advocate for their own views on issues that were related to the topic at hand but fell outside the scope of the intended discussion. For example, a school official in one district shifted the focus of the interview to argue his position that public school physical education should focus on healthy living instead of team sports. He added that this was a position for which he had risked his employment in the district. A public health official in a conservative Southern California community dominated the interview by shifting the focus of his answers to criticize the political climate that appeared to blatantly ignore the public health needs of poor and immigrant communities.

Evaluators must anticipate that they will encounter some unintended responses such as these. However, the missed premise of some of the focus groups and the personal agendas offered by several of the key informants diminished the project's ability to provide the best possible picture of the issues that may underlie childhood obesity in Latino communities. Our client asked us to address specific questions; when participants deviated too much from the evaluation questions, it was difficult to ascertain how to incorporate the divergent content.

These surprises challenged the analysis and reporting stages of our project. We felt that the Sunrise staff would be best served by summarizing focus group and key informant data with a minimum of interpretation. This was significant in that there were twenty-two 45-minute phone interviews and 189 participants in the fifteen 90-minute focus groups. We felt that the summarized data were representative of the region as a whole, but less representative of specific counties, public health planning areas, or school districts. As we listened to focus group participants and key informants, we came to understand the many nuances and shades that represented the essence of their experience and understanding of problems of childhood obesity and the potential solutions. We conveyed these insights to our sponsor and pointed out the limitations of the data as we interpreted them so that the COD outreach staff could have an appreciation for the limitations and complexities of the data. For example, one of the limitations we encountered was that translation did not always suffice to give meaning to participants' responses. Therefore, we included direct quotes (in Spanish) obtained from study participants in the final report.

Reporting our findings consisted of a final report and an in-person debriefing at the administrative headquarters of Sunrise Health Systems. The final report summarized the purpose of the evaluation and our methods. Results focused on findings from the environmental scan and themes and patterns synthesized from the focus groups with members of the Latino community and telephone interviews with key informants. The report also contained an extensive set of appendices showing the data collection instruments, consent letters, and other supporting material. The Sunrise Department of Administration shared the report with key Sunrise staff members, including members of the pediatrics department, several planners and health educators, as well as a representative from the public relations and marketing department. These individuals were also invited to attend the debriefing.

We decided to organize the presentation of the findings in a way that highlighted the common perspectives shared by particular groups of study participants. Among the revelations in the study findings were the community-based health planners' and educators' (i.e., key informants') interests in having Sunrise Health Systems take a leadership role beyond the medical/clinical model. The following quotes illustrate this perspective and the community perception of the political power held by the study sponsor. "[Get involved] with environmental and policy changes, i.e., participate in collaborations to encourage activity in communities; lobby for more park space." And, given the clinical role for which the study sponsor was known, another participant expressed interest in having Sunrise doctors influence independent private doctors—"there is no consistency in referrals and follow-up of overweight or obese children; medical plans for follow-up are not known by the schools."

Focus group participants repeatedly mentioned community and school settings as places for future educational programs. We found that responses from community residents and *promotoras* (community outreach workers) intersected. Parents generally were more concerned about school meals than meals prepared at home. Parents also acknowledged fast food outlets and children's peer influences as challenges to their parental guidance about food. They discussed physical activity as something to do primarily outdoors rather than indoors. Key recommendations from the *promotoras* included a call to increase awareness of the [childhood obesity] problem and long-term effects on family life. They also recommended that Sunrise Health Systems develop a holistic approach to strategic thinking and planning.

REFLECTIONS ON EVALUATOR BACKGROUND

My role in this study was not to be just a health educator, nor just an evaluator of a particular educational program. I was a consultant on a study of a community's knowledge, attitudes, behaviors, and perceptions, in which my experiences in both roles influenced my decisions. The evaluation framework was familiar because of my professional background as a health educator and researcher.

Much of my work since this evaluation has focused on blending theoretical frameworks taken from the fields of health education, program evaluation, and business administration. What has proved most useful in communications with clients and the reports prepared for further internal dissemination is the intertwining of methodological approaches and decision-making models from these three fields.

Just as important, the community of study was familiar because of my personal background. The privilege I had in gaining access to the study community, because of a shared language and its nuances, the rapport I established and trust I gained, and the flexibility in speaking colloquially and more formally as needed enabled me to more fully inform other stakeholders who did not have the same privilege and access. My contribution back to the study community was my sharing of their ideas with individuals who are in a position to affect and influence the lives of community members.

In this evaluation, because of the need to explore how various cultural factors such as language, acculturation, income levels, civic engagement, number of children, and so forth contribute to Latino parents' perceptions of health, nutrition, obesity, and family and school environments, we felt that hearing the words of the Latino families was the best approach to take. Our study involved a group of people we anticipated would be more inclined to engage in conversations about these matters than self-report their knowledge or perceptions on written survey instruments. This is consistent with a focus group format. Additionally, we anticipated varied degrees of literacy that might affect the response rate to surveys by not providing us sufficient data to begin to notice patterns across respondents from the different counties. Indeed, our assumptions, for the most part, held.

What was interesting for me at a personal and professional level was that, unlike the study participants, I lacked experience as a parent. Although I have not been a parent, I am curious about parental attitudes toward the health of their children; their perceptions of what constitutes a healthy meal; and their understanding of social and peer pressures as disruptions and potential threats to the values they wish to establish in their families and impart to their children. For the most part, I have observed and studied these experiences from the somewhat more distant perspective of a health educator. The focus groups allowed me to gather in-depth personal and familial information in a more direct manner.

REFLECTIONS ON OUR EVALUATION PROCESS

As proponents of rigorous evaluations, my colleague Stu and I began with a formulaic response to a call for proposals that included our understanding of a community problem, descriptions of our technical backgrounds and training, proposed study design, timeline, and budget. Throughout the study, we, as co-investigators, shared a genuine interest in the community of study, the particular line of qualitative inquiry we chose to follow, examining the assumptions that we found ourselves making along the way, and the perspectives that we each brought to the project.

Did we conduct this study with a traditional scientific approach that began with a theory and was designed to prove or disprove it? No. We conducted our work with a set of assumptions that were deliberately stated by the two evaluators at the outset. We described the direction of the inquiry in the proposal we submitted to our client. We presented our professional credentials, highlighted our cultural sensitivity to the study community, and offered our client the option to include more or fewer of the type of data-collection approaches we considered most appropriate within budgetary constraints. We exhibited resourcefulness in transforming ordinary meeting rooms into dynamic information exchange settings for the focus groups (by, for example, using the standard provision of refreshments in creative and culturally appropriate ways that prompted dialogue on the study topic). We demonstrated flexibility by being willing to collect data from a wide array of Latino community members who met in a variety of places, including school and community assembly rooms and residents' backyards and basements. We framed our interview questions such that interviewees would be made welcome to express positive and negative comments about their experiences with the study sponsor. We guaranteed confidentiality and built in opt-out options for all participants. We compensated community participants for their valued opinions and remarks. We explicitly acknowledged in our written report all who contributed their time to make the study possible administratively and in the field.

One of the reasons we approached the community assessment in the manner we did was our conviction that frequently, well-intentioned people, including educators, evaluators, researchers, and organizational leaders, develop and implement programs to "fix a problem." This problem-solving orientation is particularly noticeable when using a medical model in which the "solution" is largely derived from the health professionals' viewpoint, given what is known in the particular professional discipline and as a result of the practitioners' diagnostic skills. In this project, we were fortunate to have encountered a study sponsor whose community-oriented perspective allowed us to tap into qualitative inquiry to inform future program direction. Stu and I shared a perspective that working in communities requires participatory approaches, qualitative data collection methods, and modes of exchange that are mutually beneficial to the researchers and the research sponsor. Furthermore, creating opportunities for community members to give their opinions on future programming is in keeping with our philosophical approach: to involve, in direct, in-depth, and meaningful ways, people whose lives will be affected by the evaluation and the evaluation process.

The backgrounds and philosophical orientations that Stu and I brought to the project undoubtedly informed the study design. As co-evaluators, we used a consultative approach with our study sponsor. After receiving notice of the contract award, we held several in-person meetings and telephone conference calls to confirm our understanding of the questions to be posed within the study communities and the sponsors' learning goals for the project. What resulted was an evaluation that used an iterative and consultative approach throughout to engage our study sponsor as well as agency representatives and parents.

REFLECTIONS ON OUR USE OF QUALITATIVE INQUIRY

Qualitative inquiry, in the form of semi-structured interviews with key informants and focus groups of community residents and *promotoras*, was the backbone of our community needs assessment. The most important insights generated through this project would not have been possible without such direct and open-ended communication with our study population. The flexibility inherent in the semi-structured interviews allowed the inclusion of spontaneous conversation to establish rapport between interviewer and interviewee. This created a more natural interaction in which to ask the key questions of interest to our client and was essential to inform future program planning by Sunrise Health Systems. The versatility of the focus groups allowed us to be creative in their design. We set up the sites where focus groups were held to make them appealing and welcoming. We demonstrated the importance of information exchange through relevant incentives to focus group participants.

From our perspective, the overarching goal in collecting data is to generate information that will be truthful and of utility to our client. The deliberate selection of questions that we posed, whether in the interviews or focus groups, was the result of several iterations and discussions with each other, with our client, and ultimately, as the major test, with study participants. We discovered that the Latino community residents with whom we spoke knew that there was an increasing problem related to the food to which their children were exposed and that they consumed outside their homes. We were told of numerous challenges faced by parents whose children were becoming increasingly interested in eating meals outside the home, prepared in ways vastly different from traditional meals. We learned, too, that within the Latino communities are *promotoras*, informational resources interested in and willing to complement the medical model by using a more holistic approach through community involvement and outreach.

CONCLUSION

Sunrise Health Systems, our study sponsor, incorporated our findings into their COD's framework for future program planning. We got a glimpse of that future direction when we met with them near the conclusion of our engagement. The staff members who had been our key contacts from the COD and administrative departments attended our presentation. Also present were staff members from the marketing department whom our contacts had invited. We took this as a sign that our study was a significant accomplishment of the COD and warranted the participation of others who had not sat through the laborious discussions that led to its implementation. That labor was behind us. What lay ahead were opportunities to inform future in-house program directions and possibly regional intra-agency policies.

KEY CONCEPTS

Collegiality	Focus group
Community of interest	Heterogeneity
Community needs assessment	Implementation effectiveness
Consultative approach	Intrusiveness
Cultural sensitivity	Key informant interview
Environmental scan	Modes of inquiry
Establishing rapport	Professional disciplines and alliances
External consultant	

Professional reputation

Recruitment of evaluation participants

Representative sample

Request for proposals

Response variation

Self-identification

Semi-structured interview

Stakeholder groups

DISCUSSION QUESTIONS

1. This chapter illustrates one way in which evaluators are stakeholders. As the authors prepared for, designed, and implemented their evaluation, they needed to balance their own understanding of the issues with those of the community served by the program. What are some strategies an evaluator can use to balance one's own perspective with the multiple cultures represented within a given organization, group, or community?

2. Whether to include quotes and how to translate quotes that are reported in evaluation reports is a controversial issue. Discuss the pros and cons of including untranslated quotes in the final report to the sponsor.

3. How can an evaluator utilize qualitative inquiry to give a voice to program participants and to do so in a manner that can best be heard by the client and other key stakeholders?

REFERENCES

Altschuld, J. W., & Kumar, D. D. (2005). Needs assessment. In S. Mathison (Ed.), *Encyclopedia of evaluation* (pp. 276–277). Thousand Oaks, CA: Sage.

Krueger, R. A., & Casey, M. A. (2000). *Focus groups: A practical guide for applied research* (3rd ed.). Thousand Oaks, CA: Sage.

Lara, M., Gamboa, C., Kahramanian, M. I., Morales, L. S., & Hayes Bautista, D. E. (2005). Acculturation and Latino health in the United States: A review of the literature and its sociopolitical context. *Annual Review of Public Health, 26*, 367–397.

SB 697. (1994). Chapter 812 Statutes of 1994. Available at http://leginfo .ca.gov/blinfo.html

9

Whose Story Is This, Anyway?

Navigating an Ethical Conundrum

Sharon F. Rallis

Key Ideas

- Ethical dilemmas can arise when those involved in a qualitative evaluation have conflicting norms around practice. Evaluators must consider their own ethical practice as well as the ethical practice of stakeholders and others who are peripherally connected to the program.

- Evaluators often have to deal with surprises, particularly when stakeholders fall short of the evaluator's expectations or standards.

- Ethical challenges can arise when qualitative evaluators are navigating the following:

    Creating the context for evaluation

    Negotiating multiple evaluator roles

    Engaging program participants

    Clarifying project purposes, benefits, and risks

    Confronting a lack of methodological expertise among stakeholders

    Representing participant voice

Maintaining relationships with stakeholders and others peripherally connected to the program

On August 14 in the early afternoon, the director of one participating school in *Bridging the Gap: Innovation for Achievement* (pseudonym of a federally funded initiative to study and disseminate findings regarding successful innovative schools) sent this e-mail to the executive director of the sponsoring agency:

Subject: instr/concl chapters from [the book[1]]
Norman, Please do what you need to do to remove Horizon School from the [research team's] study. We have consensus that we want to pull out. Do what you have to do to ensure that our rights to do so are respected. Please reply as soon as possible as to my request. TC[2]

The request in the e-mail represents an ethical dilemma that emerged from conflicting norms between two cultures in a quasi-ethnographic study of innovative schools that was one component of the larger initiative. The conflicting norms were the researchers' culture and the cultures of the participant schools. Specifically, the researchers valued the norms of academia and scholarship (such as following stipulated protocols and publishing results), whereas the schools valued practical action to meet students' needs. As in the case of sociologist Carolyn Ellis's study of the Virginia Tidewater Guineamen (Ellis, 1986), the two cultures differed on what defines the *truth* and on the ethics underlying the discovery of any truth. Ellis's judgments that the fisher culture was deficit (defined as a lack or impairment in a functional capacity) were based on her western white worldview; that is, she saw a culture lacking social mechanisms she considered necessary to function and prosper in the modern world. Similarly, the judgments made by the university researchers regarding aspects of the schools in the study are based on their own academic values, not the values that drove schools' operations. And, like Ellis's fisher folk community, the schools had opened doors and taken the research team into their lives with the expectation that their voices would be heard and respected. However, unlike Ellis, the members of the research team were novice ethnographers who did not practice the *caring reflexivity* (see Guillemin & Gillam, 2004; Rallis & Rossman, 2010) necessary for a qualitative study to be ethical and thus trustworthy.

As is often the case in federally funded education initiatives that include research as well as dissemination, evaluation is required. As the project evaluators, we found ourselves entangled in ambiguous role delineations while also addressing conflict and inexperience. At times we saw ourselves playing the guide for ethical decision-making. This chapter tells the story of the project through the eyes of the evaluator, using a moral lens and organized by the challenges we faced. We follow the development of our role as evaluators and explore the implications of our actions within multiple contexts. That both the methods used by the research team and the primary tools used by the evaluators were qualitative holds potential for dual insights into what contributes to ethical qualitative evaluation practice.

THE CONTEXT: WHO'S DOING WHAT?

Bridging the Gap (BTG) was a replication and dissemination grant project funded by the US Department of Education (DOE) through a nonprofit State Association of Innovative Schools (henceforth to be called the association). Specifically, the association received the funding to carry out the project, which brought together a variety of players. BTG began with three questions:

- What are the common elements of success (as measured by standardized tests and graduation rates) in high-quality innovative schools serving students at educational risk in high-need communities?

- How do we share this information with a broad audience of educators and policy makers?

- How can states disseminate and replicate these common elements to create more highly successful schools?

To find answers, BTG put forth goals to: *identify* high-quality innovative schools in the state that serve students at risk of educational failure in high-need communities; *research* and *document* the common elements of success in these schools; *disseminate* findings nationally through a variety of media; and conduct trainings to *replicate* best practices. To meet these goals, a mix of people interacted: the association director and project coordinator, innovative school leaders and staff, university researchers, a filmmaker, personnel from the professional development organization that would support dissemination activities, and two evaluators. Each stakeholder group brought to the project its own agenda, particular interests, and individual perspectives.

The first task was to identify and select five innovative public schools in which student performance on a variety of academic scales (i.e., state high-stakes standardized tests, graduation rates, college acceptance) outperformed the demographics of each school's surrounding district. Each of the selected schools wrote *whole school papers* explicating the philosophy and practices that they believed contributed to the high achievement of their students. The association contracted a university researcher specifically designated by the funder to research the schools and document what these schools did to produce such positive results. The research team (one faculty member and five graduate students) was to collect data and produce a book for dissemination. The project also contracted an independent filmmaker to produce a film illustrating what he saw as elements contributing to the high performance of the students; the film was to be suitable for dissemination through public broadcasting and other public venues. An agency with expertise in providing professional development was contracted to design and lead study tours of the schools in the final year of the project as a means of demonstrating best practices. Finally, the association chose my colleague Andy and me, of the Education Evaluation and Policy Research Group, to evaluate the BTG project.

Regarding evaluation of the project, the association wrote in the proposal: "We believe that staffing for [the evaluation] tasks requires a combination of sophisticated evaluation design skills (benchmarks, protocols, etc.), high-level personal interaction skills with senior personnel (school leader interviews, review panel recruitment and facilitation, and research and project team), and regular, ongoing availability to manage logistics, attend meetings, schedule interviews, collect and write up data, provide editorial support, synthesize findings, etc." Indeed, in our roles as evaluators, we drew on all those skills and more. BTG's goal was to produce knowledge for dissemination and replication, so throughout we found ourselves challenged ethically and logistically with these enduring questions: *Whose knowledge is captured? How is it captured and represented? Does the story that unfolds realistically relate participants' experiences?*

THE MORAL LENS ON QUALITATIVE INQUIRY: PRINCIPLES AND ETHICAL THEORIES

As a program evaluator who relies on qualitative methods to inform questions about the program, I recognize that I am the means through which the data are collected, analyzed, and interpreted. Essentially, I am constructing new or confirming extant knowledge; as such, I continually and consciously make decisions about conceptualizing, designing, conducting, interpreting, and writing up findings. To ensure that my decision-making is both competent and ethical, I establish my moral position—that all evaluation should have a goal of improving some social circumstance (Rossman & Rallis, 2003), specifically to "improve policy and programming for the well-being of all" (Weiss, 1998, p. ix)—and I draw on moral principles that direct me to act as I would want everyone else to act in any given situation (Kant, 1788/1956): *justice* (fairness and equity), *beneficence* (risks and benefits, reciprocity), and *respect* for persons (participants are seen as autonomous agents) (see Hemmings, 2006).

Nearly all aspects of qualitative inquiry are governed by ethics, which are standards of conduct based on moral principles. "The point of moral principles is to regulate interactions among human beings" (Strike, Haller, & Soltis, 1998, p, 41). Thus, my ethical keystone is relationships, not procedures. A social activity, evaluation is naturally interactive and dialogic; ethical evaluators seek out and listen carefully to the voices embedded in the social context (Taylor, 1994). "Good qualitative [evaluators] are adventurous in their pursuit of thick descriptive data on how [actors] make sense of their worlds; . . . and do their best to forge rapport with participants in order to capture their 'emic' viewpoints on various social phenomena" (Hemmings, 2006, p. 12). We engage in the reflexive reasoning that is central to any trustworthy evaluation. Reflexive reasoning is relational; it is multifaceted and iterative, moving back and forth between the details and the whole, between the evaluator's questions, the participants' knowledge, and the evaluator's interpretation of that knowledge. We ask: *What do I see? How and why do I see this? How might others see it? What does it mean to me? To others?* Put simply, reflexivity is "looking at yourself making sense of how someone else makes sense of her world" (Rossman & Rallis, 2003, p. 49).

Reflexivity recognizes that the evaluator and the participants are involved in continual and changing interaction. The evaluator asks: What is happening in this relationship? Is it fair? What might be possible consequences of my actions? Of my interpretations? What rights of participants might I violate or potential harms might result? Are the participants likely to benefit in any way—and are they likely to agree on the benefit? What burden might my inquiry lay upon participants? Equally important is that we question our own actions: Do I act according to my principles?

Building an ethical relationship with participants may not be easy or happen immediately, but I do believe that it becomes easier when we articulate (at least explicitly to ourselves) the moral principles we intend to use. Not all moral principles are compatible, and contradictions even lie within some. Moral principles form ethical theories that can be grouped into two broad categories: consequentialist and non-consequentialist. Consequentialist ethical theories focus on the results of actions in determining their rightness or wrongness. Any particular action is neither intrinsically good nor bad; rather, it is good or bad because of its results in a particular context—its consequences. From a consequentialist perspective, the evaluator considers the results over the process; means are less important if the end has value; for example, utilitarianism advocates that one's behavior should result in the greatest good for the greatest number. Using this moral principle, an evaluator's work would be more summative; she might document the impact of the program on a majority of participants.

In the other major category, non-consequentialist ethical theories derive from the moral principle that universal standards exist to guide human behavior and interaction. Two non-consequentialist theories on which we as qualitative evaluators claim to operate are the ethic of individual rights and responsibilities and the ethic of justice (see, for example, House

& Howe, 1999). The first upholds the unconditional worth of the individual and judges actions by the degree to which they respect a person, not by its outcomes or consequences. The protection of these rights may not be denied, even for the greatest good for the greatest number. Ethics of justice go beyond individual rights and responsibilities to espouse the redistribution of resources and opportunities to achieve equity above equality. The goal is to ensure that everyone is better off, even though the allocation of some benefits may differ; rightness or wrongness of actions is judged through principles of fairness and equity. The moral principles of non-consequentialist ethics argue that people must be treated as an end in themselves, not as a means to an end. According to Rawls (1971), the benefit or welfare of the least advantaged, not that of the majority or average, must drive any action. His view maintains that improving the welfare of the least advantaged ultimately benefits everyone because the communal resources of society and future generations will grow.

Principles of justice and individual rights consider questions of power and representation: Who defines what is right in a given situation? Whose values are used in rating on criteria? Are all voices given opportunity to be heard? Other perspectives situate morality within the context and relationship. Communitarianism (MacIntyre, 1981) acknowledges that communities differ on what is morally good or right. Evaluators often find that not all stakeholders share fundamental values, and that those values may conflict with the evaluator's own values. So whose values define the research, guide decisions, and shape interpretations? A postmodern response would posit that power and dominant versions of "truth" shape the relationships and thus the research (Foucault, 1970).

Knowing ethical theories and the principles on which they rest can help evaluators analyze and understand their choices for action, but theory is abstract and therefore may not be practically helpful. The AEA *Guiding Principles for Evaluators* codifies ethical theories into a collection of principles to guide evaluation practice; for example, evaluators will: "conduct systematic, data-based inquiries"; "provide competent performance to stakeholders"; "display honesty and integrity"; "respect the security, dignity, and self-worth" of all involved; and "take into account the diversity of general and public interests and values" (www.eval.org). Not standards or directives, each principle must be explicated and applied to the relevant situation in practice. From a moral perspective, the danger in applying any set of externally generated theories to real-life settings, that is, translating abstract principles into practical actions, is the establishment and imposition of one-size-fits-all rules. Thus, evaluators are still challenged not to simply follow procedures but to consider what any action may mean for the relationships present in the evaluation setting.

The *ethic of care* is an alternative perspective that offers a potentially powerful and practical way to operationalize the moral and ethical aspects of the evaluation process. *Caring* argues that the core of morality must be the relationship itself. "Ethical decisions must be made in caring interactions with those affected by the discussion. Indeed, it is exactly in the most difficult situations that principles fail us. Thus, instead of turning to a principle for guidance, a carer returns to the cared-for" (Noddings, 1995, p. 187). This approach emphasizes concrete circumstances over abstract principles: What does *this* person need in *this* moment? Care theory emphasizes the moral interdependence of people: "Our goodness and our growth are inextricably bound to that of others we encounter. As researchers, we are as dependent on our [participants] as they are on us" (Noddings, 1995, p. 196).

From these ethical theories and their corollary moral principles emerge two practical tensions that offer a framework for analyzing our ethical and logistical challenges: harm versus care and burden versus benefit. As evaluators of BTG, our overall goal was to contribute to improving aspects of the initiative so that the initiative could, in turn, contribute to the improvement of the social circumstance: education. In achieving this goal, we sought to avoid doing harm, both in our own work and in the work of the various other players; to encourage care and respect for all participants; and to minimize burden while promoting benefit. We knew that in qualitative evaluation potentials for harm "are often quite subtle and stem from the nature of the interaction between researcher and participant" (Guillemin & Gillam, 2004, p. 272). Thus we strove for conscious reflexivity, which included reflection both on and during action, as antidote to harm. Our reflexivity, driven by our ethical stance, drew both from principles and from reciprocal and caring relationships unique to the contexts. We believe we practiced caring reflexivity to conduct ethical evaluation and to monitor for ethical research. To summarize, in all decisions and interactions with participant individuals and groups, we considered principles of justice, beneficence, and respect for persons.

CHALLENGES: ETHICAL AND LOGISTIC

Challenge 1: Creating the Context for Evaluation and Negotiating the Evaluator's Role

As an evaluator, especially one who uses primarily qualitative tools, I am used to negotiating my role. This project was no exception. As noted earlier, federal research grants often require an independent evaluation of the research, thereby relegating the evaluator to a role of compliance monitoring (e.g., did the project meet benchmarks/do what they promised?). As an evaluator, I prefer to inhabit a role that works with the program people to consider the merit or worth of the program or of the study being conducted about the program. Defining the scope and activities of the evaluation emerged as a challenge during early conversations among ourselves in the Evaluation Group and between us and the association. At the outset, we wondered why we were not conducting the research on (i.e., evaluating) what made these schools effective. While evaluators might seem the natural choice to study the schools with the aim of identifying elements that contributed to school success, for later dissem- ination through book, film, and tours, the federal request for proposal (RFP) separated the research role from the evaluation role, and the grant officer specified that the researchers were to be recruited from a specific institution. Thus, the association had already contracted "researchers" to complete that task as well as to produce the book.

So what was our role to be? The grant defined evaluation as monitoring to ensure that tasks were completed as described in the proposal, but we demurred because we could not see ourselves as police. Thus, we re-negotiated the purpose and conditions of the evaluation. First, we established our approach to evaluation: interactive and participatory, grounded in an ethic of care (Noddings, 1984). Although we recognize that outcomes are important, we choose to focus on what happens to reach those outcomes (a more non-consequentialist stance). We proposed that we do more than monitor benchmark achievement and instead suggested the role of evaluator as *critical friend* (see Rallis & Rossman, 2000, 2001), that is, observing, interacting across the players, providing feedback, and asking multilayered questions about intents and impacts. This enactment of our role, while drawing on mixed-methods tools, places strong emphasis on the more dialogic reporting strategies common in qualitative or participatory studies.

While still stipulating the monitoring role, the association warmed to our proposed expanded role, so the contract between the group and the association defined the evaluation scope of work as the following:

- Work with program staff and research team to clarify research goals and project benchmarks

- Develop protocols for collecting qualitative and quantitative data on process, product quality, and project outcomes

- Document research and project progress according to benchmarks

- Independently review data used in the selection process (including US Census, state education department files, and school records)

- Interview school leaders to ensure that the research accurately represents the schools profiled

- Assemble, convene, and synthesize feedback from a review panel to evaluate quality of products

- Monitor and document progress on book, video, website, ads, institutes, and other documentation, dissemination, and replication products

- Provide editorial feedback on research, documentation, and dissemination products

- Provide data and feedback to program staff on a regular basis, for reporting and program improvement purposes

■ Produce a quantitative and qualitative summative evaluation report

Thus began a three-year relationship with the many players involved with BTG. Initially our efforts were directed toward building a trustworthy relationship with the association director (Norman) and project coordinator (Alice), based on the mutual goal of ensuring that the project be the best it could possibly be. Our part of the bargain was to provide evidence-based feedback, facilitate interpretations, summarize findings, and raise questions. One of the first e-mails between the project coordinator, Alice, and me illustrates the tone of our interactions. Note that we clarified how the knowledge produced is theirs, not ours:

> Alice and Andy,
>
> Great—albeit brief—talk just now. To summarize, the point is that we need to modify the task/activity-timeline chart to add two columns: completion and quality. We can then check off and add footnotes to explain or inform any deviations (to quote you, Alice!) in the completion column. For quality we agree that to check off we need to be sure we have discussed and agreed—and reference any formal assessments leading to judgments of quality. Note that we, as evaluators, are not the determinants of quality, but serve to help you make quality judgments (i.e., are you pleased and why or why not?)
>
> The three of us may choose to meet to review—or we may agree that face-to-face meeting is not necessary.
>
> Thanks, Alice, for your persistence and patience.
>
> Sharon

At each step along the way, we had a set of questions that guided our behaviors. The questions we pondered are boxed near each of our challenges.

Challenge 2: Engaging Participants and Clarifying Project Purposes, Benefits, and Risks

Our second challenge arose in ensuring that the "right" innovative schools were chosen and brought on board. This task was tricky because the schools did not initiate the project and initially saw project activities as potentially more intrusive than beneficial. However, were project involvement to become seen as

BOX 9.1. **Questions We Used to Guide Our Qualitative Inquiry and Actions (Challenge 1)**

- What moral principles do we expect will guide our practice?

- What approach and tools will best serve this evaluation? How do we describe these to stakeholders?

- Can all parties agree on our role and expectations for the evaluation? Can all reach consensus on expectations for activities and events?

- What is the nature of the relationships we are building (e.g., *critical friend*)? How will we interact with the players?

advantageous or selection as an honor, competition to be chosen would result. Thus, the association realized that both school selection and entry/access would be complicated and difficult. Andy and I helped Alice, the project coordinator, specify and promulgate selection criteria and then verified that the selection process was transparent and matched the criteria. For this task, we used primarily qualitative methods: interviews and reviewing descriptive documents about the schools, both to select and to verify.

Once the five schools had been selected and agreed to join, questions of power, authority, and representation surfaced (questions qualitative researchers learn to notice). Andy and I brought evidence of the schools' interest and their concerns to Alice's attention. The schools expressed reasons why they were willing to participate: recognition; promised resources; embedded professional development; opportunity to "tell our story." They also intimated the kinds of knowledge they hoped the research would produce: their strengths; their struggles (e.g., long hours, burn-out); their successes. The first general meeting was held at the university where the researchers were located; the schools appeared impressed to be part of the "research agenda" of a professor at a prestigious institution. They were excited about being filmed and about the concept that they would serve as "laboratories for innovative developers and district schools identified for improvement, corrective action, or restructuring." They expressed concerns about the time that might be required of them and of their staff and students. Although BTG made clear that involvement would entail additional time, promises were made that the schools' needs and integrity would be respected.

Gradually, what became clear to us was that not all parties shared common perspectives of participation and product. In hindsight, we now realize that as evaluators we should have asked that both sides make more explicit and formally agree on their expectations and promises. The ethical challenges were those of *consequence* (would the intrusion be worth the result?), *just-ness* (would rights and expectations of individuals in the school be honored?), and *care* (what relationships would develop and what would they mean to the various parties?).

The first activity to engage the schools, the writing of the *Whole School Papers* by a team of school members, both set the tone for future engagement and provided an integral way for us to connect with people at the schools. These papers were to be based on a school-designed self-analysis, and the evaluators were supposed to ensure that this self-analysis occurred in each school, that it involved faculty and staff as well as administration, that it was conducted somewhat systematically, and, finally, that the results of the analysis were incorporated in the papers. This role provided us an opportunity to talk with the school writing team about their goals for the paper and how they could use their learning from the self-analysis to meet those goals. We also facilitated conversations between the authors and other staff members to ensure agreement on how the authors represented the school in the papers.

Our next activity was to review and comment on the professional development experts' initial plans for the study tours. The study tours (a dissemination activity) were meant to offer other schools opportunities to visit the participant schools and learn from witnessing the research findings (best practices) in action. The plan revealed that the professional development experts drew on their expertise and incorporated practical input from the participating schools and the association leadership. In an e-mail to Alice, we commented on the evidence that the experts were developing their plan in conjunction with others in the schools and thus would likely provide a strong foundation for the "replication" process. For example, we highlighted these excerpts from the draft:

- The principals noted that involving (district school) teachers throughout the dissemination process would ensure their investment in the project.

- In addition to ensuring that district school teachers are involved in all steps of the dissemination process, it might be useful to include them in meetings/outreach when initially presenting the project to prospective schools.

- Find out not only what specific district schools want to learn about/change, but what state and district mandates have been given to them.

- Approaching district leadership first will ensure that district leaders are aware of the project and its potential benefits.

Now, having come to know the school people and having seen their early interactions with other players, we felt that access to the five schools was negotiated; indeed, the host schools opened their doors to the research team, the professional development experts, and the filmmaker. As evaluators we contributed to reaching this point through drawing on multiple roles that included convening conversations and facilitating dialogue; lending our expertise to the whole school paper teams regarding case study development; reviewing and commenting on documents; and informal content analyses of work to date.

Challenge 3: Cooperating with the Research Team: Issues of Expertise, Experience, and Representation

The most extensive component of the BTG project was the work conducted by the research team to "identify common elements in the five schools that could be described for the benefit of others wishing to learn from our experience" (from the proposal). Each of the five graduate students would take the lead for one school: they chose an ethnographic approach, spending time on-site to observe actions and interactions; interviewing teachers to capture what these interactions meant to participants; and discovering

BOX 9.2. **Questions We Used to Guide Our Qualitative Inquiry and Actions (Challenge 2)**

- How do various players understand the purposes of the project? How can we facilitate shared understandings of what the work will entail?

- What potential risks as well as benefits are likely to emerge? What do they entail? Are all parties aware of these potential risks and benefits?

- What potential issues of power, authority, and representation are in play?

- Have we established workable ways to monitor promises and expectations from both sides? Do we provide evidence with our feedback? Do we summarize findings, raise relevant questions, and facilitate interpretations?

patterns. The team's findings would serve as a basis for all dissemination and replication activities, so Andy and I felt a strong sense of responsibility for ensuring that the research process was both rigorous and ethical.

The proposal described our charge under Ongoing Evaluation of Outcomes, Goal 2 (Documentation and Research):

1. Evaluate research findings.

2. Evaluator will develop a review panel consisting of innovative school authorizers, innovative school and district school leaders, legislative education staff, and higher education faculty. Researcher will present findings to review panel through oral presentation, as well as print materials (summary of conclusions and spreadsheet). Review panel will provide verbal input and written feedback; specifically, panel members will evaluate the research.

3. Evaluator will summarize verbal feedback, compile written evaluation responses, and share these with researcher and association.

4. Researcher will use input to review and refine research, determine next steps—more research, a change in approach, etc.

We became aware of potential challenges to evaluating the research activity—perhaps playing a broader role than we had planned—when Howell, the professor leading the team of five graduate students, took me aside to say, "I'm really glad you are the evaluator because I'm not really a researcher—don't know a lot about doing this." Shocked, I was unsure of how to deal with the ethical dilemma I felt I faced: the knowledge of the research team's lack of expertise and experience that might cause harm conflicted with promises made by the project to protect the schools. A non-consequentialist moral principle would ask: What is fair and just? A caring perspective would ask: What do the participants need in this relationship? Three of the American Evaluation Association (AEA) *Guiding Principles for Evaluators* mandate that I "adhere to the highest technical standards," ensure that I "provide competent performance to stakeholders," and that I "display honesty and integrity in my behavior" (www.eval.org).

Howell suggested that, given my knowledge of qualitative methods, I could provide his team with an overview. Because I teach, have written about, and have offered workshops on qualitative research, I agreed to meet with the team to do a crash course, but I wondered whether it would be enough. Practically, I did not think such quick coverage of qualitative methods would suffice, but I felt I had no choice but to work with them because their contract was established in accordance with the specifications of the granting agency. My decision was driven by a hope to meet the needs of the graduate student research team (ethic of care) and by our charge to evaluate the research process and product quality (consequentialist moral principles). Still, I wondered, what implications might arise from my adding *methods instructor* to my role?

Evaluators are often "asked" (in various ways) to take on unanticipated and additional roles. Sometimes these roles either complement or replace a designated role. Other times, they become a burden, demanding more than resources allow. In the worst cases, they may contradict what was promised. The request to help the research team get off to an informed start seemed doable and even complementary to our role as critical friend. I even felt that Howell's remark underestimated his knowledge and skills in research. In retrospect, I wonder whether providing an inadequate crash course contributed in some way to later research team actions that may have been interpreted as harmful or burdensome to the school personnel.

We set a date for me to review the basics of qualitative ethnographic research with the research team. We discussed the need for a solid conceptual framework to guide data collection and analyses. We considered what rigor and ethics might mean in this study. We talked about establishing a trustworthy and caring relationship with the school people, especially because they were generous to open their doors and give their time to the researchers. One of the students had experience doing qualitative research; another had previously worked in one of the schools. They all expressed confidence in their ability to conduct the research. Off they went to collect their data; however, I remained concerned that they were unaware that qualitative research often seems simpler in theory than it is in practice. I was left to monitor their research practice.

We turned our attention to assembling and facilitating an expert review panel, which I hoped would offer additional eyes in evaluating the research process and findings. The panel was convened in January of the second year, after the preliminary research report was completed. The review panel comprised local and regional practitioners termed "experts": three leaders of innovative schools not in the study, two public school principals, three education faculty members, and the innovative school director in the state's department of education. No national experts were able to attend (one sent his comments to the preliminary report). As requested, the research team presented the themes that emerged from their preliminary analyses: organizational practices (what); organizational assumptions (why); human side of the organization (who). The expert reviewers reacted, focusing on how these themes would be represented in the book. Their recommendations included the following:

- Clarify that members of the audience are practitioners and write for them

- Present the book as a best-practices "menu" for practitioners

- Describe specific practices with sufficient detail so the reader can "see" the practice

- Be careful not to oversell the differences between the innovative and district situations ("best practices are still best practices")

The exchange between the expert panel and research team revealed significant tensions grounded in cultural differences between the two groups. One panelist said: "I want to know what exactly CIT Prep is doing around their Saturday School model. Connect the conceptual and operational." Howell responded, "But that is not doing research." He reminded the panel that while they were experts on practice, he and his team were the experts on research. A few panelists noted that, because the team was from a university, Howell would have the last word on what constituted research. In my notes on the meeting, I wondered about Howell's rapid acquisition of expertise, given his confession several months earlier that he was not a researcher and knew little about research.

During the presentation and discussion, other panelists expressed additional concerns. Several questioned how any conclusions could be drawn after "only twenty-two days spent across all [five] schools?" Others wondered why students' input was minimal; students had not been surveyed, and, according to one of the researchers, "We did each shadow a student but have not done any formal interviews with students." One panelist said, "I need a chapter on instruction practices—curriculum, instruction, and assessment. Then I can think about how to support teachers in classrooms." Howell replied: "We have a lot on assessment, alignment, not on instructional practice." Another panelist responded, "Don't try to talk about what you don't know. If you don't have it, you don't have it." Howell noted that a focus on instruction was "beyond their charge."

Andy and I summarized the panel discussion, noting themes, questions, recommendations, and concerns. We also reiterated the purpose of the book. We forwarded this summary, along with a transcript of the panel discussion, to all who had attended—researchers and panelists—asking for a check on our interpretations of what had transpired. Our goal was transparency and agreement on representation. All agreed that the summary accurately represented all viewpoints expressed. Revealing his acceptance of my summary, Howell e-mailed me:

> Hi there, Thanks so much for sending along the summary and that set of notes from the review. We are going over them now and hope on Monday to get fairly well squared away on the format for the book. Thanks for all of your suggestions and help. When I know more I'll be in touch.

Drawing on the panel discussion and the results of a survey we conducted to collect reactions from the school personnel to the research team's preliminary research report, I met with Howell to review his plans for the book—a case study of each school with a cross-case analysis chapter. We also discussed possible publishers and dissemination. I encouraged him to choose a publisher who would not determine what was important to emphasize; as the evaluator, my effort was to ensure that the book represented actual events and activities occurring in the schools, not what a publisher thought would be marketable. Shortly thereafter, we (Alice, Andy, and I) received Howell's revised outline and a possible publisher. I e-mailed Alice:

> My thinking in response to the direction Howell seems to be taking with the book is: Whose book is this? The review panel clearly called for a practitioner-oriented book. Howell appears to be heading in a somewhat different direction (for example, it raises issues that are not illuminated by the data collected or necessarily integral to the original conceptual framework for the book). You may find [you need to confront Howell] . . . because you hold the grant and the responsibility to see that your purposes are met. I'm hoping that in our critical friend evaluator role, we can help facilitate a product that will meet the needs of both the association and Howell. You have a lot of good material in Howell's work—now the challenge is to get it out in a form that will be useful for practitioners. I look forward to the meeting with all of us (Andy, you, me, and Howell).
>   Sharon

Alice e-mailed Howell:

This project has a central focus on producing practical products. At the vetting, we consistently heard "let the reader see a practice," "how is this operationalized?" etc. Your reaction at one point ("that isn't research") worried me, as did the shift you mentioned regarding publishers being considered, and to a lesser degree your response to photographs. I think the feedback at the vetting was fairly consistent, and now I need to follow through—how is that feedback being incorporated into the next steps, into the production of the book?

Alice

Howell responded to these concerns by assuring us that "We will produce a book that you are proud of."

We waited in anticipation for the book draft, which, according to the original agreement, was to be reviewed by Norman, Alice, Andy, and myself. The original agreement also stipulated that the association, the evaluators, and the researcher were to collaborate on book goals, editing, and design. In March, before the drafts could be vetted, the graduate students uploaded papers that were versions of their draft case studies on a website for an annual conference of their professional association. One of the schools discovered that the papers had "gone public" and was very upset. Alice asked Howell to have the papers removed, which was done.

The damage, however, had begun. School people had read the material on the web and were troubled by what they read. During the next month, full drafts of the case studies were sent out; because of earlier concerns, Norman forwarded each on to its school. The director of Connection e-mailed her reaction:

> The proposal to DOE describes the process of selecting schools in urban areas who are successful in standardized testing, that success being the basis of selection for the project. We were told during the whole paper/school survey phase to look at the challenges faced by our students and at methods we employed to meet those challenges in order to close the achievement gap. Other schools, we were told, would do the same and researchers would be selected to "identify common elements in the five schools that could be described for the benefit of others wishing to learn from our experience." Based on this understanding, then, we instructed our staff and faculty to speak with researchers about how we addressed the goal of academic success for each student.
>
> We asked them to focus on how we diagnosed learning needs and then developed methods to address those needs in an effort to close the gap. This is what was expected by the association and the DOE.
>
> So what happened? [In the case study], we are described as focusing on children's deficits and somehow not respecting their

cultural heritages. Our entire community, especially our parents, is most concerned about the conclusions drawn by the researchers. We do not agree with the opinions related to our respect for the whole child. I hope you understand our concerns. TC

Alice's e-mail to Andy and me shortly thereafter seems to recognize the relational issues and what it means to produce *findings*:

> If you read the EQUAL paper, you will also find some very poorly written material, and there are some worrisome places in the Horizon paper too (but definitely fewer and less worrisome; the director is replying to those). I'm glad the other two papers are in very good shape—COL and CIT Prep—though after all this with Connection, I think I'll re-review all chapters. As David at CIT Prep put it, they and their researcher were a good match; that probably goes a long way toward making this chapter business work.

What followed was a spring and summer of often vitriolic exchanges regarding the tone and content of the case studies and the cross-case analyses that came after. As independent evaluators who had been seen as critical friends to all parties, not members of either group, we became mediators and negotiators, facilitating a co-construction of the work.

Challenge 4: Finding Balance between Perspectives: Participants' Voice or Researchers' Truth?

Two cultures at odds—*public school* versus *academic research*—had faced off. The question centered on which culture would prevail in the book: What message would be sent about the schools? How would they be represented in the images and words presented in the text? As discussed earlier, Ellis's (1986) judgments of the *Fisher Folk* were based on her worldview, which represented their culture as deficient, that is, lacking social mechanisms she saw as requisite to prospering according to western modern criteria. In the case of BTG, the judgments of the university researchers critiqued aspects of the innovative schools based on their own academic values (e.g., publishing, being recognized as experts in their field, claims of truth), not the values that drove schools' operation. What fed the conflict was the perception that the researchers' judgments were unbalanced and were over-interpretations of the data.

BOX 9.3. **Questions We Used to Guide Our Qualitative Inquiry and Actions (Challenge 3)**

- How is our role developing? Do our actions support *justice*, *beneficence*, and *respect*?

- Do we provide evidence with our feedback? Do we summarize findings, raise relevant questions, and facilitate interpretations?

- What expertise is needed? Did we appropriately facilitate the provision of expertise via the panel? What else might be needed?

- Have we established and promulgated criteria we will use to judge merit and worth of project activities and products? Do all parties understand and agree on these criteria?

- What evaluation tools are proving useful?

- Are our activity reviews/summaries revealing evaluator perceptions of activities, events, and products? What evidence do we have that these summaries are useful? What purposes are they serving?

- Whose voices are represented in project products? What voices are absent? Should more voices be included?

- What conflicting perspectives and moral stances may be in play in the project activities? What impact do conflicts have on *justice*, *beneficence*, and *respect*?

One side, the researchers, laid a claim for scientific rigor that can discover the "truth" of a situation. The research team posited that their perspective was "objective" and thus provided the true, accurate representation. (As a qualitative evaluator, I note that qualitative ethnographers do not claim to be objective, nor do they seek a single truth—we analytically describe and interpret events and interactions and make explicit our subjective perspectives.) On the other side were the schools and the association, which claimed the researchers had exceeded the scope of the project as defined in both the proposal and the contract—and as had been explained to the schools when they gave their consent. In the United States, any institution that receives federal funds must have a review board to protect human subjects from harm or other violations of their individual rights. These institutional review boards (IRBs) require that research participants give their voluntary and informed consent. This consent must document that the participant ("subject") fully understands the nature, purpose, and potential uses of the research; privacy and confidentiality are assured; participation will not adversely affect the rights and welfare of the individual; and participants may withdraw at any point without any negative consequence to themselves. (This agreement was what the opening e-mail referenced in asking to pull out.) Given the explanation by the association of the project purposes and goals, the schools expected that their voices would be heard, that the story told would be one they recognized as theirs, not one they felt was imposed on them.

The actual conflict was more complicated than the school and association personnel believing that the researchers had over-represented what had happened at the schools. They also questioned how it could have been possible for the researchers to represent the voice of the school with so little contact, thus challenging the research methods and rigor:

> These assumptions [about our schools] are presented as based on many weeks of research in these schools. We don't agree with that. We know they were not in schools that much. We need to have a clear statement of how many classes were seen, how many hours, and over what period of time. The researchers need to make it clear that they just saw a snapshot. (LT at COL)

The researchers' representation of one school's use of English as the dominant language illustrates this conflict of perspectives. The following paragraph concluded a section of one case study:

> It is important to note that these administrators' framing of their students' backgrounds causes them to focus on deficits, rather than assets. While such an intense focus on student weakness may be, to some degree, inevitable in the standards and accountability era—and while this orientation does allow for instructional

goal-setting, concentrating on a child's perceived deficits could inhibit a full understanding of a whole child—an understanding that honors the many facets of a child's identity and worth, and not just those skills that are easily measured and valued by the current testing educational system. Indeed, Connection navigates what can appear to be a cultural trade-off for some students: Standard English skills for the language spoken at home or within the home country. While the school does have cultural nights and students do receive some Spanish lessons, English instruction is, without a doubt, the focus of the staff's instructional energies, especially for students within the lower grades. Such a trade-off raises questions, questions confronting any school drawing upon a diverse student body: What are the costs of replacing the language of home with the language of school? Does the notion of "compensatory education" suggest that students must give up something worthy and valuable about their own backgrounds? (Draft of Connection chapter)

Teachers and leaders at Connection were deeply offended. They protested that the chapter did not present the whole picture. They were complying with the state's English-first policy; indeed, parents had chosen the school because of its emphasis on English. Furthermore, they argued that topics such as "costs of replacing the language of home with the language of school" were not even in the purview of the research project. In an e-mail exchange, they remarked that this section read like a "typical academic treatise." Andy and I worked closely with Howell and the graduate students to modify this and other offending sections; all agreed that the resulting modifications compromised neither the integrity of the school nor of the research.

Another illustration of conflict is the representation of cognitive demand that appeared in the chapter with the cross-case analyses. One section emphasized the low cognitive demand of the instruction and the schools' focus on the state's high stakes test (passing was required for graduation). A leader in one school reacted as follows:

Wow—This is TERRIBLE. It reads like an indictment—it seems very one-sided, meaning only negative and not balanced at all. I'm not just over sensitive here—increasing the rigor of our instruction is a constant goal and conversation for us—but the examples and analysis in this chapter doesn't accurately represent the work that goes on at Horizon. It's also completely inaccurate that we are solely focused on the [state tests] and use that as our main reference point in classrooms or at the leadership level. . . The tone of the chapter is also condescending, particularly with regard to the SAT, as if we train our kids like dogs for the state test and can't do that for the SAT because it requires too much higher-order thinking for us (perhaps she should compare SAT data disaggregated by race or first-generation college [students] as a more accurate comparison. . . there's a lot more going on in our kids' scores than [what she describes] as "low level" instruction). The conclusion over-reaches and seems biased. Seems to essentially say that the [state standardized test] is pathetic and it's the only measure by which any of our schools have had success (not true). (PJ at Horizon)

Whereas we understood the concerns expressed by the school and association staff, the research team was also a stakeholder group with which the association had entered into a contract. As our relationship with Howell was positive, he sent me this e-mail:

> Sharon, This brings into question the integrity of our work. I can't agree to withhold information that is part of why these schools are successful (even if it is not complementary [sic])

In reaction to the cross-case analysis chapter, one of the schools asked to withdraw from the study, a move that would remove their data from the book. Howell contacted his university's lawyers, claiming "breach of confidentiality" on the part of the association in sharing the case studies with the schools, although the researchers themselves had been the first to make the papers public on the aforementioned website. Again, Howell e-mailed me:

> Norman's sharing our drafts with the schools was unauthorized and completely compromises my commitment to my IRB to only share documents about the project where I said I would. Furthermore he has, by sharing these DRAFTS essentially trashed my reputation with these schools and with others in the metropolitan area. Can you imagine someone taking your first draft and sending it to your subjects without permission?? Imagine how you would feel, what it would do to your ability to work with those people in the future and your reputation. Does it make you shudder?? If not, it should in my humble opinion. I intend to make sure the Program Officer knows full well of this terrible indiscretion.

Good luck on reporting about this mess created by Norman in your overall evaluation. I have every intention of making it well known in Washington funding circles including the DOE, as well as with [others in the innovative school community] and all of the other grantees supported by this initiative from the DOE. It will already have been heard of in DC and in innovative school circles by the time your report arrives.

I was surprised by Howell's stance. After careful consideration, I sent him this e-mail on the following day:

Howell,

Let me start by repeating that the work of you and your team is quite well done. But that is why I am so surprised and concerned with your reaction—concerned because it runs counter to procedures and ethics of conducting solid qualitative research that honors the idiosyncratic and contextual nature of human experience and allows complex and dynamic interpretations of that experience. The issue is not about academic freedom—it is about rigorous and systematically conducted research and producing valid results.

You ask me to imagine how I would feel were someone to share my drafts with my "subjects." My response is that I do not have to imagine—I always share my drafts with my participants (qualitative researchers generally do not call the people in their studies *subjects*) as a validity check. The process is referred to as member checks—not so that members can change the results but so that the researcher can ensure that her interpretations are ones others share. While qualitative research embraces subjectivity (individual perspectives and interpretations), Michael Scriven (in his classic Philosophical Inquiry Methods in Education for AERA, 1988, and his Thesaurus, 1991) acknowledges a form of objectivity can be approached when multiple perspectives are integrated to fully describe the phenomena—thus the need for member checks to ensure validity and a trustworthy study (see the classic text by Lincoln and Guba, 1985, or Rossman and Rallis, 2003). Without integrating the schools' perspectives, your interpretation is as subjective as theirs.

The issue is also ethical. The IRB exists to protect the participants/subjects, not the researcher. Qualitative researchers deeply respect the voices of their participants and acknowledge that the process is as important as the outcome (re: John Rawls means must equal ends). Ethically conducted research is transparent—that is, everyone sees clearly how you arrived at your conclusions and accepts your process—not necessarily your conclusions, but the process must be transparent. Thus, sharing drafts with participants is de rigueur.

Yes, this takes time. Often unbelievable amounts of time. In fact, I recently finished a chapter for The Sage International Handbook of Educational Evaluation—the chapter is based on the work of the Connecticut Superintendents Network (the one Dick Elmore has been facilitating), and I must have run 5 or 6 different drafts by them, making many changes—both minor and major—never changing the findings but the way in which I represented them. The final result is one that they and I are deeply pleased with. And we did have a deadline but the publishers felt it was critical that the chapter offer a trustworthy representation of what actually happened in the network.

I repeat that in general you and the team have used systematic and ethical inquiry appropriate for the purposes of this study. Sharing drafts with participants should be a part of that systematic inquiry.

Sharon

While I received no direct response from Howell, the situation appeared to settle. We heard no further threats, and some revisions softened the offensive sections. Our quarterly report described the situation (Table 9.1).

Table 9.1 Quarterly Report to Funding Agency

Dates/Timeframe	Tasks/progress this quarter	Problems encountered?
Jul—Aug	Research Team work: reading and compiling joint group-association suggested edits on book chapters; phone meetings and frequent e-mail exchanges with lead researcher and her team; attempting to help negotiate different perspectives of research leader and association team	Monitoring researcher's adherence to project goals has consumed an extraordinary amount of effort and time. Lead researcher has held to an inappropriate conception of the researcher's role that is at odds with the goals of the project. The research approach has led several project participants to threaten to pull out of the project. We are concerned that this may threaten the usability of a key project deliverable—the book—but we don't know for certain as we have not seen the "final" draft to date. Further comments attached below.

BOX 9.4. **Questions We Used to Guide Our Qualitative Inquiry and Actions (Challenge 4)**

- What effects do our actions and words as evaluators have on project activities?

- What is the nature of our interactions with the various players? What moral principles guided our actions?

- How can our actions and words as evaluators facilitate dialogue across different groups? How can my practice support *justice, beneficence,* and *respect*?

- Are we using knowledge and expertise appropriately? At what points, or when, should we intervene—or should we simply report activity?

The situation was further complicated because the publisher wanted a book that raised "controversial issues," so few further changes were made. As I wrote in an October e-mail to Norman and Alice:

> As Andy put it, about 90% is good (maybe only 80%), but the front and the back (what people read when deciding whether to read more) is certainly not what you contracted for. As it appears that we are not likely to get any additional revisions from Howell, the best approach might be to ensure that potential audiences/readers hear the innovative school perspective.

The book went to press with what the schools and association felt to be unsupported judgments. The association chose to back off but to publish their own review of the book.

Challenge 5: Supporting the Filmmaking and Professional Development: Reciprocal Relationships with Other Players

Meanwhile, other components of the BTG project were moving along. The filmmaker was busy taping and editing. The professional development agency was planning and conducting the study tours. These activities differed both procedurally and substantively from the research component in that those contracted built interactive and positive relationships with the school people so that the schools felt ownership of the content in both these products (film and tours).

For both components, our role was to review and facilitate review by others and to collect data to provide feedback on participants' reactions. The filmmaker, who had no training in qualitative research methods, demonstrated a near ideal qualitative research process—filming segments and editing was an interactive data collection and analysis process using collaborative question-framing, coding, theme identification, and member checking. Working with Alice, we scheduled and facilitated viewing and review sessions to provide opportunity for representatives from various stakeholder groups to offer immediate and face-to-face feedback to the filmmaker. Through open-ended surveys, we collected brief answers, which we grouped by theme and shared with the filmmaker. Even deciding on the title became a collaborative and iterative process; judging by the e-mail exchanges and time to decision, everyone had an opinion, and all opinions were heard. Thus, no ethical challenges surfaced, because the process was truly transparent and participatory, and any concern was addressed immediately and collaboratively. The process was considered to be mutually beneficial, and the resulting film was seen as a joint effort. At the premier of the final film, leaders from the school remarked on how much they had learned about themselves because of their involvement in the filming and reviewing process. One critique remained: The length of the film was too long.

Design and implementation of the study tours followed a similar process. Again, the professional development experts who had been contracted created multiple avenues during planning and piloting for participants from the five study schools to give feedback. The process resulted in various modifications to the design that contributed to what were ultimately perceived by all as successful study tours. We collected evaluation data through various channels: surveys with rating scales; interviews with open-ended questions; web forums; focus groups; feedback loops for member checks; debriefs and conference calls with the coordinator and tour planners. The following quote was

BOX 9.5. **Questions We Used to Guide Our Qualitative Inquiry and Actions (Challenge 5)**

■ What has been the nature of our interactions in these settings? Do we provide evidence with our feedback? Do we summarize findings, raise relevant questions, and facilitate interpretations?

■ How does our role differ in the various contexts?

■ What evaluation tools best serve our efforts?

in answer to the question: *What worked well?*: "The up-front involvement of Host Schools, based on info and research—Rose and Linda asked them: 'What are you interested in presenting?' They were invested" (study-tour debrief conference call). Our evaluation summary to the association for this phase of the project was positive, emphasizing the evidence that all participants were involved and felt their voices were heard.

CONCLUSION

What makes this case both challenging and interesting is that the evaluators needed to consider ethical practice at two levels—our own and the researchers'—and the interactions between both. What moral principles were practiced? Were principles of respect, beneficence, and justice followed? Could relationships be defined as caring and reciprocal? Can the results of both the research and the evaluation be considered trustworthy? How were both care and benefits balanced with burden?

Regarding the research, the questions at first appear straightforward: In what ways did the research harm or care for participants? How did the research benefit the participants? Were individual or group rights respected and protected? What consequences resulted? Evidence indicated that the research process did indeed burden the school participants in their daily work and threatened harm. Moreover, the research team was not qualified to conduct a qualitative study; they were inexperienced and untrained; for example, as we noted in communications, descriptions were thin, and they referred to participants as "subjects". Not understanding the principles underlying qualitative research practices, the team reverted to and applied what they did know, that is, externally-generated or objectivist procedures and reasoning. Any researcher (but especially one using qualitative methods, because of the close, face-to-face interactions with participants) *will* encounter ethical issues; thus, competence in conducting research depends on adhering to agreed-on moral principles. This team's lack of skill in handling technical and procedural methods and in failing to articulate their own moral principles limited their ability to deal with ensuing ethical encounters. Put simply, technical or procedural incompetence can easily lead to ethical incompetence. The study and its results were compromised in that the product did not faithfully represent participants' actions, experiences, and intents. Although participants remained open to benefits from the research, they did express feeling both harm and burden.

Given the questionable benefit and care from researchers' interactions with the participants, we needed to question our actions along with the actions of the researchers. Because as evaluators we assumed a more etic perspective (that of a self-conscious outsider and supported by data through one of the five senses), we saw that participants carried a burden that was not seen as balanced with benefit, and we witnessed instances of harm and disrespect. In what ways did our actions facilitate or mitigate the situation? What actions did we, as evaluators, take to support or inhibit the harm–care balance or to facilitate respectful and ethical interactions? Also, the project was funded with federal money, so we questioned whether we met our responsibility to public interests and values; the AEA *Guiding Principles for Evaluators* remind us to go beyond analysis of particular stakeholder interests to consider the welfare of society as a whole.

Regarding our practices, we asked: Did our actions serve to prevent harm to participants? Did our relationships enact care and respect? Did our efforts support fairness and reciprocity, consistently ensuring that those who bore the burden of our evaluation activities also benefited? Did our decisions serve to protect or enhance the public good? Given the politics of the evaluation setting and the federal demands, could we have acted differently?

While our answers to each of these questions are not all we had hoped for, we do believe we were respectful and fair in all of our interactions.

Throughout the evaluation, we sought to act reflexively; that is, we continually examined how we were making sense of how others were making sense of their worlds (see Rossman & Rallis, 2003), recognizing that all of us—researchers, participants, and evaluators—were morally interdependent, engaged in ongoing and changing interactions that were guided by our respective ethical principles. Caring about the participants and the relationships drove many of our decisions and actions. We believe we practiced caring reflexivity.

We found ourselves taking on several roles that emerged over the course of the BTG project; at various times, we acted as: critical friend; advocate and protector; facilitator of co-construction/negotiator; coach, educator, and technical assistance provider; and ethical interpreter. We believe that acting in each of these roles served us in conducting an ethical evaluation using predominately qualitative methods—and contributed, to some extent,[3] to safeguarding respect for persons, beneficence, and justice, the "de facto Kantian" principles of justice and fairness that are meant to guide ethical deliberations of IRBs (Hemmings, 2006). That these roles were recognized and accepted was confirmed when at the final yearly gathering of the DOE grantees in Washington, DC, Alice (project coordinator) introduced us as her "critical friends. They have helped us define and re-define our work."

Andy's and my actions as evaluators can be judged according to AEA guiding principles. Certainly, our data collection and analyses adhered to *high technical standards* for qualitative methods, exploring with the client (the association) as well as the other participants the best evaluation approaches and methods to offer sufficient detail for them to understand, interpret, and critique their work. Our *performance was competent*, drawing on our long experience and training in evaluation. We continually reflected on and modified our approaches and methods. We held important the *integrity/honesty principle*: we negotiated; we disclosed; we recorded and reported; we revealed our interests; we represented accurately our procedures; and we worked to resolve the multiple conflicts (both related to any potential misunderstandings of our work and related to the research). Our overriding concern was to *respect the security, dignity, and self-worth of all participants*—including the researchers; we advocated for and provided a forum for the less powerful voices. Finally, we were guided by the project's purpose of replication and dissemination for the overall improvement of public education—another AEA guiding principle (*responsibility for general and public welfare*).

In our work with the researchers, we were, I believe, directed by non-consequentialist moral principles: our concerns focused on the experience of the participants—were the *means* respectful, caring, and beneficial? We gathered data on the process from multiple sources and continuously checked to ensure that our reading of the data was (and was perceived to be) grounded in thick descriptions. Our feedback, summaries, and questions aimed to encourage dialogic exchanges across perspectives. Our emphasis on the process provided multiple moral challenges.

In the end, the final products—book, film, study-tours— were what mattered most, so the *consequentialist* principles provide a more useful analysis. The book was published, and nearly all stakeholders agreed that the case studies told important stories of successful innovative schools. We had negotiated and brokered an acceptable understanding between researchers and program: data were revisited and some changes were made, but the final cross-case analyses chapters still represented interpretations from the particular perspective and values of the researchers and were based on what we regarded as "thin" data. Many still believed that the book exceeded the scope of the researchers' contract with the association and their agreements with the schools. Drawing on evaluation data, the association, in agreement with the schools, wrote a widely disseminated review that highlighted what they viewed as positive aspects of the book and raised questions and offered counterarguments to perceived negative aspects. The review ended with the following paragraphs:

> It is, however, the final chapter with which we, and the five schools studied, take most issue. Again, it begins well, with useful summary material. But the focus changes to a consideration and critique of standardized testing, which we feel is outside the scope of the book and might have more to say about the researcher's perspective than about the schools themselves. In addition, the author asks whether

government should support schools that focus on college success, a question we find startling, given the realities of the global economy and the high level of skills and education it requires. Finally, the last few pages of the text move into a philosophical consideration of "what should matter" in education. The implication here is that the schools are too narrowly focused on tests and standards, rather than the more "profound" goals of education. We'd argue that preparing low-income, urban students for college is profound, in fact critical, and each school's unwavering commitment to continuous improvement helps them determine and regularly evaluate "what matters."

With these caveats, [the book] is a very useful piece of research and writing. It gives us a window into five high-performing urban innovative schools, describes how they operate, and demystifies the process of closing the achievement gap. The results these schools have achieved—first generation college attendance, entrance into highly competitive high schools, laudable performance on assessments, safe and productive school environments—are impressive, and they offer hope to anyone concerned about improving education for our neediest students. (ASSOCIATION)

Ultimately, the schools were satisfied but harbored a sour feeling for academic researchers, as evidenced by their failure to invite Howell to the final gala, which was in all other ways a joyous celebration. More importantly, the other components, the film and the study tours, were seen as representing balanced views of the schools and their work as well as fulfilling the goals and scope of the project. Borrowing from the consequentialist perspective, I would be tempted to suggest that all's well that ends well. However, a fairness or caring perspective presents a different picture. As one school leader questioned after reading the final version of the book: "*Whose story is this anyway?* That is NOT what's happening at Horizon!" The question of whose story is told is one any ethical qualitative evaluator should ask.

ACKNOWLEDGMENTS

I am grateful to Andy Churchill, my evaluation teammate, for the hours of conversation and caring reflexivity we shared during the evaluation and for the insights he offered as I wrote. I also appreciate the association project coordinator, who accepted us, the evaluators, as her critical friends. Also helpful were the comments that Gary Ciarczak, Soria E. Colomer, and Edith Stevens offered during a roundtable discussion on evaluator as critical friend at the 2009 American Evaluation Association Annual Conference.

KEY CONCEPTS

Beneficence

Caring reflexivity

Coding

Consequentialist ethical theory

Critical friend

Culture

Ethic of care

Ethic of individual rights and responsibilities

Ethic of justice

Etic perspective

Feedback loops

Guiding principles for evaluators

Member checking

Non-consequentialist ethical theory

Objectivist

Quasi-ethnographic study

Reflexive reasoning

DISCUSSION QUESTIONS

1. This chapter offers an example of how evaluators encounter surprises. Evaluators can choose the evaluations they agree to conduct; however, once they have agreed to conduct the evaluation, evaluators are obligated to work with all of the stakeholders associated with the program. It is not uncommon to encounter one or more people involved in the evaluation who do not live up to the expectations or standards the evaluators hold. Discuss some strategies for ensuring that the evaluation is of the highest quality, even when one or more players fall short of the evaluator's expectations or standards.

2. The author indicates that she had needed to negotiate—and renegotiate—the scope and details of the evaluation. The

renegotiation of the evaluation resulted in a "structural" overlap between the research and the evaluation.

    a. What might be an advantage of this overlap?

    b. Given the problems that resulted, in hindsight, how might the overlap have been structured to prevent these issues?

3.   One could assume that the conflict between the school leaders and the researchers would have occurred regardless of the specific role the evaluators played. Would adhering to the original evaluation strategy have helped or hurt the final outcome of the project? Please consider all three elements of the project (research-based book, film, and professional development/study tours), as well as the overall project.

4.   Was it ethical to provide a brief training to the research team? Please justify your answer. What other alternatives might the evaluator have considered?

NOTES

1. Names of persons, institutions, and locations have been changed; pseudonyms are used in all cases except for my own name and that of my co-evaluator.
2. All e-mails reproduced here, whether directed to a specific individual or a group, were copied to at least one other person. None was a private communication.
3. Although we assert that in many aspects the research did not honor these hallmarks, we ensured that the issues were raised openly, and ultimately the offending sections were removed from the book.

REFERENCES

American Evaluation Association. (2004). *Guiding principles for evaluators.* Available at http://www.eval.org/Publications/GuidingPrinciples .asp

Ellis, C. (1986). *Fisher folk: Two communities on Chesapeake Bay.* Lexington, KY: University Press of Kentucky.

Foucault, M. (1970). *Discipline and punish: The birth of the prison.* New York, NY: Vintage Books.

Guillemin, M., & Gillam, L. (2004). Ethics, reflexivity, and "ethically important moments" in research. *Qualitative Inquiry, 10,* 261–280.

Hemmings, A. (2006). Great ethical divides: Bridging the gap between institutional review boards and researchers. *Educational Researcher, 35,* 12–18.

House, E. R., & Howe, K. R. (1999). *Values in evaluation and social research.* Thousand Oaks, CA: Sage.

Kant, I. (1788/1956). *Critique of practical reason* (J. W. Beck, Trans.). New York, NY: Liberal Arts Press. (Original work published 1788.)

MacIntyre, A. (1981). *After virtue.* Notre Dame, IN: University of Notre Dame Press.

Noddings, N. (1984). *Caring: A feminine approach to ethics and moral education.* Berkeley, CA: University of California Press.

Noddings, N. (1995). *Philosophy of education.* Boulder, CO: Westview.

Rallis, S. F., & Rossman, G. B. (2000). Dialogue for learning: Evaluator as critical friend. In R. Hopson & M. Q. Patton (Eds.), *How and why language matters in evaluation: New Directions for Evaluation* (Vol. 86). San Francisco, CA: Jossey-Bass.

Rallis, S. F., & Rossman, G. B. (2001). Communicating quality and qualities: The role of the evaluator as critical friend. In A. P. Benson, D. M. Hinn, & C. Lloyd (Eds.), *Visions of quality: How evaluators define, understand, and represent program quality* (pp. 107–120). Oxford, UK: JAI Press.

Rallis, S. F., & Rossman, G. B. (2010). Caring reflexivity. *International Journal of Qualitative Studies in Education, 23*(4), 495–499.

Rawls, J. (1971). *A theory of justice.* Cambridge, MA: Belmont Press.

Rossman, G. B., & Rallis, S. F. (2003). *Learning in the field: An introduction to qualitative research* (2nd ed.). Thousand Oaks, CA: Sage.

Strike, K. A., Haller, E. J., & Soltis, J. F. (1998). *The ethics of school administration* (2nd ed.). New York, NY: Teachers College Press.

Taylor, C. (1994). The politics of recognition. In A. Gutman (Ed.), *Multiculturalism: Examining the politics of recognition,* (pp. 25–74). Princeton, NJ: Princeton University Press.

Weiss, C. H. (1998). *Evaluation* (2nd ed.). Upper Saddle River, NJ: Prentice Hall.

10

Elements of Quality in Qualitative Evaluation

Leslie Goodyear, Jennifer Jewiss, Janet Usinger, and Eric Barela

Key Ideas

- Quality in qualitative evaluation is grounded in a cyclical and reflective process that is facilitated by the evaluator.

- Five distinct elements need to be present to achieve high-quality qualitative evaluation:

  > The evaluator first must bring a clear sense of personal identity and professional role to the process. It is a matter of understanding who you are, what you know, and what you need to learn.

  > The evaluator needs to engage stakeholders and develop trusting relationships from the outset and throughout the evaluation.

  > High-quality evaluation relies on sound methodology, systematically applied, that is explicitly shared with stakeholders.

  > Conducting quality evaluation can only be accomplished by remaining "true" to the data; in other words, hearing participants as they are, not how the evaluator wants them to be.

  > Skillful facilitation of the process by the evaluator results in learning by all involved.

■ The elements of quality often interact in a relational and iterative fashion. Awareness of these elements, and a focus on developing the skills and agility to ensure that these elements are present, robust, and well-managed, are central to becoming a skilled qualitative evaluator.

This summary chapter serves a few purposes: In addition to allowing us (the editors) to reflect on the process of putting together this volume, it gives us the chance to share with the reader some of our own stories of "practice considerations" that we have discussed while working together to develop this book. Most importantly, we take the opportunity to pull from some of the Part 1 and Part 2 chapters to illustrate what we believe are elements of quality in qualitative evaluation.

Each of the four of us came to the project with different backgrounds, experiences, and perspectives. We have learned a tremendous amount from this project, and we hope that the structure of the book (the two parts: chapters about how qualitative inquiry interacts with different evaluation approaches and theories and chapters that illuminate practices of qualitative evaluators), authors' stories, and our own reflections will set the stage for readers to learn, reflect, and improve their practice as qualitative evaluators. It has been a deeply rewarding journey for us as editors, and we are delighted to broaden the conversation and continue learning along with our readers.

As we reviewed proposals for chapters, many of which were not included in this volume, we readily identified and discussed certain elements that represented quality in evaluation; although in truth, that realization was often more apparent when quality was not in evidence than when it was. We realized quickly that to determine what would be included in this book, we needed to discuss and agree on what constitutes quality in qualitative evaluation. As part of this process, we used the 2010 American Evaluation Association conference and its theme of Evaluation Quality as an opportunity to explore these notions and further our thinking. Judging by the attendance at the session we presented, we realized that the topic of what constitutes quality in qualitative evaluation was one of considerable interest. Thus, we decided to expand on it here, as the concluding chapter in this volume.

When the authors of a chapter included in this volume described evaluations that were methodologically sound and involved open, honest communication in support of mutual learning, we all readily gave the chapter a *thumbs up*. Like Supreme Court Justice Potter Stewart said (about something completely different), "we know it when we see it." When something seemed to be missing, we had lengthy discussions about why the chapter did not appear to represent the same level of quality as others. As we discussed and analyzed the *missing* pieces, we began to more clearly identify what skilled qualitative evaluators do and how they ensure quality in the evaluations they conduct.

Perhaps typical of qualitative evaluators, we brainstormed, discussed, debated, and listed our ideas. We then grouped them into themes for further exploration and refinement. We compared these themes with examples presented in the chapters and coupled them with our own experiences to test our ideas. We concluded that quality in qualitative evaluation is grounded in a cyclical and reflective process that is facilitated by the evaluator. Within this cyclical process, we believe five distinct elements need to be present to achieve high-quality qualitative evaluation:

- The evaluator first must bring a clear sense of personal identity and professional role to the process. It is a matter of understanding who you are, what you know, and what you need to learn.

- The evaluator needs to engage stakeholders and build trusting relationships from the outset and throughout the evaluation.

- High-quality evaluation relies on sound methodology, systematically applied, that is explicitly shared with stakeholders.

- Conducting high-quality evaluation can only be accomplished by remaining "true" to the data; in other words, hearing participants as they are, not how the evaluator wants them to be.

- Skillful facilitation of the process by the evaluator results in learning by all involved.

Figure 10.1 illustrates the cycle and its elements. One way of thinking about this cycle is that the process moves from *me* to *us* to *process* to *what we find* to *what we learn*.

As readers with experience in qualitative inquiry will readily identify, hardly anything in the practice of qualitative evaluation comes about in such a clean and orderly fashion as depicted in this model. Before we dive into what we mean by the particular elements and how we have seen them play out in practice, let us take a moment to reflect on the broader roles and responsibilities of a qualitative evaluator and the contexts in which we work.

Figure 10.1 Cycle of Quality in Qualitative Evaluation

Being a qualitative evaluator is like being a circus performer in a very small circus: One needs to have a variety of skills (juggling, riding a unicycle, acrobatic tumbling, walking a tightrope, telling jokes, and so forth). Often, one is required to perform more than one of these skills at the same time (juggling while riding a unicycle, walking a tightrope while telling jokes) and make the whole thing look easy. Skillful qualitative evaluators and circus performers are multi-taskers, maintaining poise and professionalism at all times, even when knives are flying (actually and figuratively).

The elements of high-quality evaluation we discuss here are not necessarily progressive (one happens after the other) or discrete (an evaluator focuses on one at a time). Like the knives, balls, or flaming torches a juggler keeps in the air while riding a unicycle, these elements are always at play—in the air, so to speak—in a qualitative evaluation. Likewise, the elements of quality often interact with each other in a relational and iterative fashion. Although distinct, the elements of quality cannot be disentangled from each other. Awareness of these elements, and a focus on developing the skills and agility to ensure that these elements are present, robust, and well-managed, are central to becoming a skilled qualitative evaluator. And, like being in a circus, being a qualitative evaluator is fun, dynamic, exciting, and hard (exhausting) work that is rewarding not only for the audience but also for the performer. Now, on to stories and examples that illustrate how we and our chapter authors have juggled, balanced, dodged flying objects—and did it all while smiling (well, at least most of the time). In this next section, each of us shares a story or two about conducting qualitative evaluations, using our examples to illustrate the elements that we think come together to constitute quality.

UNDERSTANDING AND ACKNOWLEDGING PERSONAL IDENTITY

Qualitative inquiry is an inherently intimate process; the evaluator must directly interact with participants to gather information that often reveals personal beliefs and values.

Naturally, relationships are a two-way street. Thus, an effective qualitative evaluator brings a clear understanding of his or her own personal identity and role relative to the evaluative endeavor. As qualitative evaluators, acknowledging our strengths and limitations is key to situating ourselves in the evaluative inquiry. We need to focus on understanding the stakeholders and the context, but at the same time remain aware of our own identity, our role, and its power and challenges. Leslie Goodyear presents an example of an evaluation that challenged her to confront who she was in that particular situation.

Before becoming an evaluator, I worked in human services. First I worked as an early childhood educator (four- and five-year-olds were my specialty); then I worked in HIV/AIDS prevention; and then at a rape crisis center as a fundraiser and crisis counselor. With these experiences, the study that became the center of both my master's thesis and doctoral dissertation came naturally to me. The study was a qualitative, participatory evaluation of an HIV/AIDS prevention program. (Chouinard and Cousins discuss the many ways qualitative inquiry and participatory evaluation are compatible in Chapter 5 of this volume.) This program helped parents to become better at talking with their kids about HIV and AIDS; helping them to become comfortable dispelling the myths around HIV and to learn what is appropriate to discuss at what age level. The program trained some parents to become trainers of other parents (what is commonly called a train-the-trainer model) so that they could gather people in their own communities, organizations, and social groups to learn how to talk with their kids about HIV/AIDS. The program was implemented across New York State, but I worked with the New York City group in particular. My job was to observe the training (as a participant observer) and then follow the five women who attended the training for about six months afterward to learn how their participation affected their perceptions of themselves and their communities and their understanding of HIV/AIDS.

Because all of the women who attended the training were bilingual in Spanish and English, the training was conducted in a mix of both languages. My Spanish was basic, but serviceable; I was definitely not fluent, but could follow some of the conversation. I had to ask for explanations and translations frequently, and the participants and the trainer were patient and gracious about helping me to understand. The women were from different parts of New York City, and although they all spoke Spanish, not all were Latina. The post-training group interviews I conducted were free-flowing conversational updates on what had been happening in their lives, whether they had opportunities to deliver the training in their communities, how they had been thinking about what they learned, how it felt to try out their new skills in conversations with children, and so forth. In one of these interviews, a discussion came up about a specific concept related to sexual relations. (To be honest, I do not remember the term or the concept, just what happened in the discussion and what I learned from the experience.)

After one woman told a story related to this term, the other women all laughed and nodded and talked about how they understood what she meant.

I had a dilemma at that moment: Should I laugh along with them or break the moment and ask what this term meant and risk looking dumb? I opted for the latter. I told the group I didn't understand the term and asked for them to explain. (Mind you, this was asking them to explicitly describe a sexual act, which may have made them uncomfortable.) They looked at each other, laughed, and the woman who brought it up agreed to explain. When she did, the others all looked at her, then each other, and said, "Oh no, that's not what that means!" One interjected to say she thought it meant something else, and another said she thought it meant something different from the first two. They then got in a big discussion about what the term meant, where they grew up, and what neighborhood they were from. It turned out that the meaning of this term differed across cultural groups (Puerto Rican vs. Dominican, for example) and in which New York neighborhood one lived (Washington Heights vs. Lower East Side, for example). We all had a good laugh about how they all thought they were talking about the same thing and that my need to have the Spanish translated helped to clarify what was being discussed.

This was a big moment for me in my data collection and in learning how to be a qualitative evaluator. First, the question and the conversation ensured that I got better, more accurate data. Second, the conversation helped to uncover a very important insight, that although these women all lived in New York City and were bilingual, they had very different cultures and cultural backgrounds that meant that their experiences were not uniform. Third, it helped me to learn that asking a "stupid question" in a data collection situation is a smart thing to do.

Along with the understanding that asking stupid questions can be very smart, I also came to understand the importance of what some in qualitative inquiry call locating or situating oneself in relation to the study and the participants (see Rossman & Rallis, 2003, for more information). What I mean by this is that it might have been easy for me to pretend, or even to come to believe, that I was just another one of the participants in the training, to begin to identify with the study participants in such a way that I was *one of them*. After all, anytime they were participating in the program, I was too. To them, I was just another participant, but one who brought bagels and coffee, turned on a tape recorder, took a lot of notes—and asked stupid questions. However, I was not one of them and I needed to constantly remind myself of that. When I wrote up the results of the study and my master's thesis, I needed to admit to the reader that I was *apart* from this group, that my understanding had limitations.

I did this by explicitly claiming my identity to the participants in that situation, and, since I was describing the study participants' backgrounds in the evaluation report, I described mine as well. For example, in my writing I clarified that I am a white middle class woman raised in South Dakota who speaks a bit of Spanish because of time spent in the Peace Corps. I did not grow up in New York City, and in fact was very new to the city and the cultures there. I had worked as an HIV/AIDS prevention outreach worker and as a youth development worker, so I knew quite a bit about the content they learned in the training, but I knew nothing of the life and cultures of growing up in New York City as "Nuyoricans" or immigrants. In addition, I did not have children, so I also did not know what parenthood was like, nor did I understand first-hand what raising children in a large urban area was like.

These may seem like trivial things to articulate in an evaluation study, and particularly for quantitative researchers, they may seem irrelevant. However, making sense of the experiences of others requires that we identify with them in some way or another, or at least know our own limits with regard to how we might be able to identify with them. Qualitative inquiry demands that we regularly reflect on who we are as people and as researchers so that we might be able to bring those identities forward when appropriate—or hold them back in order to better understand those whose experiences we are trying to document. This is not just harnessing or controlling one's subjectivity. Rather, it is cultivating a level of awareness and reflexivity that allows the qualitative evaluator to probe for better information, gather better data, and carry out better analyses. This is a key element in conducting a quality qualitative evaluation.

BUILDING TRUSTING RELATIONSHIPS

Engaging in an effective evaluation that involves qualitative inquiry without developing and maintaining trusting relationships is inconceivable. Jennifer Jewiss describes how she thinks about and handles her identity as an evaluator of programs about which she has limited content expertise at the outset. Within this context, she describes how she goes about building trusting relationships that set the stage for collaborative work and strong evaluation processes.

As evaluators, many of us are all too familiar with the challenge of explaining what the heck it is we do. My family members and long-time friends readily admit that their grasp on the concept of *an evaluator* is tenuous at best—and this is only exacerbated by the fact that I work with so many different types of programs and organizations. So I should have anticipated that this confusion would come to a head when I began working on several projects with colleagues in my university's medical school. Here is a sense of how things went in a phone conversation with my mother, who has always maintained high standards for intellectual pursuits:

Mom: But you don't know *anything* about medicine!
Me: I know, Mom. And believe me, the medical school faculty members working on
        these projects are really clear about that. My job isn't to know about medicine. It's

to be able to ask the right questions of them so that together we can design the right study. Then, I go interview the doctors, nurses, and office managers involved in these quality improvement projects and ask them how it's going. Right at the beginning of the interview, I explain that I'm not in the medical field—so I'll need help understanding all the acronyms and medical terminology. I get them to walk me through the project—what's working, what's not, and how they'd suggest improving things. The med school faculty and program staff have the medical expertise covered. My job is to be the one who comes in from the outside and asks the questions that prompt them to articulate what they know based on their experience.

I am not confident that this explanation quelled my mother's understandable concern, but at least it offered a different angle for consideration.

A variation on this conversation with my mother plays out in my head each time I prepare to interact with stakeholders affiliated with a new project. I am not alone. Evaluating unfamiliar programs is fairly common; even if there is familiarity with one aspect of a program, parts of the program may be new, as revealed by Norma Martínez-Rubin (Chapter 8 in this volume), who was academically prepared as a health educator but lacked experience as a parent. Because most of the evaluations I am asked to conduct fall in programmatic territory that is new to me, I often find myself thinking, "Hmm, this will be interesting. What the heck do I know about x?" But of course, that is the source of much of the fun and the challenge; I remind myself that my role is not necessarily to know about x—at least not initially. As a qualitative evaluator, overt curiosity and a willingness to dive into unfamiliar territory are two essential assets, along with methodological prowess and an understanding of how to conduct systematic inquiry.

As I discovered back in my graduate school days, sometimes not knowing is the best entry into learning what is really going on. When I was a new graduate student, along with being green, eager, and nervous, I was terribly concerned that I did not know nearly as much as the program stakeholders knew. Initially, playing the grad student card was enormously helpful and comforting. What a magical word: *student*—a card-carrying learner. But then I transitioned into a research faculty role. Another wave of fear arose. Now, I was really supposed to know what I was doing. Gradually, several important connections arose that helped me find my way forward.

Having been trained as a qualitative researcher first, and having learned about evaluation second, I approach the notion of stakeholder engagement through the lens of rapport building. As Corrine Glesne observed, "Rapport is an attribute that is instrumental to a variety of professional relationships, from used-car salesperson to marriage counselor. Its function, however, varies with each relationship. . . In qualitative research, rapport is a distance-reducing, anxiety-quieting, trust-building mechanism . . ." (Glesne, 2006, pp. 109–110). As an evaluator, I consider it my responsibility to orchestrate interactions—some quite spontaneous and informal, others more structured and facilitated—that reduce distance, quiet anxiety (theirs and mine), and build trust. One of the ways I do this is through humor. I often use humor to establish right upfront just how much I need to learn from the study participants and other stakeholders. For instance, I have used the aforementioned conversation with my mother in many other projects (thanks, Mom!) as I entered the setting, introduced myself and my role, and started building relationships with those involved.

As I look back on the first few evaluation projects I conducted many years ago, I am aware that the mind-set and skills of a qualitative researcher are put to good use in navigating the initial interactions that set the tone for the whole evaluation project. The role of interviewer is woven into initial conversations with the *point person* and a small evaluation committee that often works closely with me to shape and shepherd the evaluation process along. Gradually, this core group of stakeholders and I learn a bit more about each other and about each other's worlds relative to the program and the evaluation task at hand. I do not believe I have ever successfully engaged stakeholders without first demonstrating my engagement in understanding who they are and what they are trying to achieve, appreciating their state of affairs. Time is tight, everyone is busy, programs are complex—and let's face it—so are we as individual stakeholders. Needless to say, I do not get all the way there, but I can at least signal my genuine interest. When it works well and relationships are nurtured, a comfort emerges from a shared desire to learn together through the evaluation process. We are aligned around a common interest in the greater good that the program is trying to achieve. The program is still their baby and I am still the evaluator, but we have developed a rapport and identified a shared commitment that extends beyond the boundaries of the program. Most importantly, we have created an explicit commitment to understanding the program as it actually functions and determining how to enhance the program for the benefit of the greater good.

The importance of relationship building is addressed in the theoretical perspectives featured in Part 1 and the cases presented in Part 2 of this volume. In keeping with the iterative nature of the model presented here, recognizing that the work of building trusting relationships does not end when they are "built" is essential. These relationships need care and feeding throughout the evaluation process for evaluations to contribute most effectively to program decision making, improvement, and learning.

REFLECTING ON AND MANAGING RELATIONSHIPS

Interviewing people who participate in social or educational programs parallels certain aspects of counseling. The interviewer needs to make sure that the interviewee feels comfortable enough to share experiences candidly and honestly; the interviewer needs to be able to listen carefully and follow up interesting and unexpected "left turns" in the conversation; the interviewer needs to be nonjudgmental, or at least defer judgment until later, during data analysis; and he or she needs to be able to ask good questions and let the interviewee do nearly all of the talking. Interviewing is a two-way street: Interviewees should also feel good about the discussion after an interview, and in the best of all possible worlds, should feel as though the interview helped them better understand their own experiences in the program. Just as a counselor needs good data to be able to make a diagnosis and develop a plan for treatment, an evaluator needs good data to develop a theory or description of how the program operates or whether it is successful.

This description assumes that the evaluator and the stakeholders or participants share an understanding of the purpose or the significance of the evaluation being conducted. The challenge, of course, is when relationships must be built when there is underlying tension from either the participant or the evaluator. Janet Usinger had the experience of doubting both herself and some of the adolescents who were part of a longitudinal study of the process that adolescents undertake as they socially construct their career aspirations and the role that education plays in that process. The study was part of an evaluation of a State Gaining Early Awareness and Readiness for Undergraduate Programs (GEAR UP) project. GEAR UP is a federally funded project to increase the college-going rate by providing academic and financial support to first-generation college-going students. For this portion of the evaluation, sixty adolescents were interviewed twice a year for six years, from seventh grade through their senior year of high school. The students lived in urban, rural, and isolated remote communities; all communities were economically disadvantaged. The students were broadly represented racially and ethnically. A deliberate effort was made to recruit students who were leaders in their class, students who struggled socially or academically, and "under the radar" students who did not stand out or take center stage for one reason or other. She recounts two situations that greatly informed her practice of qualitative inquiry.

It did not take long, perhaps the second or third interview, to realize that I was experiencing self-doubt and concern about conducting the study. There were two specific concerns: one student just made me mad and another student chronically lied.

You Make Me Mad . . .

Although my feelings fell along a continuum, I liked all of the students in the study. I always looked forward to going out into the field to collect data. In fact, friends and colleagues frequently commented that I was always happy and in a good mood after "visiting my kids." I thoroughly enjoyed learning how they were navigating their lives and dealing with their various trials and tribulations.

Perhaps it was inevitable, but there was one particular exception to my general joy in catching up with the students. During the second interview, I started feeling ill at ease with Bob (pseudonym). My discomfort stemmed from his ability to "push my buttons" in several ways. Fundamentally, I felt that he discounted me as a person. He also took issue with most of the questions I asked, as if he was accusing me of nefarious motives in my inquiry. During some interviews, I felt that he was deliberately baiting me to see my reaction; this was even more unsettling for me.

At one point, I felt vindicated in my negative reaction to Bob. All of the interview audio-tapes were transcribed by two undergraduate student workers. They very rarely commented on the content of the tapes; they just listened to and typed words. Yet both transcribers independently commented about this student. They both stated that they thought that this student was rude and basically a jerk. *Ahhhh, validation of my feelings!*

I increasingly found it difficult to schedule a time to interview him; I found myself avoiding the school that Bob attended. I just did not want to interview him and subject myself to his attitude. I seriously thought about "losing" him; actually, it would have been quite easy. Of the sixty students, ten moved out of state, dropped out of school, or were expelled during the course of the study. I could just decide that Bob moved and take him off my list. Of course, that would have been unethical. After all, I had not written into my IRB application that I could remove someone from the study because I did not like him or her. So much for that idea! I also thought about having someone else interview him. However, this would not be consistent with the value I held in establishing and maintaining trust with the students. I felt stuck, wanting to adhere to principles of an ethical evaluation but feeling uncomfortable with my feelings about Bob.

At the beginning of the third year of the six-year study, as I scheduled visits to schools to conduct fall interviews, I suddenly realized that my thinking about Bob was both ridiculous and unethical. It did not matter if he pushed my buttons or I did not like him; my job was to hear what he was saying and try to understand his perspective. At the point when I started focusing on Bob rather than my own (bruised) feelings, I realized that he was actually one of the most important participants in the study. He represented an extreme case of other students whose approach to life was similar to Bob's; they just were not as good at pushing my buttons.

Grasping this rationally was simple, but I still had to engage with Bob to conduct interviews twice a year for the next four years. I had to mentally prepare myself before subsequent interviews to not react to his statements. In essence, I had to leave my ego at the door. I did this by becoming immensely curious about how someone, so early in his life, could approach the world in such an oppositional manner. Why was this apparent desire to manipulate our interaction so important to Bob?

The result of rethinking my approach to and interaction with Bob was that, very shortly, interviews with him became much deeper. I became intensely curious about every aspect of my interviews with him. I thought about how he might interact with others; was it different from his interaction with me? I also thought more deeply about my reactions during interviews with other students. How did my feelings affect the depth of the probes I used to explore ideas? In effect, I became much more attuned to my role in the interview process.

I never really looked forward to interviewing Bob, as I did other students. I never came to a sense of ease and mutual comfort with him. Nevertheless, beyond learning about my own reactions to an interview, I learned a great deal about his worldview, specifically because I consciously did not confront him. I was always prepared to dig deeper and ask him to elaborate upon his thoughts and ideas, rather than react to them. I also became fascinated in observing him with others. Although I never explicitly sought information about him from others at the school, I frequently overheard conversations with counselors and teachers about him. I came to learn that Bob interacted with almost everyone in the same manner he did with me. At one level, I was happy to learn that I was no more special than anyone else when it came to a relationship with Bob!

Why Do You Keep Telling Me Lies?

My second dilemma in developing rapport with students was that one girl had a tendency of telling fantastic tales. I kept a running story of all of the students. Before each interview, I reviewed transcripts and memos to pick up the conversation where we ended six months before. The running story involved the accomplishments and celebrations in the students' lives, the struggles they were tackling, the development of their interests, and the changes in their families and community. Note that all interviews were conducted from the stance that statements made by the students represented their interpretation of the truth. No attempt was made to verify or validate their statements. The focus was always on how the student represented himself or herself and the student's interpretation of his or her unique world.

I always expected that some of the stories students told me stretched the truth, but Mary (pseudonym) went beyond describing situations that placed her in a positive light; she made up fantastic stories. To give some examples, during the second interview, I opened up with my standard question, "So, how are things going?" She proceeded to tell me in detail about how her mother had just gotten out of the hospital after having given birth to twins. Her mother was unable to take care of these twins; Mary was staying up all night, taking care of the twins. As a result, her grades were suffering and she was just exhausted.

I had no reason to doubt story of the twins, although I had met the mother (to obtain consent for her daughter to be in the study) and had interviewed her. There was no indication of the mother being pregnant, but it was at least six months before hearing the story of the twins from Mary, so maybe she had been early in her pregnancy. However, the story she presented about the twins was never referenced in subsequent interviews. I even conducted one of the interviews at her house; no twins were in sight.

In a later interview, Mary talked about being a contestant on the television program, *American Idol*. Mary lived in Las Vegas, and the idea that *American Idol* auditions were being conducted there was perfectly plausible. But the fact that Mary was selected for an audition was a bit harder to believe; nevertheless, Mary described the audition in great detail, including the band that she met during the audition and their subsequent work to get a recording contract. During almost every interview, Mary had many stories: meeting famous people; working in the recording industry; having been in foster care in the country where she was born; family members who were engaged in illegal activity; how she got to the United States; alcoholic boyfriends; and so forth.

Although I was thoroughly entertained by her stories, I quickly started questioning everything Mary told me. The pattern of creating her own reality became problematic for two reasons: At one point, it was confusing because she told me that her stepfather had died. Because I noted all of the major events in the students' lives, (e.g., deaths of family members, incarceration of family members, divorce, milestones in the adolescent's life), recording her stepfather's death was important; but I was not sure whether it was true. Should it be noted? Should I let it go as I had so many of her other stories? How should that information be treated? Because of the implications (she had not been born in the United States and therefore the death of her [US citizen] stepfather could have profound implications about her legal status), this was the only time I tried to validate a student's statements. The story was true; her stepfather had died.

The second, and more important, problem of her fantastic tales was that I found myself focusing on the stories rather than the factors that might be contributing to her need to portray her life as extremely colorful. Like my interaction with Bob (described earlier), I had to accept Mary's presentation of her life as her own truth; the story details were not necessarily related to the purpose of the evaluation. The study did not seek to explore the veracity of what was actually happening to the students, it was to explore how the students were constructing their career aspirations and the role that education played in the process. Therefore, my job was to try to uncover why telling these entertaining, albeit fantastic, stories was important to Mary.

The significance of redirecting *my* thinking was that Mary's behavior was not unique. Other students created stories to make sense of what was happening to them in their lives; Mary was just doing it at a more extreme level. I realized Mary provided me a wonderful opportunity to explore the concept of creating a vivid and alternative reality in which the adolescent can be the *hero* of his or her own story, which is what Mary was doing beautifully. In each of her stories, she emerged as the person who rescued others or had the solution to intractable situations; she could be the hero to others. As I gained an understanding of Mary's approach to the world, the same pattern, albeit more nuanced, was found in other students. I became very comfortable with how students might be inventing stories about themselves as a means of shaping their thinking about their world.

As with Bob, Mary represented an extreme of a particular tendency. I was very fortunate to have these extremes in the data so I could locate tendencies that were revealed in a more subtle fashion in others. However, to be able to capitalize on both of these situations, I had to redirect my own thinking.

EMPLOYING SOUND AND EXPLICIT METHODOLOGY, AND BEING TRANSPARENT ABOUT IT

There are many ways to conduct evaluations; qualitative inquiry is inherent in some methodological approaches (e.g., participatory evaluation described in Chapter 5), foundational to others (e.g., theory-driven evaluation described in Chapter 4), and a component of mixed methods approaches as described by Grob in Chapter 3. Although we subscribe to Bledsoe's argument (Chapter 4) that credible evidence can only come from methods that are considered viable in the practical setting, the four of us see the question "why?" as a central characteristic of evaluations that incorporate qualitative inquiry. Each of us has had the experience of stakeholders wanting "hard numbers to prove" the importance of a program; however, when all is said and done, the hard numbers seldom answer that pesky "why?" question. Qualitative inquiry sheds light on the nuances of a program and its impact; it can help illuminate some of the thorny issues associated with the complex social problems that many programs are designed to address. Indeed, our experiences indicate that "*hard numbers* people" ultimately want to understand why things are happening in addition to demonstrating the impact of a program.

During our many rich discussions about the intersection of qualitative inquiry and evaluation practice, we have found ourselves focusing on a single word, *inquiry*. One of the definitions Merriam-Webster (Merriam-Webster.com) lists for inquiry is, "a systematic investigation often of a matter of public interest." Because so many of the programs we evaluate are conducted in service of the public good, many program designers and evaluators embrace the "matter of public interest" part of the definition. However, one fundamental tenet of all scientific inquiry, including evaluation—and within that, qualitative evaluation—is that one's work be conducted in a systematic and transparent manner. Conducting inquiry in this fashion leads to trustworthy findings. Employing sound and explicit methodology, transparently, is a key element of high-quality qualitative evaluation.

Eric Barela's entire life as an evaluator has been in service of K–12 education. In that high-stakes setting, transparency and credibility are of paramount importance.

As a proud qualitative evaluator, it is important for me to show that I am conducting a systematic investigation whenever I can in an evaluation. If I cannot show that my work is systematic, independent, and replicable, my work may well not be a matter of public interest. This is why I think about transparency often while I am at work.

An effective qualitative evaluator should attend to transparency during any and all stages of the evaluation. We can be transparent with stakeholders about who we are, our influences, biases, and, as Jennifer alluded, lack of program knowledge during the question formation process. We can be transparent with our participants about the potential uses of the data they so willingly provide. We can be transparent about what we observe in the field. We can be transparent about how we analyze our data. We can be transparent about the story we are telling from the data we gather. The following example illustrates why I feel clarity and openness about what evaluators do and why we do it is important to understanding qualitative inquiry in evaluation practice.

This example comes from my previous work as an internal school district evaluator. In that role, I evaluated a variety of programs and initiatives, from charter school renewals to instructional strategies in high-achieving, high-minority, high-poverty schools. One of my evaluations was of school-level use of Title I[1] funds. The school district's director of Title I Fund Distribution and Monitoring (not a real title) wanted me to focus on budgetary practices in two types of schools: those that were achieving academic Adequate Yearly Progress[2] (AYP) and those that were not. What I discovered was that the two types of schools allocated their Title I funds in different ways. I examined the demographic characteristics of each type of school to see whether that helped to explain their different budgeting patterns. I discovered that the two types of schools were fundamentally different in several ways. The schools not achieving AYP enrolled significantly more English learners (students whose first language is not English) and had significantly fewer teachers deemed to be highly qualified to teach in their subject area.

The emergence of these findings led me back to the director. I wanted to add a qualitative component to this evaluation that would focus on the instructional practices of each type of school. The director was hesitant. When I asked for an explanation, she told me that she did not trust qualitative findings because she never knew how they had been developed. Previous evaluators had given her reports whereby the methodology of the qualitative component of the evaluation was insufficiently explained. I was given some of the old reports to read and I found that their methods sections were full of holes. Interviews were conducted, but the number of interviews was never listed. There was no evidence of an interview protocol. The reports indicated that classrooms were observed, but there was no indication of when, how many, or how often observations occurred. In three reports written by three different evaluators, each contained only one sentence describing the technique used to analyze the collected qualitative data. Each cited content analysis as the analytic method, with no further explanation. After reading the reports, I could understand why the director had been skeptical.

With this understanding, I called a meeting with the director so I could discuss with her what to expect from my qualitative evaluation. In the report, the methodology would be explained in sufficient detail for her to understand what I did and how I went about doing it. I would provide a thorough description of the sample and the tools I used to collect the data. I would provide details about the analysis process so that she could see how I arrived at my conclusions and recommendations. I even showed the director a previous qualitative evaluation report I had written so she could see what I would provide to her. By showing her that qualitative evaluations can be explicit and transparent about methodology, she finally agreed to fund a qualitative evaluation focused on explaining the fundamental differences between high-achieving and low-achieving Title I schools.

Adding a systematic and transparent qualitative component to the evaluation was ultimately beneficial in two ways. First, it allowed for a more complete investigation of the differences between the schools. Not all schools receiving Title I funding are created equal. The low-achieving schools had to address more basic student needs, such as physical and mental health. These schools spent a much larger proportion of their Title I funds on nurses and psychologists. The leaders and teachers at these schools saw themselves not only as educators, but also as protectors. Their top priority was to help their students to be physically and psychologically ready to learn. This left less money to be earmarked for instructional purposes. The high-achieving schools spent a much higher percentage of their Title I funds on instructional supplements. The leaders and teachers at these schools were able to focus on instruction and learned that the district-mandated curricula would not support all of their students equally. Providing a complete and easy-to-understand illustration of the differences between the two types of schools was an anticipated benefit of being explicit and transparent in the qualitative evaluation component.

The unanticipated benefit of being explicit and transparent concerned my credibility as an evaluator. While the director appeared to understand how I generated my findings and recommendations, she was not pleased with the results. After completing the evaluation, I learned that the director had her own ideas about why the two types of schools performed differently. She intended to use my findings to create policies designed to push the Title I schools toward her notion of how schools should be allocating their funds. My evaluation findings did not support her ideas, which led her to attack my credibility as an evaluator.

While I have taught at the university level, I am not a certificated K–12 classroom teacher. The director attempted to discredit my findings by claiming I could not possibly understand what goes on in a K–12 classroom because I had never been a certificated teacher. My only defense was my transparent description of my data collection and analysis processes. My supervisors were able to defend my work to higher-level district administrators, and my findings were determined to be credible. Without careful attention to both conducting and reporting this systematic inquiry, my evaluation may have been deemed unacceptable and inadequate. The director and I did not work together again after this incident. However, my supervisors, other district administrators, and I knew that my qualitative evaluation work was sound.

STAYING TRUE TO THE DATA

Denzin and Lincoln (2000) described qualitative research as "an interpretive, naturalistic approach to the world. This means that qualitative researchers study things in their natural setting, attempting to make sense of, or to interpret, phenomena in terms of the meanings people bring to them" (p. 3). To make sense of the meanings derived from program stakeholders' experiences, a qualitative evaluator needs to be able to hear the various and nuanced ways people portray those experiences. First, as we discussed, one must bring a clear sense of identity and role to the process; nurture trusting relationships; and apply sound and transparent methodology. With these elements in mind, staying true to the data means knowing what you bring to the situation, yet holding that subjectivity in abeyance; respecting the meanings participants articulate; and endeavoring to represent those perspectives as accurately as possible. We have two examples of this: Eric Barela describes his experience in hiring a data collector; Janet Usinger describes her experiences in data analysis.

When I (Eric Barela) began to work for the school district as an internal evaluator, many of our qualitative data collectors were former teachers, because they quickly established a perception of credibility. Teachers who were being observed appeared to feel more comfortable when they knew an experienced teacher was observing them. Indeed, over the years, some of the best qualitative data collectors with whom I have worked were classroom teachers. They had an easier time focusing on teacher–student interactions and could take very detailed notes about classroom practices, oftentimes capturing interactions that I missed! They made meaning of the observation data in powerful ways by seeing patterns that only trained teachers would notice. These teachers were then able to assist other data collectors by teaching them about these interactions and patterns. Their guidance has made me both a better qualitative, and a better educational, evaluator.

However, I quickly learned that there is a tradeoff when trying to establish immediate credibility. A deep understanding of context does not automatically lead to richer data collection; unfortunately, some of the worst qualitative data collectors I have worked with also were classroom teachers. These teachers are unable to stay true to the data. They had a very clear idea of what it means to be an effective classroom teacher, and their observations reflected these ideas. The observed teachers were judged on overall performance as defined by the data collector, regardless of whether teacher performance was actually being assessed as part of the evaluation. On the first evaluation project I led, I hired several data collectors (from other evaluations) who came highly recommended by their supervisors. One of these individuals was a former teacher named James (pseudonym). James commanded respect whenever he entered a classroom. He had been teaching for over twenty years and would let observed teachers know this at the outset of data collection. Even though I was the evaluator and his supervisor, I was excited to learn from James . . . until I received his first set of classroom fieldnotes. James was supposed to observe a teacher for the entire school day, and he ended up leaving the classroom after morning recess. I will never forget his fieldnotes from that observation. The first line he had written was, "I don't know why you sent me into this classroom because this teacher is awful." The last lines he had written were, "I can't stay in this classroom anymore because this teacher is doing everything wrong. I might just tell her to get out of teaching altogether." Thankfully, James did not speak to the teacher after the shortened observation. James was supposed to be collecting observation data on instructional delivery strategies, not judging it based on his notion of what effective instructional delivery was. James had given me nothing I could use to analyze instructional delivery strategies. After giving him one more chance and coaching him to collect higher-quality data, James was still unable to separate his judgment of a teacher's performance and the implementation of instructional delivery strategies. Unfortunately, I had to fire James after strike two.

From this experience, I learned that a qualitative evaluator should strive for both deep contextual knowledge and an awareness to keep that knowledge from interacting with qualitative data collection. While deep contextual knowledge can speed up the credibility process, it can actually interfere with the process if one does not use the knowledge to gather useful data. In the examples, the "great" qualitative evaluator was able to minimize subjectivity and bias while also using deep contextual knowledge to find patterns in the data that had not yet emerged. Contextual knowledge served to expand the meaning of the findings. The "not-so-great" qualitative evaluator was unable to separate his thoughts on what *should* be observed as opposed to what *was* observed. Contextual knowledge served to limit the meaning that could be made from the data.

In each of our professional lives, we have encountered evaluators who are more interested in presenting their own thoughts and perspectives in the final report rather than gathering and understanding the perspectives of others. Eric's examples of teachers as data collectors illuminate the challenges in corralling one's subjectivity during data collection and reporting. Janet Usinger has an example of analysis from the same adolescent study described previously that illustrates how understanding stakeholders' views and developing a positive relationship with the stakeholders does not have to get in the way of hearing the "truth."

Although I (Janet Usinger) conducted all of the interviews with the adolescents to maintain trust and continuity with the students, the data have been analyzed for different purposes by several individuals, including graduate students. Isabel (pseudonym), a doctoral student, was interested in exploring the theory of possible selves among the Latina girls of the study. Isabel was Latina and the first person in her family to attend college; therefore, the topic (possible selves[3]) and the population (Latinas) from whom the data was obtained were of personal interest to her. I gave Isabel all of the transcripts and access to the original audiotapes. After conducting her own analysis, Isabel's first comment was, "Oh my gosh, this is amazing. I can see myself in every single one of these girls." We discussed her reaction at great length. Specifically, we discussed how easy it is to see the *familiar* in data. What is more difficult is to find discrepant statements and look for how the young girls of the study were different as well as why they might be different from Isabel. Fortunately, Isabel was very comfortable with the discussion and did not fall into the trap of over-identification; nevertheless, she talked about how easy it was for her to zero in on the portions of the data that were familiar and affirmed her own experiences and aspirations.

Feeling a sense of familiarity with the person being interviewed is not the only pitfall. Another student analyzed some of the data for a qualitative methods class. Ron (pseudonym) was exploring the role that education plays in the career aspirations of the students. As with Isabel, I gave Ron the transcripts of a subset of adolescents. After conducting his own analysis, his immediate comment was, "Wow, some of these kids don't get it, do they?" He focused on the misconceptions about college the students had expressed. Again, we talked.

In the initial phases of analysis, it is very common to make judgments about data; it is part of the sorting process. After all, the initial task is to find patterns in the data; spending too much time trying to explore the depth of the statements does not allow the evaluator to see the data holistically. But once the initial sorting is complete, focusing on what the individual is saying—from the participant's perspective, not the evaluator's perspective—is essential. It was important for Ron to redirect his thinking from what he considered to be immature or naïve ideas to recognize that the students were presenting what they considered to be legitimate—from their perspective. After all, it was their life. Indeed, because I interviewed the students for six years, I can safely say that the students would be adamant in their insistence that they were quite serious about their ideas and expectations. They would add, "And who are you to second-guess *my* understanding of *my* future?"

For me, the analysis was not difficult because I overidentified with the students or judged their thoughts and ideas. Rather, it was that I really liked some of the students. Because I liked them as individuals, I found myself wanting to read things into their statements that were not there. For instance, one student, Brenda (pseudonym), had very definite goals. She stated that her parents had instilled in her that she was special and she had embraced that self-definition. Typical of many of the students in the study, Brenda had a number of cousins whom she described as "ne'er do wells," and she was determined to break out of the mold and make something of herself. She was very pretty, gregarious, and just a delightful young person. Our interviews went very well, and I was able to dig into her thinking about herself and her future. However, once I started the analysis, I realized that I had overestimated her strategies and how she was thinking about her path toward the future. I was imagining perseverance that was not there. I had to reflect on my own feelings about her as a person, put these feelings on the back burner, and simply look at the data. What did she actually say? What were the data—not my imagination—telling me about her?

Qualitative inquiry provides richness and understandings that cannot be derived from closed-ended survey questions, test scores, demographics, and other quantitative data. It is difficult to uncover nuances and subtleties in understandings without actually hearing the words selected by the interviewee, rather than the words selected for a survey by an evaluator. Conversely, it is necessary to simultaneously be aware of your own biases. Yet it goes beyond knowing your biases; being true to the data involves constantly challenging yourself as an evaluator and deliberately reflecting on your reaction to the people who so generously share their lives. I overcome these pitfalls by posting a sign on my desk that says:

It's their story, not yours.

Evaluators do not own the truths and realities of the people from whom they gather data. Whether the evaluator is comfortable with what the participant says is irrelevant. What is *owned* is the responsibility to reflect what is communicated as honestly and respectfully as possible. The magic of capturing how individuals are framing and interpreting their world, as they understand it, is finding the subtleties that exist through different interpretations that individuals hold of the same thing.

These different interpretations and perspectives can be brought from data collection and analysis into the reporting phase of an evaluation as well. As mentioned in Leslie Goodyear's example in this chapter, this could include explicitly acknowledging the evaluator's background and perspective as well. Although it can be tempting to tie up an evaluation into a tidy bow, compiling interpretations and findings into a representative and complete story, qualitative evaluation offers the opportunity to consider presenting evaluation findings in ways that are not tidy, and that represent the cacophony of program stakeholders and the voices that are represented by them. This can mean creating a report that brings rich descriptions and quotes from participants to the fore. Or it could mean creating an opportunity (like Baur and Abma did in Chapter 7) to share evaluation findings in a public forum and engage in dialogue with stakeholders. Colleagues have experimented with such formats as poetry, performance, comics, dramatic readings, and even interpretive dance (see Dance Your Ph.D. from the American Association for the Advancement of Science for a great example of a very creative way to communicate findings that complement a more traditional written format: http://news.sciencemag.org/biology/2013/11/dance-your-ph.d.-finalists-announced). After completing the evaluation of the HIV prevention program in the story above, Leslie Goodyear created a performance that represented the different perspectives of the women involved and presented it to the program staff, the funders, other policy makers and evaluators, and even to the participants themselves. Each audience had different reactions to evaluation findings presented performatively, but all felt they learned something new and informative about the program and its participants (see Goodyear, 2007).

FOSTERING LEARNING

Evaluations are designed to provide important information to stakeholders about their program. Every program has many stakeholders: program staff, program participants, funders, policy makers, community members and leaders, and more. Each stakeholder group usually wants different information about the program because their stake in the program comes from a unique perspective. As a result, there are many different approaches to evaluation to meet the many diverse questions and information sought by stakeholders.

As we suggested earlier in this chapter, evaluators who favor a qualitative approach to evaluation tend to be somewhat obsessed with the question "*why?*" It is not enough for us to gather data about whether a program is effective; we want to understand why it was meaningful (or not) for this group of people versus another group of people. As Schwandt and Cash explained in Chapter 1, qualitative inquiry was incorporated into evaluations to move beyond simply determining whether the program was implemented as intended. Indeed, a qualitative evaluator also serves as an educator, helping program staff and participants understand the evaluation process and ways in which they can use that process for their own learning.

Answering the all-important "why?" question generally involves developing relationships with people connected to a program in many different ways. The relationships that are formed are intentional; they serve the purpose of directly learning about the experiences of the people most affected by the program, as illustrated in Jennifer Jewiss's example. The cases presented in Part 2 of this volume present a variety of different learning that occurred. In some instances, the learning was directed toward the people who sought to design educational programs that would be meaningful for specific populations. In other instances, learning was directed at the different "factions" that had formed within the program. In some cases, learning was also directed to deepen the understanding of policy makers or to give voice to a specific group. Let us take these separately to explain our thinking about how learning is inherent in high-quality evaluation that uses qualitative inquiry.

In Chapter 7, Baur and Abma deliberately sought to have the staff and members of the resident councils learn together about their different perspectives of the same phenomenon. Their experiences as evaluators and deep knowledge of the role power plays in organizations informed their interactions with the Board of Directors and the learning direction they pursued. Their evaluation set the stage for the two groups to initially examine their own understandings of the workings of the resident councils and in turn share their perceptions with the other group. The intent was to allow for the two groups to learn from each other to arrive at a solution to the problem together. The goal was for everyone to "win" through mutual learning, as opposed to the evaluators submitting a report with the "solution" to be imposed upon the staff and council members.

Martínez-Rubin described learning at many levels in Chapter 8. The various staff members of Sunrise Health Systems did not want the results of the community assessment simply to comply with the law; they wanted the findings to inform the development of their educational programming. In many ways the staff knew what the Latino families "needed" with regard to the actual program content; what they sought was an understanding of how information could be tailored to facilitate the families' actual use of nutrition information; they wanted to learn the nuances of how the various Latino communities understood their children's health needs so health promotion efforts would be effective. Martínez-Rubin was perfect for this role. Although she had no children herself, she was Latina and understood the tensions between cultural practices and health. She wanted to portray the subtleties of the living conditions of the families, not merely collapse the issues into one or two obvious, but superficial, statements such as "parents need to provide their children with more fruits and vegetables." Only through qualitative inquiry could the lives of the families be adequately represented.

Sharon Rallis (Chapter 9) was the metaphorical circus performer we described at the beginning of this chapter—juggling the needs and desires of the school personnel and the needs and desires of the research team. She and her colleague, Andy, found themselves in a very tenuous situation; the overall design of the endeavor was fixed by the granting agency. It must be noted, however, that evaluators usually find themselves in "prescribed" situations. It is not uncommon for a granting agency to have specific requirements for the project or to require the involvement of certain individuals (or organizations/institutions). Sometimes the granting agency staff have had positive experiences with individuals and insist that they be involved in the project. Granting agencies are not the only "culprit" in establishing specific demands or expectations that may not align with the goals of the program. Sometimes program staff insists that someone or something be included in the project, again whether there is programmatic alignment or not.

Because of their specific role in the process, evaluators must be consummate learners to make sense of complex (and sometimes confusing) situations and ascertain how all of the "pieces" fit together. Evaluators who use qualitative methods assume their role in a different manner than evaluators who use predominantly quantitative approaches. As we have described, qualitative evaluators develop relationships with an array of stakeholders; they look stakeholders, including participants, "in the eye" and gather personal reflections from people. As Rallis (Chapter 9) described, their ethical stance often focuses on the principle of *respect* found in the Belmont Report.[4] The concept of respect is that weight must be given to all persons' opinions and choices. Rallis and her colleague directed their learning on how to make the extremely sensitive situation ethical relative to the participating school staff. Their goal was to leave the situation better than they found it. Learning, indeed.

Social and educational programs serve all kinds of people. As evaluators—and particularly, as qualitative evaluators—our job is to be able to talk with them about their life experiences and their experiences in the program we are evaluating. Evaluations do not simply fulfill a funding requirement; they serve as tools to improve the lives of the people associated with the program: participants, staff, funders, and yes, even the evaluators. The responsibility of a qualitative evaluator is to leave the setting enriched for having conducted the evaluation.

KEY CONCEPTS

Belmont Report	Personal identity
Biases	Professional role
Contextual knowledge	Public good
Credibility	Rapport building
Deferring judgment	Reflection
Enriching the setting	Reflexivity
Mutual learning	Respect
Personal beliefs and values	Sense-making

Situating oneself

Sound, systematic, and explicit methodology

Stakeholder engagement

Staying "true" to the data

"Stupid questions"

Subjectivity

Transparency

Trusting relationships

NOTES

1. Title I funding is federal support of schools located in economically disadvantaged communities.
2. AYP is the measure used to hold schools and school districts accountable under the No Child Left Behind Act; schools and school districts must meet or exceed specific targets in terms of the percentage of students who are proficient as measured through standardized tests.
3. Possible selves is the theory advanced by Markus and Nurius (1986) that explores personal representations of the self in the future.
4. The Belmont Report provided guidance in the federal regulation of the ethical treatment of human subjects in research.

REFERENCES

Denzin, N., & Lincoln, Y. (2000). Introduction: The discipline and practice of qualitative research. In N. Denzin & Y. Lincoln (Eds.), *Handbook of qualitative research* (pp. 1–30). Thousand Oaks, CA: Sage.

Glesne, C. (2006). *Becoming qualitative researchers: An introduction* (3rd ed.). New York, NY: Pearson.

Goodyear, L. (2007). Poetry, performance and pathos in evaluation reporting. In S. Kushner & N. Norris (Eds.), *Dilemmas of engagement* (Volume 10 of the Advances in Program Evaluation Series). Oxford, UK: JAI Press.

Markus, H. R., & Nurius, P. (1986). Possible selves. *American Psychologist, 41*(9), 954–986.

Rossman, G., & Rallis, S. (2003). *Learning in the field*. Thousand Oaks, CA: Sage.

INDEX

27–28; integrity/honesty, 244; respect, 275, 276n4; T-PE's concept and practice, 103–107

Problems, 209–210; engagement of stakeholders for solving, 68–69; reason for consensus of unsolvable, 59–60

Process: dimensions of, 106–107; emancipatory, 104–105; evaluation, 42; liberatory, 105; qualitative evaluation's cyclical, 253–254. *See also specific process*

Process data, 42–43

Process studies, 25, 45; evaluation priorities clarified by, 41–43; psychology practice as utilizing, 41; qualitative inquiry's appropriateness for, 42

Professional competence, 148, 150–152

Professional development, 240–242

Professional disciplines and alliances, 195

Professional domain, 153

Professional practice: competencies in, 142–144, 150–152; program evaluation criteria for, 144–145; taxonomies as adopted in, 143–144

Professional reputation, 195

Professional role, 251, 253

Professionalism, 144–145, 255

Program evaluation scenario: participatory approach as COPE, 100–102; participatory approach of Phoenix Rising as, 101–102; WIN in participatory approach as, 101–102

The Program Evaluation Standards, 144

Program theory, 31, 79, 81, 90, 93; qualitative inquiry as developing,

92; TDE stakeholder theory or, 80, 84

Programs, 46–47, 92, 122, 144–145; child health, 67; communities affected by, 1; disability, 85; evaluation priorities clarified in study, 41–43; evaluators' observance of operating, 63–67; focus groups and educational, 205–206; focusing on diversity and comparison of, 44–45; human element in, 1; intended users' queries on, 43–44; process data permitting judgments on organization, 42–43; sensitivity in process evaluation of, 42; stakeholders' interest in improving, 1. *See also specific programs*

Project design: emergent design dynamics in, 174; mutual understanding and, 175–184; of nursing home project, 174–175; storytelling in, 170, 174–175

Project evaluation, 221–223

Prominent evaluation, 4

Promotoras (community outreach workers), 194, 205, 209–210

Pseudonyms, 248n1

Psychology: process studies utilization and, 41; of use, 27, 41; utilization-focused evaluation informed by, 27–28

Public cholesterol screenings, 64–66

Public good, 266

Q

Qualitative: data, 142–143, 162, 208, 267–269; paradigms, 141–142, 151, 154–156, 160, 162

Qualitative analysis: evaluators providing both quantitative and,